Integrating Reading and Writing Through Children's Literature

Related Titles of Interest

Getting It Together: A Process Workbook for K–12 Curriculum Development, Implementation, and Assessment
Judy F. Carr and Douglas E. Harris
ISBN: 0-205-14173-0

126 Strategies to Build Language Arts Abilities: A Month-by-Month Resource
Cathy Collins
ISBN: 0-205-13025-9

Integrated Language Arts: Controversy to Consensus
Lesley Mandel Morrow, Jeffrey K. Smith, and Louise Cherry Wilkinson (Editors)
ISBN: 0-205-14735-6   Paper   0-205-14736-4   Cloth

Literacy Development in the Early Years: Helping Children Read and Write, Second Edition
Lesley Mandel Morrow
ISBN: 0-205-14043-2

Developing Cultural Literacy Through the Writing Process: Empowering All Learners
Barbara C. Palmer, Mary L. Hafner, and Marilyn F. Sharp
ISBN: 0-205-13989-2

A Handbook for the K–12 Reading Resource Specialist
Marguerite C. Radencich, Penny G. Beers, and Jeanne Shay Schumm
ISBN: 0-205-14081-5

A Green Dinosaur Day: A Guide for Developing Thematic Units in Literature-Based Instruction, K–6
Patricia L. Roberts
ISBN: 0-205-14007-6

Integrating Reading and Writing Through Children's Literature

Kathy Everts Danielson
University of Nebraska at Omaha

Jan LaBonty
University of Montana

Allyn and Bacon

Boston   London   Toronto   Sydney   Tokyo   Singapore

Library of Congress Cataloging-in-Publication Data

Danielson, Kathy Everts.
  Integrating reading and writing through children's literature /
Kathy Everts Danielson, Jan LaBonty.
     p.   cm.
  Includes bibliographical references and index.
  ISBN 0-205-15314-3
  1. Reading (Elementary)   2. English language–Composition and
exercises.   3. Literature–Study and teaching (Elementary)
4. Children–United States–Books and reading.   I. LaBonty, Jan.
II. Title.
LB1573.S26   1993
372.4–dc20   93-14086
                                                          CIP

Credits:
page 179: Quote from *The Devil's Arithmetic* by Jane Yolen. Copyright © 1988 by Jane Yolen. Used by permission of Viking Penguin, a division of Penguin Books USA Inc.
page 180: Quote from *Esteban and the Ghost* by Sibyl Hancock. Copyright © 1983 by Sibyl Hancock. Used by permission, Dial Books for Young Readers, a division of Penguin Books USA Inc.
page 180: Quote from *How the Stars Fell into the Sky* by Jerrie Oughton. Text copyright © 1992 by Jerrie Oughton. Reprinted by permission of Houghton Mifflin Co. All rights reserved.
page 188: *The Quicksand Book,* © 1977 by Tomie dePaola, published by Holiday House.
page 191: Reprinted with permission of Atheneum Publishers, an imprint of Macmillan Publishing Company from *Deadly Animals* by Martha Holmes. Copyright © 1991 Martha Holmes.
pages 221 and 222: From *Wild Animal Families* by Margaret Davidson, copyright © 1980 by Margaret Davidson. Used by permission of Scholastic, Inc.

Printed in the United States of America

10 9 8 7 6 5 4 3 2 1   97 96 95 94 93

For Steve and Jacob:
My greatest support team.   K. E. D.

For André and Elizabeth:
Always my most appreciative and
appreciated audience.   J. L.

Contents

Chapter 3   Teaching Beginning Reading   43

Chapter 4   Teaching Reading Comprehension   63

Chapter 5   *The Writing Process   85*

Chapter 6 *Writing in Response to Literature* 117

Preface

What a wonderful time to be teaching! Children's literature is a growing field and many quality books are now available for children. Children's literature is the basis of a reading and writing classroom. It provides a good model for students. They learn from it and they are motivated to read and write because of it.

This book focuses on ways in which literature can be used in the integration of reading and writing. Student examples and lesson plan ideas have been included to give a practical focus to the book.

The first chapter provides an overview of why the use of quality children's books is imperative. Organizing a literature-based classroom is offered in Chapter 2. Ideas for grouping students beyond traditional reading groups are described, as well as other elements to consider in planning for instruction. Chapter 3 describes how children's books are critical in the process of beginning reading. Chapter 4 offers many examples of how literature can be used to enhance reading comprehension before, during, and after reading.

The writing process is examined in Chapter 5, with various links to literature provided throughout. Chapter 6 extends the process of writing to the response aspect of writing about literature. Chapter 7 explores the importance of poetry in a reading program, with varied examples of types of poetry and ways to involve students with this infectious aspect of language. A description of teaching skills within this context is covered in Chapter 8, with many examples based on children's books. Finally, Chapter 9 examines the issue of assessment within the context of a reading-writing classroom.

This book is meant to help you to prepare a literature-based classroom that encourages reading and writing. It is our hope that the many examples and lists of books will be helpful as you begin to think about how literature can be infused throughout the classroom, particularly to enhance reading and writing.

Acknowledgments

Although we have done the actual writing of this book, many people have influenced our beliefs and ideas about how reading and writing must be taught with children's literature. First, we wish to thank our own students (graduate, undergraduate, and elementary), who have taught us about the learning process and the love of books. Thanks also to university colleagues Carolyn Colvin, University of Iowa; Sue Dauer, Western Oregon State College; Mary Lickteig, University of Nebraska-Omaha; Sheri Rogers, University of Nebraska-Lincoln; and Karla Hawkins Wendelin, University of Nebraska-Lincoln, for their shared love of books and enthusiasm for quality literature and life-long learning.

We would also like to thank Sue Hutchinson at Allyn and Bacon for her help throughout this process. We appreciate the careful reviews written by Karen Bromley from the State University of New York at Binghamton and Susan Trostle from the University of Rhode Island. They helped us to refine our writing and look at the book with a fresh perspective.

Finally, we would like to thank our families for their love, support, and distractions.

1

Introduction

Whole language, holistic instruction, integrated language arts, and literature-based reading and writing are all terms currently used to describe child-centered reading and writing programs. Although no two teachers, administrators, or college professors would have the same definition of the above terms, all would agree that the four language arts (reading, writing, speaking, and listening) must be taught in an integrated manner to make learning enjoyable and meaningful for students and teachers.

Regie Routman, elementary language arts resource teacher, defines whole language in this way:

> *Perhaps, more than anything else, whole language is about all learners feeling whole and able and part of a community of learners. It is about belonging and risk taking and feeling successful as teachers and learners. It is about the power of collaboration to break down the isolation of teachers and to establish communities of belonging and learning for all students and teachers. (Routman, 1991, p. 4)*

Another way to define this philosophy is to examine the teacher's role. Bobbi Fisher, kindergarten teacher, has defined her role in this way:

> *I view my role as planner, observer, and teacher so that my beliefs about how children learn are realized in my classroom. I plan so children develop as authorities of their own learning. I organize the physical environment and daily routine in my classroom to encourage participation in a variety of experiences that are interesting, meaningful, and developmentally appropriate. I plan opportunities that offer rich literacy, math, social studies, and science experiences, and which facilitate the children's social, emotional, and physical growth. (Fisher, 1991, p. 2)*

Eighth-grade teacher Linda Rief thinks about whole language in terms of what she wants for her students:

> *What do I want for my students? I want them to leave my classroom knowing they are readers and writers, wanting to learn more, and having a number of strategies for that learning in any field. I want them to like learning and to like themselves. I want them to know they have important things to say and unique ways of saying them. I want them to know their voices are valued. I want learning to be fun. Most importantly, I want them to gain independence as learners, knowing and trusting their own choices. (Rief, 1992, p. 4)*

Former middle school teacher Nancie Atwell focuses on the importance of the teacher being able to change and adapt to his or her classroom:

When I stopped focusing on me and my methods and started observing students and their learning, I saw a gap yawning between us—between what I did as language teacher and what they did as language learners. I saw that my creating manipulated kids so they bore sole responsibility for narrowing the gap, and my students either found ways to make sense of and peace with the logic of my teaching, or they failed the course. In truth, it was I who needed to move, to strike out for some common ground. I learn in my classroom these days because I moved, because the classroom became a reading and writing workshop, a new territory my students and I could inhabit together. (Atwell, 1987, p. 4)

Writing expert Donald Graves describes the importance of teacher modeling:

Children learn from our demonstrations about reading, writing, and learning. We show how we read, write, and solve problems. This means that we regularly read and write with the children. (Graves, 1991, p. 13)

Calkins and Harwayne describe the importance of community building through literature:

Those of us who have written within a community of writers and read within a community of readers know that these communities have a different feel. They have a sense of intimacy and of adventure. The most important thing to do in September, then, is not to establish routines and rituals but to nurture the intangible spirit that can matter more than anything. Surely one way of doing this is to share incredible pieces of literature with our children. (Calkins & Harwayne, 1991, pp. 20–21)

Children's literature is the foundation of this type of philosophy because students (and adults) need real stories to read in order to be discerning readers and writers. To develop a love of reading and writing, quality literature must be used. This need for quality children's literature in classrooms has been addressed by several recent recommendations.

Recent Recommendations Regarding Literature

The recommendations to use literature have come from many sources based on research-supported practices. In *Becoming a Nation of Readers: The Report of the Commission on Reading*, these two specific recommendations were expressed:

Children should spend more time in independent reading. Independent reading, whether in school or out of school, is associated with gains in reading achievement. By the time they are in the third or fourth grade, children should read independently a minimum of two hours per week. Children's reading should include classic and modern works of fiction and nonfiction that represent the core of our cultural heritage. . . .

Schools should maintain well-stocked and managed libraries. Access to interesting and informative books is one of the keys to a successful reading program. As important as an adequate collection of books is a librarian who encourages wide reading and helps match books to children. (1985, p. 119)

More recently, the following recommendation came from *New Policy Guidelines for Reading:*

Reading instruction should include a wide variety of materials and reading experiences. Teachers should maintain and use, as an integral part of the reading program at all grade levels, a wide-stocked classroom library which includes poetry, newspapers, and trade books as well as content-area books and magazines. Fiction and nonfiction materials should be selected on the basis of quality and student interest and should represent a wide range of difficulty. (Harste, 1989, p. 52)

Benefits of Literature

There are numerous reasons for using literature as the foundation of a reading-writing classroom. Consider the following benefits:

1. *Quality children's picture books celebrate the artistic process.* Caldecott Medal winning books such as *Tuesday* (Wiesner, 1991) *Black and White* (Macaulay, 1990), or *Lon Po Po: A Red-Riding Hood Story from China* (Young, 1989) are visually captivating and add much to the stories that they accompany and tell. There are many other picture books with outstanding illustrations of varied artistic style. *Family Farm* (Locker, 1988), for instance, is an exquisite example of impressionist paintings. Egg tempera is the base of the paintings in *Good Dog, Carl* (Day, 1985), which is a wordless book that tells the story of a dog babysitting for a baby.

Other picture books with varied art styles include Chris Van Allsburg's *The Polar Express* (1985) and *Jumanji* (1981), both Caldecott Medal books. *Jumanji* is illustrated with pencil, whereas *The Polar Express* is rich with color paintings. Lois Ehlert uses bold colors and cut-out shapes to form animal faces in *Color Zoo* (1989) and *Color Farm* (1990). Collage constructions are used in *Window* (Baker, 1991) as the changes of a young boy's life are chronicled through wordless scenes observed from the window of his room. And Ann Jonas has created books that not only create stories and illustrations right side up but also upside down in her books *Round Trip* (1983) done in black and white and *Reflections* (1987) done in full color.

2. *Vocabulary and concept development are learned within the rich context of a meaningful story or genre.* Alphabet books such as *Alison's Zinnia* (Lobel, 1990) or *Eating the Alphabet: Fruits and Vegetables from A to Z* (Ehlert, 1989) show a variety of different names, flowers, and fruits and vegetables as they demonstrate the alphabet. These books allow students to explore new words in a meaningful manner, adding to their own knowledge of these concepts. Other books develop the meaning of a concept within the context of the story. For instance, *The Principal's New Clothes* (Calmenson, 1989) uses the terms "sharpest dresser," "tailors," "tricksters," and "measurements" as it tells the current-day version of "The Emperor's New Clothes." These terms are easy for children to understand once they have read the story and see how they relate to the plot and the concept of clothing. Other books develop a child's understanding of shapes, colors, and textures, such as Tana Hoban's books *Spirals, Curves, Fanshapes & Lines* (1992), *Exactly the Opposite* (1990), *Of Colors and Things* (1989), and *Look Up, Look Down* (1992).

3. *Predictable and repetitive texts give early readers confidence in their reading abilities.* Books such as *Moo Moo, Brown Cow* (Wood, 1992), *Polar Bear, Polar Bear, What Do You Hear?* (Martin, 1991), or *My Brown Bear, Barney* (Butler, 1989) encourage young readers to make predictions about the text and invite them to join in with the reading of the story or its refrain. Because

picture clues are often given, students can make good guesses about what will be coming next in the text. There is also much repetition, which allows readers to feel confident about their abilities to read or chant along. Other good predictable and repetitive books for young readers are *I Went Walking* (Williams, 1989), *Spots, Feathers, and Curly Tails* (Tafuri, 1988), *What Do You Like?* (Grejniec, 1992), *The Chick and the Duckling* (Ginsburg, 1972), *All I Am* (Roe, 1990), *Mary Wore Her Red Dress* (Peek, 1985), *The Jacket I Wear in the Snow* (Neitzel, 1989), *The Dress I'll Wear to the Party* (Neitzel, 1992), and *My Brown Bear Barney in Trouble* (Butler, 1993).

4. *Literature allows readers to learn about other people in other settings with other perspectives.* Sami, from *Sami and the Time of the Troubles* (Heide & Gilliland, 1992) lives in present-day Beirut. His story of fear and ruins contrasts his memories of good times and helps readers to think about other worlds and perspectives. *Over the Green Hills* (Isadora, 1992) tells the story of a journey in South Africa. *Hopscotch Around the World* (Lankford, 1992) displays the many different ways the common childhood game is played around the world, thus expanding a reader's horizons about a familiar experience. *On the Pampas* (Brusca, 1991) describes living on a ranch in Argentina. And the various cultural aspects of cooking rice are explored in *Everybody Cooks Rice* (Dooley, 1991) as a young girl visits the houses in her culturally diverse neighborhood during meal time and discovers how each family is cooking rice in a different manner. All these picture books are important in helping students to explore a global perspective.

Learning about history from novels is another aspect to learning about other perspectives. Readers will root for Annemarie's family to escape from the Nazi soldiers in 1943 in Lois Lowry's *Number the Stars* (1989). Readers will hope along with Anna and Caleb that the mail-order bride, Sarah, will stay with them on their farm in the early 1900s on the prairie in *Sarah, Plain and Tall* (MacLachlan, 1985). Good literature builds a perspective of history too.

5. *Literature generates interest in the real world and how people in other places live and work, as well as how things work.* Informational books, such as the incredible *The Way Things Work* (Macaulay, 1988), leave readers with not only answers to how many mechanical things work but also questions about other marvels of our computer age. *Nature by Design* (Brooks, 1991) examines the wonder of nature, from the oyster's shell to the beaver's dam. And Gail Gibbons gives a description of construction in *How a House Is Built* (Gibbons, 1990). All of these books helps students to understand the processes of nature and mechanical creations. Books such as *Hats, Hats, Hats* (Morris, 1989) and *Bread, Bread, Bread* (Morris, 1989) show the many ways that people around the world live and work as they examine the similarities and differences in food and clothing in various cultures.

6. *Literature involves readers and listeners with the infectious nature of language.* *Chicka Chicka Boom Boom* (Martin & Archambault, 1989) is such an infectious book. The refrain of this rollicking alphabet book is positively catching: "Chicka chicka boom boom! Will there be enough room?" *Is Your Mama a Llama?* (Guarino, 1989) is another "chant-along" book. Readers or listeners can easily make predictions about the different animals by noting the clues and the rhyme of the contagious text. Other books with infectious lyrics are *Thump, Thump, Rat-a-Tat-Tat* (Baer, 1989), *Cat Boy!* (Lockwood, 1989), *Bears in Pairs* (Yektai, 1987), *Sheep in a Jeep* (Shaw, 1986), *Jesse Bear, What Will You Wear?* (Carlstrom, 1986), and *One Cow, Moo Moo* (Bennett, 1990).

7. *Literature allows the reader to empathize with characters' problems and*

life-styles. Contemporary realistic fiction exposes students to many different problems that real people face. Picture books dealing with divorce and stepfamilies help students see the many types of families that exist, such as *Charlie Anderson* (Abercrombie, 1990), *My Mother's House, My Father's House* (Christiansen, 1989), and *Diana, Maybe* (Dragonwagon, 1987). Relationships with older people are examined in the picture books *Sea Swan* (Lasky, 1988) and *Wilfrid Gordon McDonald Partridge* (Fox, 1985). Adjusting to a new sibling is addressed in the picture books *Don't Touch My Room* (Lakin, 1985), *Everett Anderson's Nine Month Long* (Clifton, 1978), *Waiting for Baby* (Birdseye, 1991), and the novel *Dear Baby* (Rocklin, 1988).

Reading difficulties are dealt with in the picture book *The Wednesday Surprise* (Bunting, 1989) and the novel *Mostly Michael* (Smith, 1987). Being homeless is dealt with in the picture book *Fly Away Home* (Bunting, 1991) and the novel *The Leaves in October* (Ackerman, 1991). Saying good-bye to a farm and moving away are dealt with in the picture book *Time to Go* (Fiday & Fiday, 1990) and the novel *Good-bye My Wishing Star* (Grove, 1988). Saying good-bye to a person or a pet after death are dealt with in the picture book *Goodbye, Max* (Keller, 1987) and the novelette *Blackberries in the Dark* (Jukes, 1985). All these books give readers insight into a variety of life experiences.

8. *Literature allows reading for enjoyment.* Students will laugh with and enjoy books such as *The True Story of The Three Little Pigs* (Scieszka, 1989). This book tells the story of the Three Little Pigs from the wolf's point of view and is a natural read-aloud book for all ages! Similar retelling of folktales with humorous results are *The Frog Prince Continued* (Scieszka, 1991) and *The Stinky Cheese Man and Other Fairly Stupid Tales* (Scieszka, 1992). Enjoyment of word play is found in the reading of *Chortles* (Merriam, 1989) and *Fighting Words* (Merriam, 1992). Literal interpretations of figurative language is another example of enjoying literature. Books such as *Amelia Bedelia Goes Camping* (Parish, 1985) and *Amelia Bedelia's Family Album* (Parish, 1988) celebrate the use of literal interpretations of figurative language. Fred Gwynne's books *The King Who Rained* (1970), *A Little Pigeon Toad* (1988), and *A Chocolate Moose for Dinner* (1976) are other examples of this same type of humor. These picture books invite the life-long pursuit of reading for enjoyment for all ages.

9. *Literature provides models for writing.* Patterned language books give readers ideas for writing formats. Books such as *The Z Was Zapped* (Van Allsburg, 1987) show how an alliterative alphabet book can be written about any subject. Good writing in general gives readers models of various literary devices, such as two-level stories, unique points of view, and descriptive writing. For example, *Meanwhile, Back at the Ranch* (Noble, 1987) is a great example of a two-level story with two settings and stories told simultaneously. Different points of view are used in the picture book *Two Bad Ants* (Van Allsburg, 1988) and the novel *Shoebag* (James, 1990). *Two Bad Ants* is told from the ants' point of view, and *Shoebag* is told from a cockroach's point of view. Descriptive writing about simple things is evident in *Woodpile* (Parnall, 1990) and *Under Your Feet* (Ryder, 1990). All these books provide excellent models for readers and writers of all ages.

10. *Literature allows for the exposure to multicultural issues.* Multicultural literature can be a powerful vehicle for "the underlying purpose of multicultural education, to change the world by making it a more equitable one" (Bishop, 1992, p. 51). Picture books featuring African Americans, such as *Amazing Grace* (Hoffman, 1991), *BigMama's* (Crews, 1991), and *Aunt Flossie's Hats (and Crab Cakes Later)* (Howard, 1991), focus on common literary themes. Novels such as *The*

Friendship (Taylor, 1987) and *The Road to Memphis* (Taylor, 1990) deal with the struggles of racism in the United States.

Some picture books with Asian-Pacific American characters are *The Paper Crane* (Bang, 1985) and *The Lost Lake* (Say, 1989). Novels include *In the Year of the Boar and Jackie Robinson* (Lord, 1984) and *Grandfather's Journey* (Say, 1992). Native-American picture books include *The Legend of the Bluebonnet (dePaola, 1983), Itkomi and the Ducks* (Goble, 1990), *The Story of Jumping Mouse* (Steptoe, 1984), and *Dancing Teepees* (Sneve, 1989). Novels include *Indian Chiefs* (Freedman, 1987) and *Happily May I Walk* (Hirschfelder, 1986). These books are critical for inclusion in a classroom to support a celebration of diversity and pride in cultural heritages.

11. *Literature spans and enriches the entire curriculum.* Children's books enhance the study of content areas. For instance, the mathematical concept of multiplication and division is explored in *The Doorbell Rang* (Hutchins, 1986). Other picture books with mathematical concepts are *How Much Is a Million?* (Schwartz, 1986), *If You Made a Million* (Schwartz, 1989), *Ed Emberley's Picture Pie* (Emberley, 1984), *The Great Take-Away* (Mathews, 1980), *Fish Eyes: A Book You Can Count On* (Ehlert, 1990), *Eyewitness Books: Money* (Cribb, 1990), *26 Letters and 99 Cents* (Hoban, 1987), *Time to . . .* (McMillan, 1989), *All in a Day* (Anno et al., 1986), *Up to Ten and Down Again* (Ernst, 1986), *Ten Black Dots* (Crews, 1986), *Ten Potatoes in a Pot and Other Counting Rhymes* (Katz, 1990), and *Farmer Mack Measures His Pig* (Johnston, 1986).

For integration with social studies, *A Clearing in the Forest* (Henry, 1992) gives readers real insight into settling the frontier. Other pioneer historical fiction books include the following picture books: *Cassie's Journey* (Harvey, 1988), *My Prairie Year* (Harvey, 1986), *My Prairie Christmas* (Harvey, 1990), *Log Cabin in the Woods* (Henry, 1988), *Going West* (Van Leeuwen, 1992), *Lottie's Dream* (Pryor, 1992), and *Aurora Means Dawn* (Sanders, 1989). Novels include *Prairie Songs* (Conrad, 1985), *Westering* (Putnam, 1990), and *Grasshopper Summer* (Turner, 1989).

No study of dinosaurs in a science unit would be complete without enjoying and learning from the poems about dinosaurs in *Tyrannosaurus Was a Beast* (Prelutsky, 1988). Other dinosaur books for use in a dinosaur unit are picture books *Dinosaur Bones* (Aliki, 1988), *Dinosaur* (Hopkins, 1987), *Dinosaurs Walked Here and Other Stories Fossils Tell* (Lauber, 1987), *Patrick's Dinosaurs* (Carrick, 1983), and *Prehistoric Pinkerton* (Kellogg, 1987). Novels include *My Daniel* (Conrad, 1989) and *The Bone Wars* (Lasky, 1988).

12. *Literature allows readers to do more than just read a story; it also nurtures their imaginations.* Readers must add sounds, tastes, smells, and individual responses to the reading process, as Gary Paulsen (1989) points out in his introduction to *The Winter Room:* "If books could have more, give more, be more, show more, they would still need readers, who bring to them sound and smell and light and all the rest that can't be in books. The book needs you" (p. 3).

Books such as *Listen to the Rain* (Martin & Archambault, 1988), *Rain* (Spier, 1982), and *Rain Talk* (Serfozo, 1990) give the reader the sights, sounds, and smells associated with rain. And books such as Chris Van Allsburg's mysterious *The Wretched Stone* (1991) stretch readers imaginations and invite them to truly experience a book with all of their senses.

Reading is much more than decoding words on a page. Reading should be not only a process of making meaning but also *wanting* to read great books and to write about and discuss them with fellow readers. This definition of reading must alter the traditional teaching of reading and must include quality literature for students.

Organization of Book

This book will focus on ways in which literature can be used in the integration of reading and writing. Student examples and lesson plan ideas have been included to give a practical focus to the book.

Organizing a literature-based classroom is offered in Chapter 2. Ideas for grouping students beyond traditional reading groups are described, as well as other elements to consider in planning for instruction. Chapter 3 will describe how children's books are critical in the process of beginning reading. Chapter 4 will offer many examples of how literature can be used to enhance reading comprehension before, during, and after reading.

The writing process is examined in Chapter 5, with various links to literature provided throughout. Chapter 6 extends the process of writing to the response aspect of writing about literature. Chapter 7 explores the importance of poetry in a reading program, with varied examples of types of poetry and ways to involve students with this infectious aspect of language.

A description of teaching skills within this context is covered in Chapter 8 with many examples of children's books. Finally, Chapter 9 examines the issue of assessment within the context of a reading-writing classroom.

Many children's books are mentioned and included throughout this book. Extensive children's literature bibliographies can be found within or at the end of each chapter. Books noted with an asterisk (*) indicate multicultural themes. It is our belief that quality children's books make the difference in providing successful learning experiences for children.

References

Atwell, N. (1987). *In the middle: Writing, reading, and learning with adolescents.* Portsmouth, NH: Heinemann.

Becoming a nation of readers: The report of the commission on reading. (1985). Washington, DC: The National Institute of Education.

Bishop, R. S. (1992). Multicultural literature for children: Making informed choices. In J. V. Harris (Ed.), *Teaching multicultural literature in grades K–8* (pp. 37–53). Norwood, MA: Christopher-Gordon Publishers.

Calkins, L. M., & Harwayne, S. (1991). *Living between the lines.* Portsmouth, NH: Heinemann.

Fisher, B. (1991). *Joyful learning: A whole language kindergarten.* Portsmouth, NH: Heinemann.

Graves, D. H. (1991). *Build a literate classroom.* Portsmouth, NH: Heinemann.

Harste, J. C. (1989). *New policy guidelines for reading: Connecting research and practice.* Urbana, IL: National Council of Teachers of English.

Rief, L. (1992). *Seeking diversity: Language arts with adolescents.* Portsmouth, NH: Heinemann.

Routman, R. (1991). *Invitations: Changing as teachers and learners K–12.* Portsmouth, NH: Heinemann.

Children's Books

Abercrombie, B. (1990). *Charlie Anderson.* New York: McElderry.

Ackerman, K. (1991). *The leaves in October.* New York: Atheneum.

Aliki, (1988). *Dinosaur bones.* New York: Harper & Row.

*Anno, M., Carle, E., Briggs, R., Popov, N. Y., Hayashi, A., Calvi, G., Dillon, L., Dillon, D., Cheglian, Z., & Brooks, R. (1986). *All in a day*. New York: Philomel.

Baer, G. (1989). *Thump, thump, rat-a-tat-tat*. Ill. by Lois Ehlert. New York: Harper & Row.

*Baker, J. (1991). *Window*. New York: Greenwillow.

*Bang, M. (1985). *The paper crane*. New York: Greenwillow.

Bennett, D. (1990). *One cow, moo, moo*. Ill. by Andy Cooke. New York: Holt.

Birdseye, T. (1991). *Waiting for baby*. Ill. by Loreen Leedy. New York: Holiday House.

Brooks, B. (1991). *Nature by design*. New York: Farrar, Straus, Giroux.

*Brusca, M. C. (1991). *On the pampas*. New York: Henry Holt.

Bunting, E. (1989). *The Wednesday surprise*. Ill. by Donald Carrick. New York: Clarion.

Bunting, E. (1991). *Fly away home*. Ill. by Ronald Himler. New York: Clarion.

Butler, D. (1989). *My brown bear, Barney*. Ill. by Elizabeth Fuller. New York: Greenwillow.

Butler, D. (1993). *My brown bear Barney in trouble*. Ill. by Elizabeth Fuller. New York: Greenwillow.

Calmenson, S. (1989). *The principal's new clothes*. Ill. by Denise Brunkus. New York: Scholastic.

Carlstrom, N. (1986). *Jesse bear, what will you wear?* Ill. by Bruce Degen. New York: Macmillan.

Carrick, C. (1983). *Patrick's dinosaurs*. Ill. by Donald Carrick. Boston: Houghton Mifflin.

Christiansen, C. B. (1989). *My mother's house, my father's house*. Ill. by Irene Trivas. New York: Atheneum.

*Clifton, L. (1978). *Everett Anderson's nine month long*. Ill. by Ann Grifalconi. New York: Henry Holt.

Conrad, P. (1985). *Prairie songs*. New York: Harper & Row.

Conrad, P. (1989). *My Daniel*. New York: Harper & Row.

Crews, D. (1986). *Ten black dots*. New York: Greenwillow.

*Crews, D. (1991). *Bigmama's*. New York: Greenwillow.

*Cribb, J. (1990). *Eyewitness books: Money*. New York: Knopf.

Day, A. (1985). *Good dog, Carl*. New York: Simon and Schuster.

*dePaola, T. (1983). *The legend of the Bluebonnet*. New York: Putnams.

*Dooley, N. (1991). *Everybody cooks rice*. Minneapolis: Carolrhoda.

Dragonwagon, C. (1987). *Diana, maybe*. Ill. by Deborah Kogan Ray. New York: Macmillan.

Ehlert, L. (1989). *Color zoo*. New York: Lippincott.

Ehlert, L. (1989). *Eating the alphabet: Fruits and vegetables from A to Z*. San Diego: Harcourt Brace Jovanovich.

Ehlert, L. (1990). *Color farm*. New York: Lippincott.

Ehlert, L. (1990). *Fish eyes: A book you can count on*. San Diego: Harcourt Brace Jovanovich.

Emberley, E. (1984). *Ed Emberley's picture pie*. Boston: Little, Brown.

Ernst, L. C. (1986). *Up to ten and down again*. New York: Lothrop, Lee & Shepard.

Fiday, B., & Fiday, D. (1990). *Time to go*. Ill. by Thomas B. Allen. San Diego: Harcourt Brace Jovanovich.

Fox, M. (1985). *Wilfrid Gordon McDonald Partridge*. Ill. by Julie Vivas. New York: Kane/Miller.

*Freedman, R. (1987). *Indian chiefs.* New York: Holiday House.

Gibbons, G. (1990). *How a house is built.* New York: Holiday House.

Ginsburg, M. (1972). *The chick and the duckling.* Ill. by Jose and Ariane Aruego. New York: Macmillan.

*Goble, P. (1990). *Itkomi and the ducks.* New York: Orchard.

Grejniec, M. (1992). *What do you like?* New York: North-South Books.

Grove, V. (1988). *Good-bye my wishing star.* New York: Putnams.

Guarino, D. (1989). *Is your mama a llama?* Ill. by Steven Kellogg. New York: Scholastic.

Gwynne, F. (1970). *The king who rained.* New York: Prentice Hall.

Gwynne, F. (1976). *A chocolate moose for dinner.* New York: Prentice Hall.

Gwynne, F. (1988). *A little pigeon toad.* New York: Simon and Schuster.

Harvey, B. (1986). *My prairie year.* Ill. by Deborah Kogan Ray. New York: Holiday House.

Harvey, B. (1988). *Cassie's journey.* Ill. by Deborah Kogan Ray. New York: Holiday House.

Harvey, B. (1990). *My prairie Christmas.* Ill. by Deborah Kogan Ray. New York: Holiday House.

*Heide, F. P., & Gilliland, J. H. (1992). *Sami and the time of the troubles.* New York: Clarion.

Henry, J. L. (1988). *Log cabin in the woods.* Ill. by Joyce Audy Zarins. New York: Four Winds Press.

Henry, J. L. (1992). *A clearing in the forest.* New York: Four Winds Press.

*Hirschfelder, A. B. (1986). *Happily may I walk: American Indians and Alaska natives today.* New York: Scribners.

Hoban, T. (1987). *26 letters and 99 cents.* New York: Greenwillow.

Hoban, T. (1989). *Of colors and things.* New York: Greenwillow.

Hoban, T. (1990). *Exactly the opposite.* New York: Greenwillow.

Hoban, T. (1992). *Look up, look down.* New York: Greenwillow.

Hoban, T. (1992). *Spirals, curves, fanshapes & lines.* New York: Greenwillow.

*Hoffman, M. (1991). *Amazing Grace.* New York: Dial.

Hopkins, L. B. (1987). *Dinosaurs.* Ill. by Murray Tinkelman. San Diego: Harcourt Brace Jovanovich.

*Howard, E. F. (1991). *Aunt Flossie's hats (and crab cakes later).* New York: Clarion.

Hutchins, P. (1986). *The doorbell rang.* New York: Greenwillow.

*Isadora, R. (1992). *Over the green hills.* New York: Greenwillow.

James, M. (1990). *Shoebag.* New York: Scholastic.

Johnston, T. (1986). *Farmer Mack measures his pig.* Ill. by Megan Lloyd. New York: Harper & Row.

Jonas, A. (1983). *Round trip.* New York: Greenwillow.

Jonas, A. (1987). *Reflections.* New York: Greenwillow.

Jukes, M. (1985). *Blackberries in the dark.* Ill. by Thomas B. Allen. New York: Knopf.

Katz, M. J. (1990). *Ten potatoes in a pot and other counting rhymes.* Ill. by June Otani. New York: Harper & Row.

Keller, H. (1987). *Goodbye Max.* New York: Greenwillow.

Kellogg, S. (1987). *Prehistoric Pinkerton.* New York: Dial.

Lakin, P. (1985). *Don't touch my room.* Ill. by Patience Brewster. Boston: Little, Brown.

*Lankford, M. D. (1992). *Hopscotch around the world.* New York: Morrow.

Lasky, K. (1988). *The bone wars.* New York: Morrow.

Lasky, K. (1988). *Sea swan*. Ill. by Catherine Stock. New York: Macmillan.

Lauber, P. (1987). *Dinosaurs walked here and other stories fossils tell*. New York: Bradbury.

Lobel, A. (1990). *Alison's zinnia*. New York: Dial.

Locker, T. (1988). *Family farm*. New York: Dial.

Lockwood, P. (1989). *Cat boy!* Ill. by Clara Vulliamy. New York: Clarion.

*Lord, B. B. (1984). *In the year of the boar and Jackie Robinson*. New York: Harper & Row.

*Lowry, L. (1989). *Number the stars*. Boston: Houghton Mifflin.

Macaulay, D. (1988). *The way things work*. Boston: Houghton Mifflin.

Macaulay, D. (1990). *Black and white*. Boston: Houghton Mifflin.

MacLachlan, P. (1985). *Sarah, plain and tall*. New York: Harper & Row.

Martin, B. (1991). *Polar bear, polar bear, what do you hear?* Ill. by Eric Carle. New York: Holt.

Martin, B., & Archambault, J. (1988). *Listen to the rain*. New York: Holt.

Martin, B., & Archambault, J. (1989). *Chicka chicka boom boom*. Ill. by Lois Ehlert. New York: Simon and Schuster.

Mathews, L. (1980). *The great take-away*. Ill. by Jeni Bassett. New York: Dodd.

McMillan, B. (1989). *Time to . . . .* New York: Lothrop, Lee & Shepard.

Merriam, E. (1989). *Chortles*. Ill. by Sheila Hamanaka. New York: Morrow.

Merriam. E. (1992). *Fighting words*. Ill. by David Small. New York: Morrow.

*Morris, A. (1989). *Bread, bread, bread*. Photos by Ken Heyman. New York: Lothrop, Lee & Shepard.

*Morris, A. (1989). *Hats, hats, hats*. Photos by Ken Heyman. New York: Lothrop, Lee & Shepard.

Neitzel, S. (1989). *The jacket I wear in the snow*. New York: Greenwillow.

Neitzel, S. (1992). *The dress I'll wear to the party*. Ill. by Nancy Winslow Parker. New York: Greenwillow.

Noble, T. H. (1987). *Meanwhile, back at the ranch*. Ill. by Tony Ross. New York: Dial.

Parish, P. (1985). *Amelia Bedelia goes camping*. Ill. by Lynn Sweat. New York: Greenwillow.

Parish, P. (1988). *Amelia Bedelia's family album*. Ill. by Lynn Sweat. New York: Greenwillow.

Parnall, P. (1990). *Woodpile*. New York: Macmillan.

Paulsen, G. (1989). *The winter room*. New York: Orchard.

Peek, M. (1985). *Mary wore her red dress*. New York: Clarion.

Prelutsky, J. (1988). *Tyrannosaurus was a beast*. New York: Greenwillow.

Pryor, B. (1992). *Lottie's dream*. Ill. by Mark Graham. New York: Simon and Schuster.

Putnam. A, (1990). *Westering*. New York: Lodestar.

Rocklin, J. (1988). *Dear baby*. New York: Macmillan.

Roe, E. (1990). *All I am*. New York: Bradbury.

Ryder, J. (1990). *Under your feet*. New York: Four Winds.

Sanders, S. R. (1989). *Aurora means dawn*. Ill. by Jill Kastner. New York: Bradbury.

*Say, A. (1989). *The lost lake*. Boston: Houghton Mifflin.

*Say, A. (1992). *Grandfather's journey*. Boston: Houghton Mifflin.

Schwartz, D. M. (1986). *How much is a million?* Ill. by Steven Kellogg. New York: Lothrop, Lee & Shepard.

Schwartz, D. M. (1989). *If you made a million*. Ill. by Steven Kellogg. New York: Lothrop, Lee & Shepard.

Scieszka, J. (1989). *The true story of the three little pigs.* Ill. by Lane Smith. New York: Viking.

Scieszka, J. (1991). *The frog prince continued.* New York: Viking.

Scieszka, J. (1992). *The stinky cheese man and other fairly stupid tales.* Ill. by Lane Smith. New York: Viking.

Serfozo, M. (1990). *Rain talk.* New York: McElderry.

Shaw, N. (1986). *Sheep in a jeep.* Boston: Houghton Mifflin.

Smith, R. K. (1987). *Mostly Michael.* New York: Delacorte.

*Sneve, V. D. H. (Ed.). (1989). *Dancing teepees: Poems of American Indian youth.* Ill. by Stephen Gammell. New York: Holiday House.

Spier, P. (1982). *Rain.* Garden City, NY: Doubleday.

*Steptoe, J. (1984). *The story of jumping mouse.* New York: Lothrop, Lee & Shepard.

Tafuri, N. (1988). *Spots, feathers, and curly tails.* New York: Greenwillow.

*Taylor, M. D. (1987). *The friendship.* New York: Dial.

*Taylor, M. D. (1990). *The road to Memphis.* New York: Dial.

Turner, A. (1989). *Grasshopper summer.* New York: Macmillan.

Van Allsburg, C. (1981). *Jumanji.* Boston: Houghton Mifflin.

Van Allsburg, C. (1985). *The polar express.* Boston: Houghton Mifflin.

Van Allsburg, C. (1987). *The z was zapped.* Boston: Houghton Mifflin.

Van Allsburg, C. (1988). *Two bad ants.* Boston: Houghton Mifflin.

Van Allsburg, C. (1991). *The wretched stone.* Boston: Houghton Mifflin.

Van Leeuwen, J. (1992). *Going west.* Ill. by Thomas B. Allen. New York: Dial.

Wiesner, D. (1991). *Tuesday.* New York: Clarion.

Williams, S. (1989). *I went walking.* Ill. by Julie Vivas. San Diego: Harcourt Brace Jovanovich.

Wood, J. (1992). *Moo moo, brown cow.* San Diego: Harcourt Brace Jovanovich.

Yektai, N. (1987). *Bears in pairs.* Ill. by Diane deGroat. New York: Bradbury.

*Young, E. (1989). *Lon Po Po: A Red-Riding Hood story from China.* New York: Philomel.

*Indicates multicultural focus.

2

Organizing a Literature-Based Reading-Writing Classroom

Conditions for Learning

Theoretical aspects of encouraging language learning must be considered in the organization of a reading-writing classroom. Cambourne (1988) describes the conditions for learning that exist for children learning to speak in a nonthreatening, natural home environment. These conditions for learning to speak can also be thought of as the theoretical conditions necessary for children's reading and writing development. These conditions are: immersion, demonstration, engagement, expectation, responsibility, approximation, use, and response.

Immersion refers to the way in which babies are immersed in oral language. Babies hear oral language from family members and other adults, television, radio, and so on. This immersion exposes them to a variety of different types of language. Reading and writing programs should immerse students in print as well. Books, magazines, writing materials—are all important in this condition of learning.

Demonstrations occur when babies are shown objects and given the label for them. "Here is your bottle," parents tell children as they hand them the bottle. Teachers need to demonstrate language in a similar way. Demonstrations could include sharing a reading strategy, introducing an unfamiliar concept, or shadowing the print as the teacher reads a big book aloud to young children.

Meaningful activities that encourage *engagement* provide successful and enjoyable experiences for children. Teachers need to provide these experiences with print and allow students to be successful in reading and writing to encourage this engagement with print.

All parents have the *expectation* that children will learn to talk. The same should be true of writing and reading. Teachers should expect students to be readers and writers, not only allowing them time every day for choice reading and writing but also treating them as real readers and writers.

Responsibility includes the right to make some choices about reading and writing. Children must read and write in the manner that is developmentally appropriate for them. Children can be responsible for being engaged in a variety of reading and writing activities.

Parents accept *approximations* of children as they begin to speak. When a young child says "ball," parents often hand them the ball and say "Throw me the ball." This expansion and extension of language occurs naturally. No parent expects a child to utter grammatically correct complete sentences when they are just learning to speak. The same attitude of acceptance is needed with children's approximations of written language as well. Developmental spellings must be encouraged and accepted for younger children as they develop the conventions of print.

Children will learn to read and write by *using* print. Reading and writing breed reading and writing. Thus, purposeful reading and writing must be the core of a reading-writing program.

Response includes feedback, such as the positive reinforcement parents give young children as they begin to speak. Teachers need also to respond positively to what children are trying to do by reinforcing the children's attempts and allowing them time to share their reading and writing with others.

These conditions of learning can be incorporated into classroom organization plans. Fisher (1991) describes the way in which she organizes her whole-language kindergarten class by including shared reading and choice reading. *Shared reading* includes teacher modeling and demonstrations in whole-group settings. *Choice reading* allows students to select books of their own for reading. Students are engaged in reading in a variety of ways and for a variety of purposes.

Shared writing and choice writing are two other ways to think of classroom organization. *Shared writing,* like shared reading, includes teacher modeling and demonstrating strategies of writing. *Choice writing* gives students time to write about topics of importance to them individually. Some examples of activities to include in these four organizational categories (shared reading, choice reading, shared writing, and choice writing) follow.

SHARED READING ACTIVITIES

1. *Familiar stories and poems.* Show the illustrations of a familiar story in big-book format, such as *Rosie's Walk* (Hutchins, 1968) and have the students recite Rosie's actions around the barnyard.

2. *Reading aloud.* Ask students to make predictions about what will happen in the book. Have them examine the cover of the book, the title, the title page, and other parts of the book to help them in their predictions. While reading the book aloud to students, revise the predictions as necessary. The following picture books are especially good for this because they have clues on the cover yet have a twist to the story:

- Bunting, E. (1989). *The Wednesday surprise.* New York: Clarion. (The cover shows a young girl and her grandmother reading a book. The twist is that the young girl teaches her grandmother how to read.)
- Calmenson, S. (1989). *The principal's new clothes.* New York: Scholastic. (The cover shows the principal being fitted for new clothes. The twist is that the book is a contemporary version of "The Emperor's New Clothes" set in an elementary school.)
- Marshall, J. (1986). *Yummers too: The second course.* Boston: Houghton Mifflin. (The cover shows Emily and Eugene eating in a Chinese restaurant. The twist is that that book is a sequel to *Yummers* [Marshall, 1973] and is about Emily trying to work off a debt to Eugene and to control her overeating.)
- Wild, M. (1991). *Let the celebrations begin!* New York: Orchard. (The cover

shows some thin children playing with home-made toys. The twist to the story is that the children are celebrating the liberation of their concentration camp after World War II. This would be a good picture book to use with older students.)

3. *Storytelling.* Tell stories to children and use simple props. For instance, a basket of goodies and a red scarf could be on hand while telling the story of "Little Red Riding Hood." Nesting cats could be used to tell the story of the enlarging cat in *The Fat Cat* (Kent, 1971). Encourage students to use simple props as they retell their favorite stories.

4. *Poetry and songs.* At least one poem or song should be shared daily with all children. Poems can be displayed on charts, bulletin boards, or the overhead projector so that all students can see and recite the poem together. (See Chapter 7 for recommended poetry books and strategies.)

5. *Puppetry.* Puppetry can be used as a way to involve all children in the reading of a book. After reading the book the first time, have the students make puppets for each of the characters. Students can then manipulate the puppets and read the parts of the characters during a second reading of the book. Or students could be encouraged to write their own stories or plays for their puppets to perform. *The Little Pigs' Puppet Book* (Watson, 1990) includes directions for putting on a puppet play, including writing a script and making puppets. This helpful resource should be made available for young children. See Figure 2–1 for puppetry examples.

Books for puppetry involvement should include much dialogue and repetition for younger children. Although most children's books can be easily adapted for puppetry, the following are good choices for beginning puppetry with students:

- Aliki. (1984). *Feelings.* New York: Greenwillow.
- Aliki. (1990). *Manners.* New York: Greenwillow.
- Carle, E. (1977). *The grouchy ladybug.* New York: Scholastic.
- Fox, M. (1987). *Hattie and the fox.* New York: Bradbury.
- Kellogg, S. (1985). *Chicken little.* New York: Morrow.
- Wood, J. (1992). *Moo moo, brown cow.* San Diego: Harcourt Brace Jovanovich.

CHOICE READING ACTIVITIES

1. *Book Talks.* Short commercials for books or book talks encourage students to read a variety of different books. For example, for younger children, encourage them to bring a teddy bear to school. Display the teddy bear with a variety of books about bears. Introduce the books by showing the covers and giving a brief summary of each of the books. Encourage students to read the books during their choice reading time.

Bear Books
- Asch, F. (1982). *Happy birthday, moon.* New York: Prentice Hall.
- Bellows, C. (1991). *The grizzly sisters.* New York: Macmillan.
- Bond, M. (1992). *Michael Bond's book of bears.* New York: Aladdin.
- Browne, A. (1989). *Bear goes to town.* New York: Doubleday.

Figure 2–1 Puppetry Examples

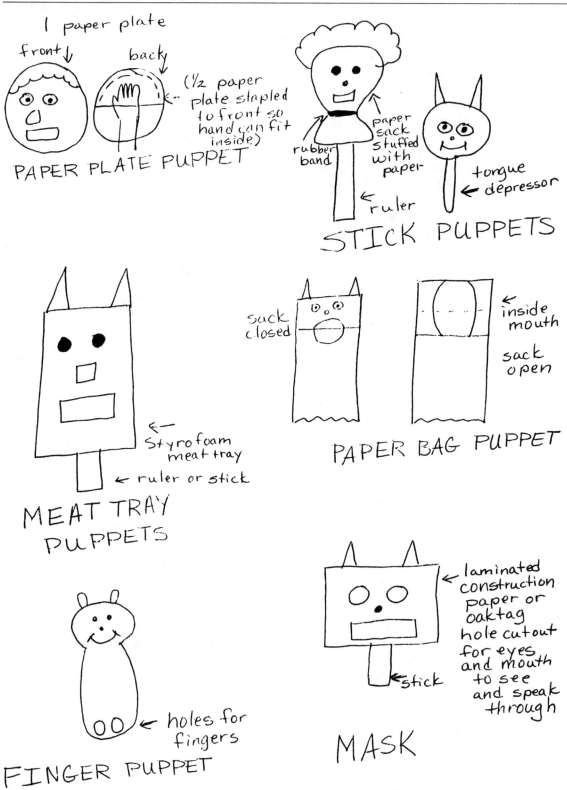

- Butler, D. (1988). *My brown bear, Barney.* New York: Greenwillow.
- Butler, D. (1993). *My brown bear Barney in trouble.* New York: Greenwillow.
- Goldstein, B. S. (1989). *Bear in mind: A book of bear poems.* New York: Viking.
- Gretz, S. (1986). *Teddy bears ABC.* New York: Four Winds.
- Gretz, S. (1986). *Teddy bears 1 to 10.* New York: Four Winds.
- Hague, K. (1989). *Bear hugs.* New York: Henry Holt.
- Inkpen, M. (1991). *Threadbear.* Boston: Little, Brown.
- MacGregor, M. (1987). *Helen and the hungry bear.* New York: Four Winds.
- Patent, D. H. (1987). *The way of the grizzly.* New York: Clarion.
- Wells, R. (1983). *Peabody.* New York: Dial.
- Yektai, N. (1987). *Bears in pairs.* New York: Bradbury.
- Yolen, J. (1990). *Baby bear's bedtime book.* San Diego: Harcourt Brace Jovanovich.

For older students, the following items could be put in a large bag: a sleeping bag, alarm clock, flashlight, peanut butter, and two slices of bread. Pull these items out of the bag and tell the students that all of these things mysteriously disappear from Marcus Mullen's house in *Is Anybody There?* (Bunting, 1988). Invite students to read the book and find out who took the items and why. Display this book with other mystery books for older students.

Mystery Books
- Base, G. (1989). *The eleventh hour.* New York: Abrams.
- Brittain, B. (1989). *My buddy, the king.* New York: Harper.
- Bunting, E. (1988). *Is anybody there?* New York: Harper.
- Conford, E. (1988). *A case for Jenny Archer.* Boston: Little, Brown.
- Conrad, P. (1990). *Stonewords.* New York: Harper.
- DeFelice, C. C. (1988). *The strange night writing of Jessamine Colter.* New York: Macmillan.
- Haas, E. A. (1982). *Incognito Mosquito, private insective.* New York: Random House.
- Haas, E. A. (1985). *Incognito Mosquito flies again.* New York: Random House.
- Haas, E. A. (1986). *Incognito Mosquito takes to the air.* New York: Random House.
- Howe, D., & Howe, J. (1979). *Bunnicula.* New York: Atheneum.
- Howe, J. (1982). *Howliday Inn.* New York: Atheneum.
- Howe, J. (1983). *The celery stalks at midnight.* New York: Atheneum.

- Howe, J. (1987). *Nighty-nightmare*. New York: Atheneum.

- Van Allsburg, C. (1984). *The mysteries of Harris Burdick*. Boston: Houghton Mifflin.

- Yolen, J. (1987). *Piggins*. San Diego: Harcourt Brace Jovanovich.

- Yolen, J. (1988). *Picnic with Piggins*. San Diego: Harcourt Brace Jovanovich.

- Yolen, J. (1988). *Piggins and the royal wedding*. San Diego: Harcourt Brace Jovanovich.

Another way to invite students to read books during their free time is simply to read the first page of a picture book or the first chapter of a novel. This often whets students' appetites for reading a book on their own. Students should also be encouraged to do book talks and to tell others about good books they have read.

2. *Silent reading time.* Set aside 15 to 30 minutes each day for silent reading time when students chose what they want to read. Adopt a name for this time, such as SSR (Sustained Silent Reading), BEAR (Be Excited About Reading), SQUIRT (Super Quiet Uninterrupted Reading Time), or DEAR (Drop Everything and Read). During this time, students and the teacher should be quietly reading for pleasure a book of their own choosing.

3. *Children's magazines.* Many fine children's magazines are available for children's reading during choice time. These magazines range from science magazines, such as *Ranger Rick* for younger students and *National Geographic World* for older students, to literary magazines with quality stories, such as *Ladybug* for younger children and *Cricket* for older students. (See the References section for a list of children's magazines.)

4. *Children's paperback book clubs.* Encourage parents and students to order their own copies of quality children's books at reduced prices in book clubs. An accompanying note about the highest-quality books or recommended titles along with the order forms would be helpful to parents and children as they decide which books they might like to order. (See the References section for addresses of book clubs.)

SHARED WRITING ACTIVITIES

1. *Mini-lessons.* Mini-lessons teach a skill or strategy of writing in a short period of time. Calkins (1986) suggests they be used to address a writing issue for the whole class or several writers in the class. For instance, if students are trying to write dialogue in their own writing and are having difficulty with quotation marks and punctuation, the teacher may want to do a mini-lesson on the use of quotation marks. Books with much dialogue in them provide wonderful examples for students. For younger children, *Hattie and the Fox* (Fox, 1987) has much repetition of dialogue and examples of quotation marks and punctuation marks. For older students, *Attaboy, Sam* (Lowry, 1992) provides rich dialogue that could also serve as an example to students.

Mini-lessons can also focus on stretching vocabulary or generating interest in words in general. For instance, books such as *Alison's Zinnia* (Lobel, 1990), *Counting Wildflowers* (McMillan, 1986), *Planting a Rainbow* (Ehlert, 1988), and *Chrysanthemum* (Henkes, 1991) feature flower names. Students could bring in other unusual flower words and add to a bulletin board or chart. These words can serve as a vocabulary lesson for students or as spelling words that students may want to learn.

2. *Literature examples or models.* Many books model a type of writing that children may want to try themselves. Teachers should first do some whole-group writing with students before having students write on their own in this manner. For example, *In a Dark, Dark, Wood* (Carter, 1991) follows a repetitive pattern. As a whole group, students might write another story with this pattern:

> In a red red school,
> There was a big big library,
> And an old old book,
> With yellow yellow pages,
> And on the last last page
> Was a furry furry spider!

Chocolate Chip Cookies (Wagner, 1990) tells how to make cookies using verbs alone. Students might try writing riddles about other tasks using only verbs, such as:

collect	*agitate*
sort	*spin*
dump	*transfer*
add	*dry*
rinse	*fold*

(Answer: Doing the laundry)

3. *Response to literature.* Children's books often serve as a stimulus for writing about similar or common experiences. For instance, Judith Viorst's *Earrings!* (1990) tells about a girl who desperately wants earrings. Figure 2–2 shows what a third-grade boy was inspired to write after the reading of this book.

CHOICE WRITING ACTIVITIES

1. *Silent writing time.* Time should be set aside every day for students and the teacher to write for their own purposes. This may take the form of a personal journal, poetry, or another form of writing. The form and topic of the writing should be left up to the child. The time set aside for daily silent writing must be a constant. Children must know that every day they will have the time to write whatever they would like. This time might be 5 to 10 minutes for younger children and 10 to 20 minutes for older students.

2. *Sharing.* Students must have an opportunity to share what they have written in a writers' workshop. This sharing can be done formally, such as in the author's chair, or informally with students reading their writing to a partner. (See Chapter 5 and 6 for further details.)

Ability Grouping

Traditional classroom organization for reading and writing focused on grouping children for reading according to their ability and on teacher selection of

Figure 2–2 Third-Grader's Response to *Earrings* (Viorst, 1990)

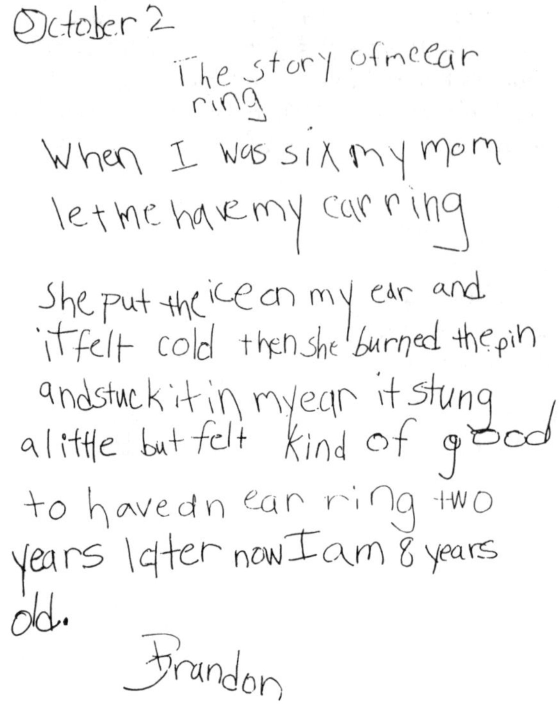

October 2

The story of me ear ring

When I was six my mom let me have my ear ring

She put the ice on my ear and it felt cold then she burned the pin and stuck it in my ear it stung a little but felt kind of good

to have an ear ring two years later now I am 8 years old.

Brandon

topics for writing. Reading groups based on reading ability have recently been questioned in terms of the effectiveness of that practice. Ability grouping does not increase students' achievement; in fact, it may have a very negative impact on self-concept and potential achievement of students in lower groups (Morgan, 1989; Slavin, 1987).

> *Having three reading groups makes sense only if a teacher believes in the assumptions underlying ability grouping: that all learning should progress in a linear manner, that a teacher has the sole responsibility for supporting each student in the class, and that the stigma attached to being grouped is negligible. . . . We hold the beliefs that learners need to have choices that allow them to make connections and develop their own courses for learning, that learners in a community should support one another, and that every student brings a unique and equally valuable contribution to the dynamics of the learning community. (Berghoff & Egawa, 1991, p. 537)*

Literature Discussion Groups

An alternative to traditional ability grouping is literature discussion groups. Literature discussion groups occur when students work in heterogeneous groups to discuss the books that they are reading. The placement in groups can be done randomly or according to the number of students reading the same book at a given time. Students read the books independently and then meet together in literature discussion groups to talk about what they have read. Literature logs may be used for students to record their comments and questions about the reading prior to coming to the group to discuss it. These literature logs allow students to write about what they read in meaningful manner (Danielson, 1992).

Figure 2–3 is a transcript of a fifth-grade literature discussion group about *The Not-Just-Anybody Family* (Byars, 1986). Descriptions of the responses are noted in brackets throughout the transcript. In order to understand the context of the discussion, a brief summary of the book is necessary. *The Not-Just-Anybody Family* is about the Blossom family, which is composed of Pap, his grandchildren (Maggie, Vern, and Junior), and his daughter-in-law, Vickie, who is currently on the rodeo circuit. In the chapter that is being discussed in Figure 2–3, Pap has been arrested after a series of unusual circumstances. He was driving his pickup truck loaded with bags of empty cans when he had to stop suddenly to avoid hitting a car. He slammed on his brakes, which caused the bags of cans to fall out of his pickup. Then two teenagers in a Toyota ran over the bags, sending the cans all over the street. Pap grabbed for his gun to hit the retreating Toyota when he accidently hit the stoplight instead. The people on the street went wild and called the police.

Figure 2–3   Transcript of Fifth-Grade Literature Discussion Group

Teacher: Let's look at the chapter called "2,147 Beer and Pop Cans." What were some of your feelings about this chapter?

[THE TEACHER BEGINS THE DISCUSSION WITH AN OPEN-ENDED INVITATION TO RESPOND.]

Ann: They shouldn't have arrested Pap.

Tom: Yeah, it wasn't his fault.

Susan: But he shot a gun!

[STUDENTS VOICE THEIR OWN OPINIONS ABOUT THE EVENTS OF THIS CHAPTER.]

Teacher: Why did he shoot the gun? Can you find the part in the book that describes that?

[THE TEACHER DIRECTS STUDENTS BACK TO THE TEXT TO SUPPORT THEIR OPINIONS.]

Ann: See on page 21 (she reads): "At that moment two teenaged boys in a Toyota cut around the corner. Pap turned with a frown. The boys ran into the bags like kids hitting a leaf pile. It looked to Pap like they had done it on purpose.

"The boys were laughing. The driver threw the Toyota into reverse, U-turned, and took off.

"Pap reached into the back of his truck for his shotgun. He fired one shot at the retreating Toyota, but he hit the traffic light down the street. It exploded and left some wires sizzling and popping over the Sumter Avenue intersection.

"Two of the bags were busted, and Pap was standing over them, worrying about his $107.35, when he saw some people on the sidewalk. He turned to the people with a frown. He was thinking about asking for some help, even though asking for help was hard for him.

"The people, however, thought he was pointing the shotgun at them" (p. 21).

[STUDENT REREADS PORTION OF THE CHAPTER FOR A PURPOSE—FOR CLARITY IN UNDERSTANDING THE CONTEXT OF THE SITUATION.]

Peter: He shot at the air and missed.

Ann: I think he was shooting at the tires.

Susan: He shot at the taillights of the Toyota.

John: No, I think he was shooting at the driver.

[STUDENTS VOICE DIFFERENCES IN INTERPRETING THE STORY EVENTS.]

Teacher: Does Pap seem like the type of person to do that?

(Continued)

Figure 2–3 *(Continued)*

Susan: I can't see him being like that.

Teacher: From what we've read about Pap, I can't picture him doing that either.

[TEACHER AND STUDENTS VOICE OWN OPINIONS OF CHARACTER'S ACTIONS BASED ON WHAT THEY KNOW ABOUT HIM FROM THE TEXT.]

Tom: I felt sorry for Pap. Nobody gave him a chance to explain.

Teacher: Did anyone feel angry in this chapter?

Susan: Yeah, when they put him in jail.

Teacher: I was mad at the boys who ran into the trash cans and then drove away. How would the story have been different if they hadn't come along?

Ann: I would have yelled, "Why don't y'all help me here!"

[STUDENT SHOWS PERSONAL ENGAGEMENT WITH THE TEXT.]

Peter: Maybe they would have helped him pick up the cans and he wouldn't have been thrown in jail.

[STUDENT MAKES A PREDICTION BASED ON A DIFFERENT INTERPRETATION OF THE TEXT.]

Teacher: Another group mentioned that Pap used a single-barrel shotgun.

[TEACHER SUBTLY ADDS AN IMPORTANT PIECE OF INFORMATION.]

Tom: That means he can only shoot one bullet at a time.

Susan: So he couldn't have been shooting at the people, just the car.

[STUDENTS ARE ALLOWED TO INFER AND COME TO THEIR OWN CONCLUSIONS ABOUT THE SITUATION.]

Teacher: Would you take time to look at the shotgun if you were being shot at?

Susan: No.

Tom: The people must not have noticed that. They were too scared.

Teacher: Any other comments on this chapter?

Susan: Yeah, look on page 21 at the bottom (she reads): "He was trying to gather up the cans and get them back into the truck by himself when the police arrived—two carloads, sirens screaming." When I read that, it sounded like the people were all gathering around him. That was a good description.

[STUDENT REREADS THE TEXT FOR PURE APPRECIATION OF DESCRIPTIVE LANGUAGE.]

John: Yeah, Betsy Byars is a good writer—she makes you feel like you were there.

[STUDENT MENTIONS AUTHOR'S NAME AND MAKES A JUDGMENT ABOUT HER WRITING ABILITY.]

Routman (1991) cites the following as beneficial outcomes of literature discussion groups: Listening skills and comprehension improve, at-risk and low-ability students succeed, students take ownership, and the teacher has time for critical observation of the discussions. In addition, Short (1990), Eeds and Wells (1989), Harste, Short, and Burke (1988), and O'Flahavan (1988) also describe the benefits and varied uses of these discussion groups.

When organizing such groups, the following suggestions are offered:

1. The group size should be between four to six students so that all students will feel comfortable participating.

2. Meetings among literature discussion groups should occur as often as necessary. For novels, students could meet twice a week to discuss several chapters. For picture books, students could also meet twice, once before the reading to make predictions and to draw on prior knowledge, and then after the reading to discuss their impressions.

3. The teacher is the facilitator of the group. The teacher models by responding to the literature with his or her opinions. Written responses that students have kept in a literature log can be the stimulus for the discussion. The students themselves can guide the discussion with their own comments. With older students, a leader or recorder can be selected to report back to the teacher what the group has discussed.

4. Provide some suggestions or prompts for writing to facilitate student engagement in the literature logs. Students who are not used to writing about literature often have difficulty understanding what it is they are supposed to write. These students need some guidance in terms of possible writing responses. Figure 2–4 shows some sample questions that might provide a model for students to follow as they write in their literature logs. These questions should be seen as possibilities only, not as assigned questions. If students are having difficulty deciding what to write or talk about in their literature groups, they could, as a group, decide on two or three questions to respond to in their journals and then discuss their responses to these questions in their discussion groups.

5. Quality literature must be used for the discussion groups so that students are exposed to engaging texts that encourage discussion. Books with trite plots or very little character development do not lend themselves to literature discussion.

Figure 2–4 Literature Log Questions and Prompts

1. What do you notice about this book?
2. How does the story make you feel?
3. What does the story remind you of?
4. If you were going to tell someone about this book, what three things would you tell them and why?
5. Did your feelings about what you were reading change as you read the book? If so, why?
6. What would you ask the author about this story?
7. What was your favorite part of this book? Why was it your favorite part?
8. Where do you think the story takes place? How do you know?
9. When does the story take place? How do you know?
10. How does the author create suspense in this book?
11. Who is your favorite character? Why?
12. Who do you think was the most important character in this book? Why?
13. Do any of the characters remind you of characters in other books? Which ones and why?
14. What is the mood created in this story? How is it done?
15. Is this story like any other story you have read? How?
16. What do you think will happen next in the story? Why?
17. Who tells this story? Would the story be different if someone else told it? How?
18. Did the author give you clues about the ending of the story? If so, what were they?
19. Does the story end the way you expected it to? Why or why not?
20. If a friend asked you about this story, what would you say?

Source: Adapted from Sloan (1984), Kelly (1990), Bleich (1978), and Kelly and Farnan (1991).

Text Sets

Text sets could also be used for the grouping of students, as they read books with common themes. In the References section, several lists of books are organized by theme and grade levels. Students could read one or more of the books on the list and then meet with students who have read other books on the list. Using the prompts or questions listed in Figure 2–4, each student could write entries in literature logs about the story. Or students could complete a comparison chart (Wendelin & Danielson, 1991), like those in Figures 2–5 and 2–6. Figure 2–5 shows a comparison chart that could be used for a specific fairy tale, such as "Little Red Riding Hood"; Figure 2–6 shows a comparison chart that could be used for any story. These charts or literature logs could then be discussed in a literature discussion group. Refer to the lists of books that have related themes (in the References section). These books could be used in conjunction with the chart shown in Figure 2–6.

Themed Web

Another way to organize instruction in a literature-based classroom is through the use of a themed web. One topic can provide a variety of related activities and books. The teacher can design the web and then present it to students. Students could choose to read several of the books and complete some of the activities or they could be invited to come up with their own ideas related to the topic to add to the web. Some activities of the web could be done with the whole class, whereas others could be projects for small groups or individual students to complete. (Note: *The Web* [Wonderfully Exciting Books], published by Ohio State University, is an excellent resource. Many examples of thematic webs for various grade levels are included.)

A themed web may be done with an author, a content area topic to integrate the language arts, or a book. An example of each of these follows.

Figure 2–5 Comparison Chart for "Little Red Riding Hood"

Book Title	Characters	Setting	Items in Basket	Ending	Illustrations

Figure 2–6 Comparison Chart for Other Stories with Similar Themes

Book Title	Characters	Setting	Plot/ Problem	Resolution/ Ending	Illustrations

MEM FOX WEB

Figure 2–7 shows a web for primary grades that focuses on an author – Mem Fox.

Information about the Author

1. Watch "Trumpet Video Visit: Mem Fox" and list five things learned about Mem Fox.

2. Write to a publisher of Mem Fox's books and ask for any free information on the author. (Harcourt Brace Jovanovich, 1250 Sixth Avenue, San Diego, CA 92101)

3. Write Mem Fox a personal letter or send a class letter to her via her publisher. Remember to send a stamped, self-addressed envelope.

Resources

"Trumpet Video Visit: Mem Fox"
Dear Mem Fox, I Have Read All Your Books, Even the Pathetic Ones

Australia

1. Mem Fox lives in Australia. Read other books written by Australian authors.

2. Make a list of words learned from these books that relate to Australia. Categorize them according to animals, food, cities, and so on.

3. Locate a map of Australia. Find the cities mentioned in the book *Possum Magic* (Fox, 1987). Taste some of the Australian food in this book, if possible.

Figure 2–7 Mem Fox Web

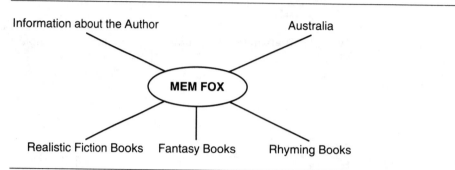

Resources
   Possum Magic
   Koala Lou
   Wombat Stew
   Happy Birthday, Wombat!
   My Grandma Lived in Gooligulch
   Kangaroos
   The Country Mail Is Coming: People From Down Under Where the Forest
      Meets the Sea
   Window
   Educating Arthur
   Who Wants Arthur?
   The Idle Bear
   Farmer Schultz's Ducks
   My Place
   The Very Best of Friends
   The Sugar Gum Tree
   Grandad's Magic
   Koala
   Australia

Realistic Fiction Books

1. Read *Wilfrid Gordon McDonald Partridge* (Fox, 1985) and *The Remembering Box* (Clifford, 1985). What are the similarities and differences of these books?
2. Vote on which book is the favorite and why.
3. Create memory boxes as Wilfrid did in *Wilfrid Gordon McDonald Partridge*.
4. Read *Night Noises* (Fox, 1989) and write about a special birthday surprise.
5. Create a list of other sound words, as in *Night Noises*.

Resources
   Wilfrid Gordon McDonald Partridge
   Night Noises
   The Remembering Box

Fantasy Books

1. Read *With Love, at Christmas* (Fox, 1988) and then tell or write about a favorite Christmas present.

2. Read *Hattie and the Fox* (Fox, 1987) and talk about surprises. Write about a special or unusual surprise.

3. Read *Koala Lou* (Fox, 1988) and discuss sibling rivalry. Write about what makes each person unique and special.

Resources
   With Love at Christmas
   Hattie and the Fox
   Koala Lou

Rhyming Books

1. Read *Shoes from Grandpa* (Fox, 1990) and list different types of clothes.

2. Read other stories told in rhyme.

3. Write a class story told in rhyme, such as:
   Once upon a time,
   David found a dime.
   He put it in his shoe.
   And bought a stick of glue.

Resources
   Shoes from Grandpa
   Sheep in a Shop
   Sheep Out to Eat
   'Twas the Night Before Thanksgiving
   Santa Cows

USA WEB

Figure 2–8 shows a web for intermediate grades that focuses on a content area—studying the United States.

Writing

1. Start a pen pal exchange with students in other states. Send objects typical of your state and ask the pen pals to do the same. (Write to Student Letter

Figure 2–8 United States Themed Web

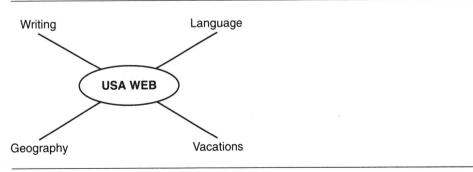

Exchange, 215 5th Avenue S.E., Waseca, MN 56093 and ask for Student Letter Exchange Order Form for information.)

2. Write an entry in your journal about the states you have been to, your favorite state, or the state you would most like to visit.

Language

1. Study the diversity of language within our country.

2. Survey 10 people to find out what they call the following terms, then discuss the diversity found.
   a. Large piece of stuffed furniture found in a living room (couch, daven-port, sofa, divan, loveseat)
   b. Carbonated beverage (pop, soda, Coke, soft drink, soda pop)
   c. Large sandwich with large rolls and many ingredients (poor boy, hero, grinder, hoagie, sub, submarine, topedo)

3. Try to determine the meaning of the Hawaiian Da Kine dialect (see Figure 2–9).

4. Research other American dialects.

Vacations

1. Collect postcards from various states.

2. Write letters or keep notes as you go on trips around the United States.

3. Make a list of items to take on a vacation.

4. Make some travel games that could be played in a car.

Resources
   Stringbean's Trip to the Shining Sea
   My Family Vacation
   The Great Skinner Getaway
   How to Travel with Grownups

Geography

1. Make slides of various pictures from all over the country. The class can then try to guess the location of the picture.

2. Make family maps that describe personal family histories (see Figure 2–10).

3. After compiling information on different states, play the states riddle game. Find five facts about a state and have others guess the state. For example:

Figure 2–9 Hawaiian Da Kine Dialect

1. Aloha	a. Delicious
2. Huhu	b. Flower wreath
3. Ho'olu'olu	c. Feast
4. Kola	d. Money
5. Lei	e. angry
6. Luau	f. Hello, Good-bye
7. Moemoe	g. Please
8. Ono	h. Sleep

Answers: 1-f, 2-e, 3-g, 4-d, 5-b, 6-c, 7-h, 8-a

Source: Hendrickson, R. *The Words and Ways of American Dialects.* New York: Viking, 1986.

Figure 2-10 Family Map

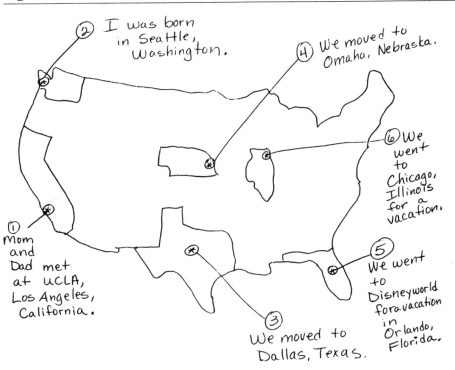

Source: Adapted from Weitzman, D. *My Backyard History Book.* Boston: Little, Brown, 1975.

> a. Its name means Land of the Indians.
> b. Its state bird is the cardinal.
> c. The state flower is the peony.
> d. James Dean was born in this state.
> e. The Wabash River is in this state.
> (Answer: Indiana)

4. Write jokes or puns about favorite states.

5. Write state poems. Use the following format to write a poem about different states.
>   Line 1: First initial of the state
>   Line 2: Four adjectives that describe the state
>   Line 3: "Next to, Bordering, North/East/West/South of . . ."
>   Line 4: "Who is proud of" three things
>   Line 5: "Who produces" three things
>   Line 6: "Home of" cities, places
>   Line 7: Last initial of the state

For instance, a poem about Nebraska might look like this:

N

Flat, windy, seasonal, midwestern

North of Kansas

Who is proud of football, Johnny Carson, Arbor Day

Who produces cattle, corn, wheat

Home of Omaha, Lincoln, and Pioneer Village

A

Resources
    America the Beautiful series
    Geographunny
    From Sea to Sea: The Growth of the United States
    Puzzle Maps USA
    Geography: The United States of America
    Anno's USA
    101 Wacky State Jokes
    A Picture Book of the USA
    Fabulous Facts about the 50 States
    We the People
    How Proudly They Wave
    A Road Might Lead to Anywhere
    My Backyard History Book

6. The Midwest: Study the distinguishing features of this part of the country. What makes it unique?

Resources
    The American Family Farm
    Farming
    Family Farm
    The Auction
    County Fair
    Prairie Songs
    Prairie Visions
    One Day in the Prairie
    Night of the Twisters
    Heartland
    Laura Ingalls Wilder Country

7. The Northeast: Study the distinguishing features of this part of the country. What makes it unique?

Resources
    The Strength of the Hills
    A Visit to Washington D.C.
    City! New York
    A Williamsburg Household
    Island Boy
    Amazing Grace

8. The South: Study the distinguishing features of this part of the country. What makes it unique?

Resources
    Appalachia
    Granny Will Your Dog Bite
    In Coal Country
    Your Best Friend, Kate

9. The West: Study the distinguishing features of this part of the country. What makes it unique?

Resources
    Kate Heads West
    Kate on the Coast

Mojave
Sierra
Eskimo Boy
The Oregon Trail

ANASTASIA AT THIS ADDRESS *WEB*

Figure 2–11 shows a web for upper grades that focuses on one book – *Anastasia at This Address* (Lowry, 1991).

Other Anastasia Books

1. Read other Anastasia books.

2. Vote on each person's favorite Anastasia book.

3. Make a poster advertising the various Anastasia books.

4. Draw a picture of what Anastasia's family looks like.

Resources
> *Anastasia Krupnik*
> *Anastasia Again*
> *Anastasia at Your Service*
> *Anastasia, Ask Your Analyst*
> *Anastasia on Her Own*
> *Anastasia Has the Answers*
> *Anastasia's Chosen Career*

5. Talk about different points of view after reading Sam's point of view of the Anastasia books. Brainstorm and discuss how a story might be written from Anastasia's mother's or father's point of view.

Resources
> *All About Sam*
> *Attaboy Sam*

Other Lois Lowry Books

1. Read other Lois Lowry books.

2. Vote on each person's favorite Lois Lowry books.

3. Categorize Lois Lowry's other books according to genre, theme, or setting.

Figure 2–11 *Anastasia at This Address* Web

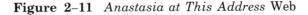
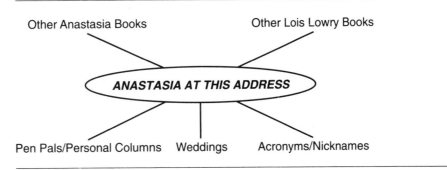

Resources
The One Hundredth Thing about Caroline
Switcharound
Your Move, J.P.!
A Summer to Die
Find a Stranger, Say Goodbye
Autumn Street
Taking Care of Terrific
Us and Uncle Fraud
Rabble Starkey
Number the Stars
The Giver

Pen Pals/Personal Columns

1. Begin a pen pal exchange with another class.
2. Write ads for a personal column, modeled after Anastasia's letter.

Resources
Dear Mr. Henshaw
Thank You, Santa
Dear Annie
Dear Emily
Dear Sarah

Weddings

1. Discuss weddings and various cultural traditions surrounding weddings. Brainstorm a list of words associated with weddings. Work in pairs to illustrate each word or concept and display.
2. Read other books about weddings and compare other characters' experiences with Anastasia's experience.

Resources
Angel's Mother's Wedding
Piggins and the Royal Wedding
Betty's Wedding
Sachiko's Wedding
Helga's Dowry: A Troll Love Story
Jafta and the Wedding
Harry Gets an Uncle
My Mother Got Married (and Other Disasters)

Acronyms/Nicknames

1. Students can find out about the history of their name. Were they named after someone?
2. Discuss nicknames. Make a list of the nicknames of the students in the class.
3. List commonly used acronyms (such as IBM, VCR, etc.). Have students add to the list as they see or hear of other acronyms.

Resources
Chrysanthemem
What's Your Name?
A Book about Names
But Names Will Never Hurt Me

Josephina Hates Her Name
A Porcupine Named Fluffy
The Adventure of Ali Baba Bernstein
The Other Emily
Orp
Turtle Knows Your Name
Acronyms, Initialisms and Abbreviations Dictionary

Other Grouping Possibilities

Students need opportunities to work in varied grouping situations. Whole groups, small groups, pairs, and independent work all have a place in the organization of a reading-writing classroom. Suggestions for using these different grouping arrangements follow.

Whole-group time is needed to "develop the learning community" and as "time to share culture and literacy" (Berghoff & Egawa, 1991, p. 538). Possibilities for whole-group time include the writing of class rules; author's chair sessions; teacher reading aloud to students; choral reading; sharing of students' favorite books; book talks; and mini-lessons on topics of interest to the whole class, such as writing good beginnings, using dialogue, and so on. Whole-group time should be a part of every day in reading and writing. It is the time to extend invitations to students about their own reading and writing, to make general announcements, and to provide an opportunity for students to celebrate their own reading and writing accomplishments with the rest of the class.

Small groups are needed when much interaction between students is the goal. Students may share common interests, be reading the same or similar books, or be working on a group project together. To encourage interaction among all of the students, no more than five or six should be placed in a small group. Literature discussion groups, mini-lessons on needed skills, writing revision groups, and groups projects are examples of when students might be placed in small groups. These groups may be formed according to shared interest, common need of skill instruction, or selected by the teacher or students, depending on the goal of the small groups' interaction.

Pairs can be used when students need one-to-one work. The teacher can select the pairs, chosing one strong reader and one weak reader, or students can select the pairs themselves. Cross-age tutors could also be utilized, such as first-graders working with fifth-graders. Pair work would include responding to a first draft of the partner's writing, reading aloud to each other, dialogue journal partners, and the like.

Students also need independent work time. This allows for them to make choices about what they are reading and writing independently. Sustained silent reading and writing are two ways to provide for this independent work daily.

Other Factors

Another factor to consider when organizing a classroom is the physical environment. Students should be surrounded by print. Books and magazines should be easily accessible to students and prominently displayed. Morrow and

Weinstein (1986) find that students choose reading during choice time and spend more time interacting with books (even poor readers) when there is an inviting reading corner for students. Routman (1991) suggests that 100 to 150 books in various genres is a good number to aim for in a classroom library. These books can come from book clubs such as Scholastic, Trumpet Club, or Troll (with teachers using bonus points to get numerous books), parents' donations, or the public library.

Parent involvement and communication is critical for the success of such a program. Weekly newsletters, invitations to class plays and presentations, volunteers for reading to students or listening to students share their own writing—all are ways to involve and inform parents of the literacy activities of the classroom.

Choosing to implement some of these suggestions depends on teachers' own personalities, scheduling flexibility, and other factors. But the final questions that teachers must ask themselves while organizing their own literature-based reading-writing classrooms are these: Are students actively involved in the language arts? Are students reading, writing, listening, and speaking in a meaningful manner every day? Is quality literature used daily in my classroom? Do students have choices about their own reading and writing? These questions should guide the organization of a classroom that encourages student involvement in literacy.

Summary

When organizing a literature-based classroom, the teacher must consider replicating the conditions of learning that exist in the home regarding oral language learning. Immersion, demonstration, engagement, expectation, responsibility, approximation, use, and response are important factors in learning reading and writing. Choice reading and writing, as well as shared reading and writing, are ways in which these conditions of learning may be replicated in a reading-writing classroom.

Alternatives to traditional ability grouping include literature discussion groups and the use of text sets. Another option to organizing such a classroom would include the use of thematic webs, based on content area topics, authors, or books.

References

Berghoff, B., & Egawa, K. (1991). No more "rocks": Grouping to give students control of their learning. *The Reading Teacher, 44,* 536–541.

Bleich, D. (1978). *Subjective criticism.* Baltimore: John Hopkins University Press.

Calkins, L. M. (1986). *The art of teaching writing.* Portsmouth, NH: Heinemann.

Cambourne, B. (1988). *The whole story: Natural learning and the acquisition of literacy in the classroom.* New York: Ashton Scholastic.

Danielson, K. E. (1992). Literature groups and literature logs: Responding to literature in a community of readers. *Reading Horizons, 32,* 372–382.

Eeds, M., & Wells, D. (1989). Grand conversations: An exploration of meaning construction in literature study groups. *Research in the Teaching of English, 23,* 4–25.

Fisher, B. (1991). *Joyful learning: A whole language kindergarten.* Portsmouth, NH: Heinemann.

Harste, J. C., Short, K. G., & Burke, C. (1988). *Creating classrooms for authors: The reading-writing connection.* Portsmouth, NH: Heinemann.

Hendrickson, R. (1986). *American talk: The words and ways of American dialects.* New York: Viking.

Kelly, P. R. (1990). Guiding young students' response to literature. *The Reading Teacher, 43,* 464–470.

Kelly, P. R., & Farnan, N. (1991). Promoting critical thinking through response logs: A reader-response approach with fourth graders. In J. Zutell & S. McCormick (Eds.), *Learner factors/teacher factors: Issues in literacy research and instruction* (pp. 277–284). Fortieth Yearbook, National Reading Conference, Chicago, IL: National Reading Conference.

Morgan, M. (1989). *Ability grouping in reading instruction: Research alternatives.* (Fast Bib No. 21 RCS). Bloomington, IN: ERIC Clearinghouse on Reading and Communication Skills.

Morrow, L. M., & Weinstein, C. S. (1986). Encouraging voluntary reading: The impact of a literature program on children's use of library centers. *Reading Research Quarterly,* 330–346.

O'Flahavan, J. (1988). *Conversational discussion groups: A study of second graders leading their own discussion.* Paper presented at the National Reading Conference, Tucson, AZ.

Peterson, R., & Eed, M. (1990). *Grand conversations: Literature groups in action.* New York: Scholastic.

Routman, R. (1991). *Invitations: Changing as teachers and learners K–12.* Portsmouth, NH: Heinemann.

Short, K. G. (Ed.) (1990). *Talking about books: Creating literate communities.* Portsmouth, NH: Heinemann.

Slavin, R. E. (1987). Ability grouping and student achievement in elementary schools: A best-evidence synthesis. *Review of Educational Research, 57,* 293–336.

Sloan, G. D. (1984). *The child as critic.* New York: Teachers College Press.

The Web. The Ohio State University, Room 200 Ramseyer Hall, 29 West Woodruff, Columbus, OH 43210. Annual subscription for four issues is $10.00.

Wendelin, K. H., & Danielson, K. E. (1991). *Developing critical thinking skills using folk tale variants: A collaboration of cross-age groups.* Paper presented at the National Council of Teachers of English Spring Conference, Indianapolis, IN.

Children's Books

Ancona, G. (1989). *The American family farm.* San Diego: Harcourt Brace Jovanovich.

*Anderson, J. (1988). *A Williamsburg household.* New York: Clarion.

Anderson, W. (1988). *Laura Ingalls Wilder country.* New York: Harper.

Andrews, J. (1991). *The auction.* New York: Macmillan.

Anno, M. (1983). *Anno's USA.* New York: Philomel.

*Argent, K. (1991). *Happy birthday Wombat!* Boston: Little, Brown.

*Arnold, C. (1987). *Koala.* New York: Morrow.

*Baker, J. (1987). *Where the forest meets the sea.* New York: Greenwillow.

*Baker, J. (1991). *Window.* New York: Greenwillow.

Base, G. (1990). *My grandma lived in Gooligulch.* New York: Abrams.

Berger, M. (1991). *101 wacky state jokes.* New York: Scholastic.

Bial, R. (1992). *County fair.* Boston: Houghton Mifflin.

Borchers, E. (1981). *Dear Sarah.* New York: Greenwillow.

Bragg, M. (1988). *Betty's wedding.* New York: Macmillan.

Bridgman, E. (1980). *How to travel with grownups.* New York: Crowell.

Brisson, P. (1989). *Your best friend, Kate.* New York: Bradbury.

Brisson, P. (1990). *Kate heads west.* New York: Bradbury.

Brisson, P. (1992). *Kate on the coast.* New York: Bradbury.

*Bryan, A. (1989). *Turtle knows your name.* New York: Atheneum.

Bunting, E. (1988). *Is anybody there?* New York: Harper.

*Burt, D. (1991). *Kangaroos.* Boston: Houghton Mifflin.

Byars, B. (1986). *The not-just-anybody family.* New York: Delacorte.

Carter, D. A. (1991). *In a dark, dark wood.* New York: Simon and Schuster.

Caseley, J. (1991). *Dear Annie.* New York: Greenwillow.

Cleary, B. (1983). *Dear Mr. Henshaw.* New York: Morrow.

Clifford, E. (1985). *The remembering box.* Boston: Houghton Mifflin.

Climo, S. (1990). *City! New York.* New York: Macmillan.

Clouse, N. (1990). *Puzzle maps, USA.* New York: Henry Holt.

*Collins, C. (1990). *Sachiko's wedding.* New York: Marion Boyars.

Conrad, P. (1985). *Prairie songs.* New York: Harper.

Conrad, P. (1991). *Prairie visions.* New York: Harper.

Cooney, B. (1988). *Island boy.* New York: Viking.

Davis, G. (1984). *The other Emily.* Boston: Houghton Mifflin.

Delton, J. (1987). *Angel's mother's wedding.* Boston: Houghton Mifflin.

dePaola, T. (1977). *Helga's dowry: A troll love story.* New York: Harcourt Brace Jovanovich.

Edens, C. (1991). *Santa Cows.* New York: Simon and Schuster.

Ehlert, L. (1988). *Planting a Rainbow.* San Diego: Harcourt Brace Jovanovich.

Engel, D. (1989). *Josephina hates her name.* New York: Morrow.

Faber, H. (1992). *From sea to sea: The growth of the United States.* New York: Scribners.

*Fatchen, M. (1990). *The country mail is coming: Poems from down under.* Boston: Little, Brown.

Field, R. (1990). *A road might lead to anywhere.* Boston: Little, Brown.

Fisher, L. E. (1990). *The Oregon Trail.* New York: Holiday House.

Fox, M. (1985). *Wilfrid Gordon McDonald Partridge.* New York: Kane/Miller.

*Fox, M. (1987). *Hattie and the Fox.* Ill. by Patricia Mullins, New York: Bradbury.

Fox, M. (1987). *Possum magic.* San Diego: Harcourt Brace Jovanovich.

Fox, M. (1988). *Koala Lou.* Ill. by Pamela Lofts. San Diego: Harcourt Brace Jovanovich.

Fox, M. (1988). *With love, at Christmas.* Ill. by Gary Lippincott. Nashville: Abingdon.

Fox, M. (1989). *Night noises.* Ill. by Terry Denton. San Diego: Harcourt Brace Jovanovich.

*Fox, M. (1992). *Dear Mem Fox, I have read all your books, even the pathetic ones.* San Diego: Harcourt Brace Jovanovich.

George, J. C. (1986). *One day in the prairie.* New York: Crowell.

Gerberg, M. (1991). *Geographunny.* New York: Clarion.

Gibbons, G. (1988). *Farming.* New York: Holiday House.

Goodman, B. (1991). *A picture book of the USA.* New York: Scholastic.

Goodman, B., & Krulik, N. E. (1991). *What's your name?* New York: Scholastic.

Graff, N. P. (1989). *The strength of the hills.* Boston: Little, Brown.

*Graham, A. (1987). *Who wants Arthur?* Milwaukee, WI: Gareth Stevens.

*Graham, A. (1988). *Educating Arthur.* Milwaukee, WI: Gareth Stevens.

*Graham, A. (1989). *Grandad's magic.* Boston: Little, Brown.

Haban, R. D. (1989). *How proudly they wave.* Minneapolis: Lerner.

Hendershot, J. (1987). *In coal country.* New York: Knopf.

*Hendrickson, R. (1986). *America talks: The words and ways of American dialects.* New York: Viking.

Henkes, K. (1991). *Chrysanthemum.* New York: Greenwillow.

Hurwitz, J. (1985). *The adventures of Ali Baba Bernstein.* New York: Morrow.

Hutchins, P. (1968). *Rosie's walk.* New York: Macmillan.

*Ingpen, R. (1987). *The idle bear.* New York: Bedrick.

*Kendall, R. (1992). *Eskimo boy.* New York: Scholastic.

Kent, J. (1971). *The fat cat.* New York: Parents Magazine Press.

Khalsa, D. K. (1988). *My family vacation.* New York: Orchard.

Kline, S. (1989). *Orp.* New York: Putnam.

Krementz, J. (1987). *A visit to Washington D.C.* New York: Scholastic.

*Lepthien, E. U. (1982). *Australia.* Chicago: Children's Press.

Lester, H. (1986). *A porcupine named Fluffy.* Boston: Houghton Mifflin.

*Lewin, H. (1983). *Jafta and the wedding.* Minneapolis: Carolrhoda.

Lobel, A. (1990). *Alison's zinnia.* New York: Greenwillow.

Locker, T. (1988). *Family farm.* New York: Dial.

Lowry, L. (1977). *A summer to die.* Boston: Houghton Mifflin.

Lowry, L. (1978). *Find a stranger, say goodbye.* Boston: Houghton Mifflin.

Lowry, L. (1979). *Anastasia Krupnik.* Boston: Houghton Mifflin.

Lowry, L. (1980). *Autumn Street.* Boston: Houghton Mifflin.

Lowry, L. (1981). *Anastasia again.* Boston: Houghton Mifflin.

Lowry, L. (1982). *Anastasia at your service.* Boston: Houghton Mifflin.

Lowry, L. (1983). *The one hundredth thing about Caroline.* Boston: Houghton Mifflin.

Lowry, L. (1983). *Taking care of Terrific.* Boston: Houghton Mifflin.

Lowry, L. (1984). *Anastasia ask your analyst.* Boston: Houghton Mifflin.

Lowry, L. (1984). *Us and Uncle Fraud.* Boston: Houghton Mifflin.

Lowry, L. (1985). *Anastasia has the answers.* Boston: Houghton Mifflin.

Lowry, L. (1985). *Anastasia on her own.* Boston: Houghton Mifflin.

Lowry, L. (1985). *Switcharound.* Boston: Houghton Mifflin.

Lowry, L. (1987). *Anastasia's chosen career.* Boston: Houghton Mifflin.

Lowry, L. (1987). *Rabble Starkey.* Boston: Houghton Mifflin.

Lowry, L. (1988). *All about Sam.* Boston: Houghton Mifflin.

*Lowry, L. (1989). *Number the stars.* Boston: Houghton Mifflin.

Lowry, L. (1990). *Your move, J.P.!* Boston: Houghton Mifflin.

Lowry, L. (1991). *Anastasia at this address.* Boston: Houghton Mifflin.

Lowry, L. (1992). *Attaboy, Sam.* Boston: Houghton Mifflin.

Lowry, L. (1993). *The giver.* Boston: Houghton Mifflin.

Marshall, J. (1973). *Yummers.* Boston: Houghton Mifflin.

McMillan, B. (1986). *Counting wildflowers.* New York: Lothrop.

Meltzer, M. (1984). *A book about names.* New York: Crowell.

*Milnes, G. (1990). *Granny will your dog bite and other mountain rhymes.* New York: Knopf.

Mossman, J. (1991). *Acronyms, initialisms and abbreviations dictionary.* Detroit: Gale.

Park, B. (1989). *My mother got married (and other disasters).* New York: Knopf.

Pilkey, D. (1990). *'Twas the night before Thanksgiving.* New York: Orchard.
Porte, B. A. (1991). *Harry gets an uncle.* New York: Greenwillow.
Ross, W. S. (1991). *Fabulous facts about the 50 states.* New York: Scholastic.
Ruckman, I. (1984). *Night of the twisters.* New York: Crowell.
*Rylant, C. (1991). *Appalachia.* San Diego: Harcourt Brace Jovanovich.
Shaw, N. (1991). *Sheep in a shop.* Boston: Houghton Mifflin.
Shaw, N. (1992). *Sheep out to eat.* Boston: Houghton Mifflin.
Siebert, D. (1988). *Mojave.* New York: Crowell.
Siebert, D. (1989). *Heartland.* New York: Crowell.
Siebert, D. (1991). *Sierra.* New York: HarperCollins.
*Spier, P. (1987). *We the people.* New York: Doubleday.
Stein, R. C. *America the beautiful* series. Chicago: Children's Press.
Stewart, F., & Stewart, C. (1990). *Geography: The United States of America.* New York: Harper.
*Stewart, M. (1986). *Dear Emily.* New York: Puffin.
*Thiele, C. (1988). *Farmer Schultz's ducks.* New York: Harper & Row.
Tolan, S. S. (1987). *The great Skinner getaway.* New York: Macmillan.
*Trumpet Club Video. (1992). *Trumpet video visit: Mem Fox.* Holmes, PA: Trumpet Club.
*Vaughan, M. (1986). *Wombat stew.* Englewood Cliffs, NJ: Silver Burdett.
Viorst, J. (1990). *Earrings!* New York: Atheneum.
Waber, B. (1976). *But names will never hurt me.* Boston: Houghton Mifflin.
Wagner, K. (1990). *Chocolate chip cookies.* New York: Henry Holt.
Watson, N. C. (1990). *The little pigs' puppet book.* Boston: Little, Brown.
Weitzman, D. (1975). *My backyard history book.* Boston: Little, Brown.
*Wheatley, N. (1989). *My place.* Long Beach, CA: Australia in Print.
Wild, M. (1990). *The very best of friends.* San Diego: Harcourt Brace Jovanovich.
*Wild, M. (1992). *Thank you, Santa.* New York: Scholastic.
Williams, V., & Williams, J. (1988). *Stringbean's trip to the shining sea.* New York: Greenwillow.
Wolf, B. (1986). *Amazing grace: Smith island and the Chesapeake watermen.* New York: Macmillan.
*Wrightson, P. (1991). *The sugar gum tree.* New York: Viking.
Yolen, J. (1988). *Piggins and the royal wedding.* San Diego: Harcourt Brace Jovanovich.

Children's Magazines

Cobblestone, 30 Grove Street, Peterborough, NH 03458
Cricket, Box 52961, Boulder, CO 80322-2961
Ebony Junior, Johnson Publishing Co., 820 S. Michigan Avenue, Chicago, IL 60605
Highlights, Box 269, Columbus, OH 43272
Kid City, Box 53349, Boulder, CO 80322
Kids Discover, Box 54206, Boulder, CO 80323-4206
Ladybug, Box 50285, Boulder, CO 80323-0285
National Geographic World, National Geographic Society, Washington, DC 10036
Pack-o-Fun, 701 Lee Street, Suite 1000, Des Plaines, IL 60016-4570
Plays, 120 Boylston Street, Boston, MA 02116-4615
Ranger Rick, National Wildlife Federation, 1412 16th Street NW, Washington, DC 20036

Stone Soup, Box 83, Santa Cruz, CA 95063
3-2-1 Contact, Box, 53051, Boulder, CO 80322-3051
U.S. Kids, Box 7133, Red Oak, IA 51591-0133
Your Big Back Yard, 1100 Waterway Blvd., Box 567B, Indianapolis, IN 46206
Zillions, Box 54861, Boulder, CO 80322-4861

Book Clubs

Scholastic Book Clubs, Jefferson City, MO 65102
Troll Book Club, 2 Lethbridge Plaza, Mahway, NJ 07430
Trumpet Club Book Club, Box 604, Holmes, PA 19043

Theme: Little Red Riding Hood (Primary to Intermediate)

Crawford, E. D. (1983). *Little red cap.* Ill. by Lisbeth Zwerger. New York: Morrow.
Emberly, M. (1990). *Ruby.* Boston: Little, Brown.
Galdone, P. (1974). *Little red riding hood.* New York: McGraw-Hill.
Goodall, J. S. (1988). *Little red riding hood.* New York: McElderry.
Hyman, T. S. (1983). *Little red riding hood.* New York: Holiday House.
Marshall, J. (1987). *Red riding hood.* New York: Dial.
*Young, E. (1989). *Lon Po Po.* New York: Philomel.

The Three Little Pigs (Primary to Intermediate)

Galdone, P. (1970). *The three little pigs.* New York: Seabury.
Hooks, W. H. (1989). *The three little pigs and the fox.* New York: Macmillan.
Marshall, J. (1989). *The three little pigs.* New York: Dial.
Scieszka, J. (1989). *The true story of the 3 little pigs.* New York: Viking.
Zemach, M. (1988). *The three little pigs.* New York: Farrar.

Camps (Primary)

Brown, M. (1982). *Arthur goes to camp.* Boston: Little, Brown.
Carlson, N. (1988). *Arnie goes to camp.* New York: Viking.
Marshall, J. (1989). *The cut-ups at Camp Custer.* New York: Viking.
McPhail, D. (1983). *Pig Pig goes to camp.* New York: Dutton.

School Stories (Primary)

Ahlberg, J. (1988). *Starting school.* New York: Viking.
Bourgeois, P. (1990). *Too many chickens!* Boston: Little, Brown.
Bunting, E. (1992). *Our teacher's having a baby.* New York: Clarion.
Carlson, N. (1990). *Arnie and the new kid.* New York: Viking.
Cazet, D. (1990). *Never spit on your shoes.* New York: Orchard.
Cohen, M. (1983). *See you tomorrow, Charles.* New York: Greenwillow.
Gantos, J. (1989). *Rotten Ralph's show and tell.* Boston: Houghton Mifflin.
Giff, P. R. (1980). *Today was a terrible day.* New York: Viking.
Hennesey, B. G. (1990). *School days.* New York: Viking.
Houston, G. (1992). *My Great Aunt Arizona.* New York: Harper.
Howe, J. (1984). *The day the teacher went bananas.* New York: Dutton.
Keller, H. (1991). *The new boy.* New York: Greenwillow.
Naylor, P. R. (1991). *King of the playground.* New York: Atheneum.

Pulver, R. (1991). *Mrs. Toggle and the dinosaur.* New York: Macmillan.
Schwartz, A. (1988). *Annabelle Swift, kindergartner.* New York: Orchard.
Stevenson, J. (1985). *That dreadful day.* New York: Greenwillow.
Van Leeuwen, J. (1990). *Oliver Pig at school.* New York: Dial.
Weiss, L. (1984). *My teacher sleeps at school.* New York: Warne.
Wells, R. (1981). *Timothy goes to school.* New York: Dial.
Woodruff, E. (1991). *Show and tell.* New York: Holiday House.

School Stories (Intermediate to Upper)

Dahl, R. (1988). *Matilda.* New York: Viking.
Gilson, J. (1982). *13 ways to sink a sub.* New York: Lothrop.
Gilson, J. (1983). *4B goes wild.* New York: Lothrup.
Herman, C. (1985). *Millie Cooper, 3B.* New York: Dutton.
Lowry, L. (1990). *Your move, J.P.* Boston: Houghton Mifflin.
Sachar, L. (1987). *There's a boy in the girls' bathroom.* New York: Knopf.

African Americans and Baseball (Intermediate to Upper)

*Golenbock, P. (1990). *Teammates.* New York: Trumpet Club.
*Lord, B. B. (1984). *In the Year of the Boar and Jackie Robinson.* New York: Harper.
*Slote, A. (1991). *Finding Buck McHenry.* New York: Harper.

Civil War/Prejudice (Intermediate to Upper)

*Murphy, J. (1991). *The boys' war.* New York: Scholastic.
*Rappaport, D. (1991). *Escape from slavery.* New York: Harper.
*Turner, A. (1987). *Nettie's trip south.* New York: Macmillan.
*Winter, J. (1988). *Follow the drinking gourd.* New York: Knopf.

Moving West (Primary to Intermediate)

Ackerman, K. (1990). *Araminta's paint box.* New York: Atheneum.
Anderson, J. (1987). *Joshua's westward journal.* New York: Morrow.
Coerr, E. (1986). *The Josefina story quilt.* New York: Harper.
Harvey, B. (1988). *Cassie's journey.* New York: Holiday House.
Pryor, B. (1992). *Lottie's dream.* New York: Simon and Schuster.
Sanders, S. R. (1989). *Aurora means dawn.* New York: Bradbury.
Van Leeuwen, J. (1992). *Going west.* New York: Dial.

Life on the Prairie (Intermediate to Upper)

Harvey, B. (1986). *My prairie year.* New York: Holiday House.
Harvey, B. (1990). *My prairie Christmas.* New York: Holiday House.
Henry, J. L. (1988). *Log cabin in the woods.* New York: Macmillan.
Turner, A. (1985). *Dakota dugout.* New York: Macmillan.

Life on the Prairie (Upper)

Conrad, P. (1985). *Prairie songs.* New York: Harper.
Conrad, P. (1989). *My Daniel.* New York: Harper.

Fleischman, P. (1991). *The borning room*. New York: Harper.
Holland, I. (1990). *The journey home*. New York: Scholastic.

Witches (Primary)

Adler, D. A. (1988). *I know I'm a witch*. New York: Henry Holt.
Balian, L. (1984). *Humbug potion*. Nashville: Abingdon.
Gunthrie, D. (1990). *The witch has an itch*. New York: Simon and Schuster.
Hautzig, D. (1984). *Little witch's big night*. New York: Random House.
Meddaugh, S. (1991). *The witches' supermarket*. Boston: Houghton Mifflin.

Thanksgiving (Primary)

Brown, M. (1983). *Arthur's Thanksgiving*. Boston: Little, Brown.
Bunting, E. (1991). *A turkey for Thanksgiving*. New York: Clarion.
Cohen, M. (1987). *Don't eat too much turkey*. New York: Morrow.
Cuyler, M. (1990). *Daisy's crazy Thanksgiving*. New York: Holt.
Pilkney, D. (1990). *'Twas the night before Thanksgiving*. New York: Orchard.
Prelutsky, J. (1982). *It's Thanksgiving*. New York: Greenwillow.
Smith, J. (1990). *The turkey's side of it*. New York: Harper.
Stevenson, J. (1986). *Fried feathers for Thanksgiving*. New York: Greenwillow.

Pilgrims (Intermediate to Upper)

*Anderson, J. (1984). *The first Thanksgiving feast*. Boston: Houghton Mifflin.
*Bunting, E. (1988). *How many days to America?* New York: Clarion.
*Cohen, B. (1983). *Molly's pilgrim*. New York: Lothrup.

Santa Claus (Primary to Intermediate)

Civardi, A. (1991). *The secrets of Santa*. New York: Simon and Schuster.
Cuyler, M. (1987). *Fat Santa*. New York: Henry Holt.
Haywood, C. (1986). *How the reindeer saved Santa*. New York: Morrow.
Pilkington, B. (1990). *Grandpa Claus*. Minneapolis: Carolrhoda.
Sharmat, M. W. (1990). *I'm Santa Claus and I'm famous*. New York: Holiday House.
Wild, M. (1992). *Thank you, Santa*. New York: Scholastic.

Dogs (Primary to Intermediate)

Brown, R. (1987). *Our puppy's vacation*. New York: Dutton.
Day, A. (1985). *Good dog, Carl*. New York: Simon and Schuster.
Day, A. (1989). *Carl goes shopping*. New York: Farrar.
Day, A. (1990). *Carl's Christmas*. New York: Farrar.
Day, A. (1991). *Carl's afternoon in the park*. New York: Farrar.
Hazen, B. S. (1987). *Fang*. New York: Atheneum.
Kellogg, S. (1979). *Pinkerton behave*. New York: Dial.
Kellogg, S. (1981). *A rose for Pinkerton*. New York: Dial.
Kellogg, S. (1982). *Tallyho, Pinkerton*. New York: Dial.
Kellogg, S. (1987). *Prehistoric Pinkerton*. New York: Dial.
Khalsa, D. K. (1987). *I want a dog*. New York: Crown.
MacLachlan, P. (1991). *Three names*. New York: Harper.

Robertus, P. M. (1988). *The dog who had kittens.* New York: Holiday House.
Thayer, J. (1985). *The puppy who wanted a boy.* New York: Morrow.

Dogs (Upper)

Cleary, B. (1991). *Strider.* New York: Morrow.
*Gardiner, J. R. (1980). *Stone Fox.* New York: Crowell.
Naylor, P. R. (1991). *Shiloh.* New York: Atheneum.
Putnam, A. (1990). *Westering.* New York: Lodestar.
Wallace, B. (1980). *A dog called Kitty.* New York: Holiday House.
Wallace, B. (1989). *Red dog.* New York: Holiday House.

Cowboys (Primary to Intermediate)

*Brusca, M. C. (1991). *On the pampas.* New York: Henry Holt.
Kellogg, S. (1986). *Pecos Bill.* New York: Morrow.
Khalsa, D. K. (1990). *Cowboy dreams.* New York: Potter.
Kimmel, E. (1990). *Four dollars and fifty cents.* New York: Holiday House.
*Medearis, A. S. (1992). *The zebra-riding cowboy.* New York: Henry Holt.
Read, L. R. (1990). *Rattlesnake stew.* New York: Farrar.
Rounds, G. (1991). *Cowboys.* New York: Holiday House.
Scott, A. H. (1989). *Someday rider.* New York: Clarion.
Sewall, M. (1985). *Ridin' that strawberry roan.* New York: Viking.

*Indicates multicultural focus.

3

Teaching
Beginning Reading

One year when I was an elementary teacher, we had the pleasure of having a professional storyteller come to our school. He made visits to each classroom, telling wonderful tales that delighted us all. The particular story he chose for my class was "The Three Little Pigs." When he announced the title, my students, much like the main characters in the story, squealed with delight. "The Three Little Pigs" was a favorite of theirs and they especially liked the part where the wolf was cooked in the stew pot at the end of the tale.

Our storyteller gathered his eager audience about him and settled himself as comfortably as possible in a child-sized plastic chair. He immediately drew the children into the story; they hung on his every word. He soon came to the part of the story where the first little pig met the villain. The storyteller looked at my students and said, "And who should Little Pig meet but a big, ugly, hairy, slobbery. . . ." "Wolf!" my 26 listeners shouted. "No," he said, "It was a *fox!*" My students murmured about this anomaly for a while and he went on with the story. But every time the storyteller mentioned the big, ugly, hairy, slobbery you-know-what, my students would shout, "Wolf!" They had all heard "The Three Little Pigs" numerous times, either at home or school, and the bad guy was always the wolf. They never did take to the idea of switching it to a fox.

Certain children's stories, often referred to as *predictable,* like "The Three Little Pigs" are typical story-time favorites for children. The repetitive nature of the story and the chant, "Little pig, little pig, let me come in! Not by the hair on my chinny-chin-chin," makes it easy for the child to know what is coming next. These predictable bits of language "enter the ear" (Martin & Brogan, 1971) and become part of the child's language repertoire. The weary parent who has read the same book seven nights in a row and who tries to accidentally skip a page or two will be caught short by the child who has already taken major chunks of the story for his or her own and recognizes anything that is a serious departure. As my students had internalized, "Big bad, hairy, ugly, slobbery *wolf,*" and recognized the insertion of the character of the fox for the fraud it was, other young listeners are expecting a perfect match between the story the parent reads tonight and the one they have nearly memorized from nights before. These early experiences with listening to stories play a critical role in emergent literacy, beginning at birth with oral language and continuing through life as we become readers and writers.

Emergent Literacy

Emergent literacy refers to the increasing awareness of the print world as young learners observe and experiment with the reading and writing process (Smith, 1991). Beginning in infancy, children have numerous occasions to witness interactions between members of their families and the print environment. They see their parents reading a newspaper, paying bills, or making a grocery list. They see an older brother or sister reading the back of a cereal box, writing out valentines or invitations to a birthday party, and reading the directions to play a new game or put a model together.

Through vicarious experiences, young children begin to conclude that what may look like scribbles and squiggles on paper to them may evoke strong emotions in someone else. Witnessing a parent's response to an unusually high phone bill or seeing someone laugh out loud at a novel reinforces the notion that what is written has meaning. The child is learning that reading and writing are tools for communication. Through this natural, emerging process, the young learner gains the confidence that he or she will need in order to become an active participant in the world of reading and writing.

Young children also become familiar with print outside their homes. They quickly learn to read environmental print, such as labels and fast-food signs. Given paper and pencils, they will model writing behavior. As the desire to communicate and to make sense of and control their world inspires the child to learn to talk, seeing the possibilities that reading and writing afford can stimulate a desire to master these skills during the school years.

Two facets of emergent literacy have particular importance in teaching beginning reading: lap reading and storybook reading.

Lap Reading

Lap reading is an important step in the development of literacy. One of the characteristics shared by children who learn to read before they enter school is that of having been read to frequently. There are several features common to lap reading, or reading to children before they enter school, that contribute to its effectiveness:

1. The child is close to the reader and can see the print and pictures while the story is being read.
2. The stories are often of a predictable nature and are easily remembered.
3. There is dialogue between the reader and the child that pertains to the story.
4. The story is often reread many times.

If we picture what might be a typical story-reading session at home, we would expect certain things to happen. Usually, the child, or children, would be sitting very close to the reader, maybe even on his or her lap—hence the term, *lap reading*. As the story begins, the reader may stop occasionally to ask the child a question or point out something interesting in the illustrations.

While the story is being read, the child has the opportunity to absorb considerable information about the process of reading. He or she notices that the pages of the book are read from front to back and that the reader says the same words for each page every night. As the reader says the words, the child is able to see the print and the illustrations simultaneously. If need be, questions can easily be asked and answered. At the conclusion of story time, the adult often asks the child for his or her own opinions about the story and whether or not he or she liked it. This ritual occurs in a nurturant, warm environment. Even as adults, many of us can still be lulled into a state of contentment by the sound of a good reader reading or telling a story.

The type of story often read to young children is also a key factor in the ability of the child to memorize the text. Many times, the reading selection from the branch of traditional literature, or stories that have their roots in oral literacy. Before people could write and before books could easily be published, the accumulated wisdom, folklore, and values of a culture were handed down by word of mouth. Everything had to be memorized and retold. In order to make their job easier, professional storytellers used linguistic crutches, or patterns of language, that made memorization easier. Perhaps the story was cumulative, such as "The House that Jack Built," or it may have had a repetitive pattern, such as "The Little Red Hen." Sequences such as days of the week, numbers, or rhymes also made it easier for the storytellers to do their jobs well. These same gimmicks make it possible for young readers to commit a storytime favorite to memory and be well on their way to becoming independent, enthusiastic readers.

Specific techniques for reading to young children yield the best results. Children will benefit most from being involved in an oral problem-solving situation in which they are asked to respond (Holdaway, 1979). For example, when the parent pauses at the part of the story where Little Red Riding Hood first meets the wolf and asks the listener if the heroine should tell the villain where she is headed, the child has an opportunity to integrate and relate details from the story and to construct meaning. The more the adult assists the child in making sense of the story based on his or her own experiences, background, and beliefs, the more productive the story reading episodes will be (Morrow, 1988). There is a positive relationship between listening to literature and the desire to learn to read (Roser, 1987). Children who enter school having had many experiences to listen to stories perform better on tests that measure vocabulary development, reading comprehension, and decoding skills (Feitelson, Kita, & Goldstein, 1986).

Because children like to hear their favorite stories over and over, rereading is also a typical component of the story reading that is done at home. Fortunately, this rereading is very beneficial (Sulzby, 1985). Hearing a story again and again provides a framework of background information and meaning that allows the child to interact with the story on a variety of levels. After hearing "Goldilocks and the Three Bears" several times, the child knows exactly what Goldilocks will do as soon as the bear family has gone for their morning stroll. Having the main points of the story well in hand, the child can begin to think about whether or not little children should go into strange houses and make themselves at home. The questions children ask and the comments they make increase and become more interpretive and evaluative after repeated readings of the same tale. With repeated readings, the behaviors of the child change. Although his or her initial attention to a story focuses on illustrations, with later enactments the child will begin to tend to print and the shape and sound of the story (Sulzby, 1985).

Storybook Reading

Storybook reading occurs when children memorize large chunks of a story or even the entire story. After subsequent readings, children will attempt to read a story for themselves. Storybook reading is the stage that bridges listening to a story and reading it for oneself. It predominantly involves memory and repetition, very similar to language development when a child repeats words and phrases he or she heard many times.

At this point, children are still unable to read the words in isolation; however, they can model reading-like behavior. They hold a book appropriately, turn the pages, and may even mimic the intonation used by the adult who reads to them. Fortified by the security of knowing what a book says, these children are then able to attend to the particulars of print and the configuration of individual words. The child may ask the parent to point out the words that say "Chinny-chin-chin." These early experiences with being read to have given the children involved an understanding of how books are handled, the realization that there is a connection between the words on the page and what someone says out loud, and a taste of the wonderful world available between the covers of a book. This awareness of books and stories is an important facet of emergent literacy.

The Traditional Curriculum

Children who have been read to and who have had opportunities to interact with reading and writing in a variety of situations come to school and formal instruction with many advantages. Their progress in reading and writing will be enhanced if early school experiences include the best of what happened at home. Children who have not shared these early literacy experiences will benefit from the teacher who takes the most beneficial preschool experiences and incorporates them into the beginning reading curriculum. For these students, to be placed in a rigid, skill-oriented program will mean skipping many important steps in the process of becoming literate. Morrow (1988) finds that five-year-olds who have the opportunity to hear a story repeatedly and to interact verbally with the reader increase the quality of their responses to the story and are subsequently able to focus on the meaning and the intricacies of print. For children from lower socioeconomic backgrounds, the method of interactive rereadings of stories is the most effective.

Unfortunately, once children begin school, their experiences with reading and writing will be very different—sometimes completely opposite of what happened at home. The Joint Statement on Literacy Development in Pre-first Grade (1986) cites areas of weakness within a traditional reading program: The rigid, formal programs have inappropriate expectations and experiences, little attention is given to individual development or learning styles, the accelerated programs do not encourage risk taking or allow children to experiment with language, too much attention is focused on skills, and there is little attention given to reading for pleasure. Mason (1985) concludes that preparation for reading is more effective when it focuses on words, book handling, letter recognition, and simulated writing than when the emphasis is on general cognitive tasks and motor skills. Instead of teaching children sounds and high-frequency words, they need to be involved in meaningful print-related activities. The natural progression for children who are read to at home is a focus on illustrations, title, characters, and story events. The last element to which children attend is print (Martinez & Roser, 1985).

Skills designed to teach the visual and auditory acuity assumed to be necessary for learning to read are less important in beginning reading than opportunities to listen to stories, to look at books, and to attempt to write. In fact, exposure to books and a chance to explore them is a better predictor than is maturity in making sense out of print (Lundsteen, 1986).

Even the materials used to teach beginning reading can be deceptively difficult. The label "Easy to Read" may look that way to adults because of the short sentences and short vocabulary words, but to many children these books become obstacles. Just as my students kept expecting a wolf instead of a fox, children will expect language that matches their own and will expect a story to make sense. The linguistic style that makes predictable books so effective is often missing in a basal reader. These plotless stories and unrelated sets of sentences fail to live up to the child's notion of what a story should be (Whaley, 1981–1982).

The most productive early reading curriculum has the following qualities:

1. The focus is on meaningful language experiences rather than isolated skill development.
2. What children already know is the basis of instruction.
3. Children are given opportunities to experience success with language.
4. The children are read to daily and have opportunities for independent reading and writing.
5. Literacy is fostered in a warm, nurturing environment that allows for individual development.
6. Children learn to read with quality literature.
7. The teacher discusses and evaluates stories with children and relates them to the child's life experiences.

Teaching Reading with Predictable Books

We know that children learn to read by reading. Like any skill, the more we practice it, the better we become. Unfortunately, in the past it has been difficult to figure out how we could teach children to read by reading when they could not yet read. The use of certain children's stories, called *predictable books,* has allowed teachers to involve children with wonderful stories in their beginning school experiences. By involving children in activities that simulate the best of what occurred with their parents or another adult during lap reading, we can teach children to read with the most productive method. The following elements of storybook and lap reading identified by research and observation as most conducive to early reading would become the core of the reading curriculum: a nurturant environment, the opportunity to hear a story more than once, and verbal interactions before, during, and after reading.

Bridge, Winograd, and Haley (1983) compared groups of first-graders who were taught with basal readers to those taught with predictable books. Children reading predictable books learned more sight words, were better able to use context to determine an unknown word, and had more positive feelings about reading out loud. Using predictable stories also yielded higher reading comprehension skills (Deford, 1981). The benefits of teaching beginning reading with predictable books are numerous:

1. The child is exposed to wonderful literature. Predictable books include many of the best books available for children today. The importance of quality

literature when children are still forming their attitudes about reading cannot be overestimated. The milk companies are right about "the formative years." We want children's initial experiences with reading to be interesting and rewarding and to instill in them a desire for more (Rhodes, 1979).

2. Predictable books can be read over and over and still be enjoyed (Sulzby, 1985). Since one of the components of teaching reading with literature is that the story is read many times, we need a story that can bear repeating. Just as the child begs the parent at home to read a certain book again and again, he or she will want to hear and read these books repeatedly. And for the teacher who has to listen and read again and again, it helps when the story is good.

3. Predictable books provide excellent practice for sight words (Bridge & Burton, 1982). Teaching children to memorize sight words can be a frustrating experience. These so-called glue words that make up the majority of the words we encounter in reading often have little meaning on their own and do not conjure up a visual picture when encountered in isolation. Words such as *on, was, from,* or *because* take their meaning from surrounding words and have little in the way of distinguishing features or uniqueness that makes them easy to recognize. Like all books, predictable books contain these same words and the children learn to read them in a supportive context.

4. Reading comprehension—the goal of reading instruction—can be emphasized (Lauritzen, 1980). In order for us to ask children to discuss a story, there must be something to the story to begin with. A justifiable criticism of basal readers in the primary grades is that the stories are merely collections of words and sentences with little plot or character development. There is nothing to be learned or experienced. It is critical that beginning readers recognize that reading can never be separated from meaning. We cannot wait until children know all the words before we start asking them to think about what has been read; making sense of print must begin with early reading.

5. Good oral reading skills are easily taught (Lauritzen, 1980). Because children will be reading stories with delightful dialogue and linguistic devices that appeal to their preference for rhyme and rhythm, the dreaded sing-song voice we so often associate with oral reading in the early grades can be extinguished. The first person who reads each story orally is the best model of good reading: the classroom teacher.

6. Predictable books provide excellent opportunities for writing activities (Cullinan, 1987). Once children have read a predictable story, the language format of the book lends itself to writing activities that are an integral part of reading.

7. Since the stories are filled with action and dialogue, predictable books lend themselves to creative dramatics. Experiences with dramatizing a story help children remember it and understand it (Pellegrini & Galda, 1982). Many of the folktales that are predictable can easily be dramatized or reenacted by using puppets or flannel figures.

8. Children have the opportunity to read what they often call "real books." The sense of accomplishment children feel when they finish an entire book is invaluable. When these books are the same ones they see in stores and libraries, their vision of themselves as true readers is enhanced. Few adults would consider a skill mastered if they could do it only in a classroom under direct supervision.

9. Predictable books allow the child to learn to read by reading. The predicting cycle (sampling, predicting, and confirming or rejecting) that is necessary for making sense occurs (Smith, 1979). Children hear a bit of the story, have

an idea of what the next word or phrase will be, and then listen to see if they were right. By using books that are predictable, we have removed an obstacle for young readers; the language patterns of these stories provide security for beginners. When children know what word will come next, they can focus their energies on the print and make the connection between the spoken word and the written word.

The Classroom

The physical structure of the classroom is an important component of an effective beginning reading curriculum. The environment should be warm and should look inviting; it should be a place where a child chooses to spend time. Consider the following:

1. There must be a classroom library. One part of the room, generally a corner, must be designated as the library. A rug or carpet is an asset, and comfortable seating (rocking chairs, beanbag chairs, or pillows) will help this corner look inviting. Few adults who read for pleasure sit upright in a chair at a desk; most of us prefer to be curled up in chairs, sprawled on couches, or snuggled in beds. Although not necessary, old bathtubs, seats from junkyard cars, and bunkbeds make excellent reading spots.

It is helpful if the library can be partially enclosed. Bookshelves or bookcases can form walls. Picture books should be displayed with their covers showing. Plastic crates or cardboard boxes can also hold books. Magazines and newspapers are important components of the literate environment and need a designated place in the library. Book posters can transform even the most sterile cement blocks. The classroom library must be kept neat; children need to learn that we care for books in a way that is different from toys. Books are not to be dumped in corners or piled on shelves. Children can assume the responsibility for maintaining the order of the library.

2. There must be a writing center. A separate portion of the room should serve as the writing center. Like the library, it must look attractive to children. A variety of types of paper, note pads, pens, pencils, and erasers should be available. Envelopes, stamp pads and stamps, and liquid correction fluid are valuable supplies. A typewriter and a supply of typing paper will also attract children. Again, the children can assume the responsibility for maintaining the writing center and keeping supplies replenished.

3. Objects and furniture in the room should be labeled in order to capitalize on any opportunity to help children make the connection between the written word and communication.

4. Charts for language experience stories, poetry, and texts of predictable books are necessary.

5. The room should be colorful and attractive. Commercially prepared bulletin boards and learning displays should be avoided. Children's work should comprise much of what hangs on the wall or is displayed. Alphabet charts and number lines made by the teacher will be much more interesting to the students.

6. The room should be neat and orderly. There is a tendency in all of us to collect far more than we could ever use. The environment is a contributing factor to the behavior of children. A room nearly suffocating in stacks of old magazines, boxes of unused materials, and faded art objects is neither efficient nor attractive.

7. The learning environment should nurture the tentative attempts of beginning readers and should be a supportive climate that encourages risk taking.

Preparing for Instruction

To begin the year, the teacher will want to have materials ready for several predictable books. Enlarged texts, often called *Big Books,* are available from catalogs and book clubs for many children's books and make excellent teaching tools. By enlarging the book, it can be used as a teaching tool for a small group or an entire class. Again, we are emulating the process that parents began in the home. The child can see the pages of the book while it is being read, and thus make matches between oral and written language and have all the clues given by authors and illustrators at his or her fingertips. If a school cannot afford to purchase commercially made Big Books, teachers can make them. Directions for making Big Books are given in Figure 3–1.

Teachers must select Big Books carefully. Merely enlarging a basal-like story will not make it an effective tool for teaching beginning reading. The best Big Books are enlarged copies of tradebooks and contain at least one of the patterns of predictability.

If possible, several paperback copies of the predictable books should be available for individual student use. This allows children to read different stories and to take the books home to read to their families. Having the stories on tape at a listening center provides additional practice for young readers.

Several different types of books are considered predictable:

1. *Repetitive stories.* Some predictable books have a set of words, such as "Little Pig, Little Pig, let me come in," that become a chorus and are repeated throughout the story. Sometimes the syntactical pattern of a story is repeated with a few word changes, as in *Mary Wore Her Red Dress* (Peek, 1985). It begins, "Mary wore her red dress, red dress, red dress. Mary wore her red dress all day long." The next story event is changed slightly: "Henry wore his green sneakers, green sneakers, green sneakers . . . ."

Figure 3–1 Making Your Own Big Books

1. Select a predictable story you like.

2. Get an end roll of newsprint from your local newspaper office. (Usually, your local newspaper office will give these to you free of charge.)

3. Cut a 36-inch length of paper for each page of the story, including the cover and dedication page.

4. Fold the sheets in half (18 inches) and staple them together on the cut side. Cover the staples with some type of tape. (Folding the sheets in half gives them more durability and prevents magic markers from bleeding through.)

5. Print the text of the story exactly as it appears in the trade book. Letters should be at least 1 inch high.

6. Illustrate the story. The students, parents, or friends may help. (If several people are assisting you, it is easier to wait until the illustrations are complete before you assemble and staple the pages.)

2. *Repetitive and cumulative stories.* Some books have a set of words that are repeated, and with each repetition, new words are added. For example, in *The Jacket I Wear in the Snow* (Neitzel, 1989), the cumulative repetition is, "This is the jacket I wear in the snow. This is the zipper that's stuck on the jacket I wear in the snow."

3. *Rhyming stories.* Some predictable books rhyme. In *Is Your Mama a Llama?* (Guarino, 1989) Lloyd tries to guess what each animal's mother is: "'Is your mama a llama?' I asked my friend *Dave.* 'No, she is not,' is the answer Dave *gave.*"

4. *Familiar cultural pattern.* Some predictable books contain the alphabet, numbers, or days of the week that make them predictable. *One Hunter* (Hutchins, 1982) shows jungle animals in a predictable sequence: "1 hunter, 2 elephants, 3 giraffes. . . ."

5. *Link wording.* In some predictable books, the words at the end of one sentence are repeated at the beginning of the next sentence, In *Brown Bear, Brown Bear, What Do You See?* (Martin, 1970) we read, "Brown Bear, Brown Bear, What do you see? I see a redbird looking at me. Redbird, redbird, what do you see? I see a yellow duck looking at me."

6. *Predictable events.* In some stories, the sequence of events in the story make it possible to guess what will happen next. For example, in *Lazy Jack* (Ross, 1985) we know that when Jack's mother chastises him for not putting a coin in his pocket, the next day when he is given a pitcher of milk, he will pour it in his pocket.

7. *Combination.* Many authors combine several of these techniques within one story.

A list of predictable books is given at the end of this chapter.

The Reading Lesson

Although we will assume that the teacher is teaching reading every day for a five-day week, this time frame can easily be modified to suit the needs of the students. The goal is to lend support to the reading process and to remove obstacles that may come between the reader and reading. The lessons are designed to become increasingly more abstract, since children learn more easily when first introduced to new ideas through concrete methods. If children experience difficulty with one level of the lesson, such as reading the phrase cards, then the teacher should repeat an earlier experience. These students may need to read along with their teacher from a Big Book again in order to gain the confidence they need to read the phrases from the story in isolation. The Big Book and the original book should be available in the classroom library for children's perusal during their free time once the teacher is through teaching from the story. Photocopies of the text of the stories can be kept in a notebook by each student. These pages may be illustrated and taken home to share with family members.

The primary focus of using predictable books is to help students understand and enjoy the story. Discussion questions that encourage the students to relate the story to their own lives and to judge and evaluate it are essential. Attention to individual words and letters is the most abstract facet of predictable reading; therefore, it takes place near the end of the sequence of lessons. The teacher can vary the lessons by choosing an art, music, or craft activity to introduce the book rather than to culminate the lessons. The use of guest speakers or field trips can provide valuable background for what will be read.

Since all the books used are picture books, the illustrations in each book also tell the story. The teacher should draw the attention of the students to the visual elements of each story so that the children become increasingly aware of what authors and illustrators do to tell their stories. Although teachers can introduce each book by reading the enlarged version, it is important that children be exposed to the original picture books. Book jackets and endpapers are works of art that students can well appreciate. Picture books come in a wonderful variety of sizes, shapes, and textures. Reading is a sensual experience and it is important for children to use as many senses as possible in exploring books.

SAMPLE ACTIVITY

Day 1
The teacher introduces the book to the class by reading the title and the names of the author and the illustrator, and asking questions that will help draw the students into the story. If the author or illustrator wrote a dedication in the book, it should be shared with children. They enjoy trying to guess who these special people may be. The teacher reads the story to the children. Reading the book to the children first provides a secure foundation for future instruction and gives children a good model of how that story should be read. At the conclusion of the story, the teacher can discuss it with the children and ask questions that require them to evaluate the story and relate it to their own lives. In the interest of variety, the teacher may introduce a story with a Book Talk or an initiating experience.

Day 2
The teacher reads the story to the children from the Big Book. He or she reminds the class that they have heard the story before and encourages them to chime in whenever they know what is being said. Guiding the reading with his or her hand or a pointer keeps the children focused and reinforces the left-to-right concept.

Day 3
Using individual copies, the children read the story with the teacher. (If this is too expensive, then the text of the story can be typed and distributed to the children.) Again, the children are encouraged to join in when they can.

The teacher introduces phrase cards to the children. It is important that children be able to read the words from the story individually, out of context. This process is initiated by taking key phrases from the story and writing them on cards. As the teacher or a classmate reads the book, children can find the matching phrase card.

Day 4

The teacher introduces word cards to the children. Certain words from the story can be printed on cards. Again, the children can match the word cards to the actual text of the story.

The teacher uses the text of the story to draw the attention of the children to word families, letters of the alphabet, or certain symbol-sound relationships.

Day 5

The teacher involves the children in some type of activity related to the story. These tasks may include writing, creative dramatics, or art projects.

Sample Lessons

- *Mary Wore Her Red Dress and Henry Wore His Green Sneakers.* Merle Peek. New York: Clarion, 1985.

Summary This is a story about animal children on their way to a birthday party. The book begins with Mary on her way to the party with her red dress being the only colored thing on the page. As each guest arrives, the pictures become increasingly colorful until the illustrations are full color.

This story is an adaptation of a Texan folksong. The endpapers are covered with balloons, which give children a hint about what will happen in the story. The book has a repetitive syntactical pattern with slight changes in wording.

Day 1

The teacher reads the title and author to the children and shows the endpapers so they can see the balloons. The children can discuss which balloon is their favorite and when and where they get balloons. The cover of the book depicts animals at a birthday party, so children can talk about their birthdays, birthday parties, what they like to eat, and so on.

The teacher reads the story to the children. At the conclusion, he or she asks the children for their opinions of it. Other concluding questions could address why Katy wore her pink hat all day. Children could tell what their favorite item of clothing is.

Day 2

The teacher reminds the students that they heard *Mary Wore Her Red Dress and Henry Wore His Green Sneakers* the day before, so they may read along if they remember any part of it. Using the Big Book, the teacher reads the text (beginning with title and author). If he or she touches lightly under each word as it is read, children can begin to focus on the left-to-right progression and make the connection between talk and print.

Day 3

The teacher hands out photocopies of the story to each child. An overhead transparency of the story text is also helpful. Children can read the story in parts or individually.

The teacher introduces phrase cards to the students. Children can match the phrase cards as they hear the story. They can be given phrase cards and can read them when they come to that part of the story. Children can also be given a phrase card for which they will draw and color an accompanying picture.

Phrase Cards
>   Mary wore her red dress
>   Henry wore his green sneakers
>   Katy wore her yellow sweater
>   Ben wore his blue jeans
>   Amanda wore her brown bandana
>   Ryan wore his purple socks
>   Stacey wore her violet ribbons
>   Kenny wore his orange shirt
>   Katy wore a pink hat
>   All day long

Day 4

The teacher introduces word cards to the students. Key words from the book can be listed. Using activities similar to what happened with phrase cards, the children can begin to focus on the individual words from the story.

Depending on the readiness of the students, the teacher can focus on the letter-sound relationship. Children can sort word cards that have the same beginning or ending letters. They can also sort color words, name words, and clothing words.

Day 5

The teacher supplements the reading with extended activities.

Writing

Children can rewrite the story by using statements from children in the class that include their name and their favorite item of clothing.

Children can write a story that has the same rhythm and syntax as *Mary Wore Her Red Dress and Henry Wore His Green Sneakers.* For example:
>   Amy ate some green grapes.
>   Joseph liked those furry kittens.

Children can write birthday party invitations for the animals who come to Katy's party.

Creative Activities

Children can draw a mural to accompany their class stories.

Children can learn the music for this story (given in the back of the book). They can also set their own stories to song and make a tape of them for the class library.

Children can make birthday hats and have a class party.

- *It's a Perfect Day.* Abigail Pizer. New York: Lippincott, 1990.

Summary   This is a rebus story about the beginning of a farm day. Each farm animal and the sound it makes is introduced on the right-hand page of the book; the accompanying rebus picture is on the left-hand page. The story begins at sunrise and ends with sunset.

This story has a repetitive and cumulative pattern.

Day 1

The teacher can introduce this story by playing "Old MacDonald Had a Farm" for the children. They can sing along if they know the song. After they listen to the record, the students can recall all the farm animals in the song and the sounds they make. The teacher can tell the students that the story they will hear is also about farm animals.

The teacher introduces the title and author of the book to the children. Using the cover of the book, the children can predict what animals they will meet in the story. The teacher can ask the children what sounds these animals make. Children who have had experiences either visiting or living on a farm can share them with the class.

After the teacher finishes the story, he or she can ask the children to discuss whether they liked it. The teacher can explain what a rebus story is.

Day 2

Using the Big Book, the teacher can read the story to the children. They can join in whenever they know what comes next. The teacher should point out how this story is arranged with the rebus story accumulating on the left pages.

Day 3

The teacher can hand out photocopies of the final rebus page of the story. Children can take turns reading the phrases and making the appropriate animals sounds.

Phrase Cards

The rooster says, Cock-a-doodle-doo!
The bee says, Buzz buzz!
The cat says, Purr purr!
The cow says, Moo moo!
The duck says, Quack quack!
The pig says, Oink oink!
The mouse says, Squeak squeak!
The goose says, Honk honk!
The dog says, Woof woof!
What a perfect day!

Day 4

The teacher can introduce word cards from the story. Children can match the animal names to their sounds. As the story is read, they can find the matching word cards. This is also a good story for teaching the sight words *the* and *says*.

The teacher may want to focus on beginning consonant sounds. This story also contains examples of when exclamation marks can be used.

Day 5

The teacher supplements the reading with extended activities.

Writing

The children can rewrite the story using other animals.

The children can make their own rebus stories to be enclosed in a class book.

Creative Activities

The children can act out the story as a play.

The children can do a watercolor of one of the farm animals in the book and an accompanying silhouette. (The back of the book shows a silhouette of all the farm animals.)

- *My Brown Bear Barney.* Dorothy Butler. Ill. by Elizabeth Fuller. New York: Greenwillow, 1988.

Summary   This is a story about a little girl and her teddy bear, Barney. Barney goes everywhere with the little girl and she is worried because she's starting school and her mother says bears can't go to school. Each story segment begins with the little girl and the beginning of a sentence, "When I go shopping, I take . . . . The following page contains a picture of each item she takes shopping with her and the corresponding words, "my mother, my little brother, my yellow basket, my red umbrella." The third page shows the shopping experience with the child and her teddy bear. Under the picture, the sentence and story segment are concluded with "and my brown bear Barney."

The story has a repetitive syntactical pattern.

Day 1

The teacher can introduce the book to the children by reading the title and author and showing them all the bears on the endpapers in the book. Since the teddy bears are in a variety of positions, the children may want to move their bodies like the bears. The teacher can ask the students to talk about their favorite stuffed animals, what their names are, what makes them special, and so on. The children can also have the opportunity to bring their favorite teddy bears to class to hear "My Brown Bear Barney." Extra bears should be available for children who forget.

After listening to the story, the children can talk about some of the places they take their stuffed animals. They may enjoy hearing about the origins of teddy bears. Also, the teacher may want to bring a bear of his or her own to show.

Day 2

Using the Big Book, the teacher rereads "My Brown Bear Barney" to the class. Children can join in whenever they feel comfortable. The students can also discuss the ending of the story and whether they think the little girl took Barney to school.

Day 3

The teacher hands out photocopies of the text of the story to the children. Choral reading can be used with groups of children or an individual can read the first two parts of each story segment and the whole class chimes in on "and my brown bear Barney."

Phrase Cards

    When I go shopping, I take
    When I play with my friend Fred, I take
    When I go gardening, I take
    When I go to the beach, I take
    When I go to my grandmother's, I take
    When I go to bed, I take
    When I go to school, next year or the next, I'll take
    and my brown bear Barney

Day 4

Word cards can be introduced. Using the Big Book, the teacher can have students match the word cards to the objects to which he or she points on each page.

The sight words *when, with, yellow, red, brown,* and *green* can be introduced. The story also contains good examples of one way that commas are used in writing.

Day 5
The teacher supplements the reading with extended activities.

Writing

The children can write an adventure of their own that involves a teddy bear.

The children can unpack their bookbags or backpacks and make a list of all the contents.

The children can write an introduction for the teddy bear to be read to the class. To be included would be the name of the bear, what is special about it, and what it looks like.

As a prediction activity, children can write invitations to their bears to come to school.

Creative Activities

Working in cooperative groups, the student can make Big Book pages like those in the stories.

Since the artwork in this story has a paper-doll format, the children may want to make clothes for a paper bear. The teacher may also want to have paper dolls for the children to cut out and play with.

The children can make movable teddy bears with construction paper and paper fasteners. These bears can be placed in positions like those on the endpapers of the book and displayed around the room.

The students may enjoy the video "Winnie the Pooh."

- *Is Your Mama a Llama?* Deborah Guarino. Ill. by Steven Kellogg. New York: Scholastic, 1989.

Summary This is a story about a llama named Lloyd who asks each animal he encounters if his or her mama is a llama. The babies respond by giving Lloyd rhyming clues about their mamas. For example, "'Is your mama a llama?' I asked my friend Dave. 'No, she is not,' is the answer Dave gave. 'She hangs by her feet, and she lives in a cave. I do not believe that's how llamas behave.' 'Oh,' I said. 'You are right about that. I think your mama sounds more like a . . . BAT!'"

The artwork in this book is extremely detailed and the pages show pictures of many mother animals with their babies. The story begins in the morning and concludes in the evening.

The story has a predictable syntactic pattern and rhymes.

Day 1
The teacher can introduce this book by asking the children to name all the animals on the front and back covers. Both the author and the illustrator have written dedications in the book and the children may want to guess who these special people are. (The information about Deborah Guarino and Steven Kellogg on the book's jacket identifies most of the people in the dedications and tells how Guarino was inspired to write the book.)

The story is told in the first person and the teacher may need to point this out to children. At the conclusion of the story, the children should know who is telling the story.

Since llamas are a bit uncommon, the teacher may want to have pictures from an encyclopedia to share with the students. Also, since this book is written like a riddle, the students should be encouraged to guess which animal is being described in each set of clues without looking at the pictures.

After hearing the story, the children can talk about other animals and their young. The teacher can have pictures of common animals (cats, dogs, chickens) and the children can match mothers to babies and label each pair.

Day 2

The teacher can read the story from the Big Book and encourage the children to join in. This time, the children can predict what animal is being described by using clues from both the author and the illustrator.

Day 3

The teacher can hand out photocopies of the stories. Since this story is told in dialogue, it can be read using a Reader's Theatre approach, with the teacher being the narrator and the childre taking the different parts.

Phrase Cards
    Is your mama a llama?
    I asked my friend
    No, she is not

Day 4

Word cards can be introduced. Students can match the rhyming words for each story segment. They can also match the pictures of each animal to the corresponding word. Since this story is told in dialogue, it is a good time to point out to the children how writers use quotation marks to enclose conversation.

Day 5

The teacher supplements the reading with extended activities.

Writing
    The students can choose an animal and write clues for the class to guess using the same pattern as the story.

    The children can practice writing dedications to books.

    The children can practice writing conversations.

Creative Activities
    The children may want to dramatize this story.

    The students can make posters of mother animals with their young.

    Children may want to explore the use of water color since it is the media used by Steven Kellogg.

    A guest speaker (perhaps a veterinarian or someone from a zoo) could talk to the children about how animals care for their babies. A field trip to a zoo or farm may provide an opportunity for children to see a variety of animals and their young.

    An appropriate video about animals may be shown.

Summary

We know that children learn to read by reading and, like any skill, the more reading is practiced, the better it becomes. However, in the past, it has been difficult to apply this information to instruction in the early grades when children did not yet know how to read; when they recognized few, if any, sight words; and when they had little understanding of the symbol-sound relationship. Fortunately, research in emergent literacy and reading aloud to young children has shed considerable light on the intriguing subject of teaching beginning reading by using tradebooks.

The following information summarizes the main points presented in this chapter:

1. *Emergent literacy* refers to an increasing awareness of the world of print.

2. One factor of emergent literacy with relevance for beginning instruction is lap reading. *Lap reading* is the term for what occurs when adults read to children. Within this warm, interactive environment, children listen to a story while they see the pictures and the words.

3. A second important facet of emergent literacy is storybook reading. This occurs when children memorize chunks of a story after hearing it several times. Storybook reading bridges the gap between nonreading and reading.

4. The traditional curriculum with its focus on letters and sounds is often devoid of the factors that make early reading experiences productive.

5. Using predictable books to teach beginning reading incorporates the best of lap and storybook reading within the curriculum.

6. Predictable books include books with repetitive patterns, cumulative and repetitive patterns, rhyming stories, familiar cultural patterns or predictable events, stories that link wording, and a variety of combinations.

7. The benefits of teaching reading with predictable books are numerous: Children read quality literature, the stories invite rereading and provide excellent practice for memorizing sight words and developing comprehension skills, good oral reading is easily taught, there are numerous opportunities for writing and creative dramatics, and children read "real books."

References

Bridge, C. A., & Burton, B. (1982). Predictable materials for beginning readers. *Language Arts, 58,* 503–507.

Bridge, C. A., Winograd, P. N., & Haley, D. (1983). Using predictable materials vs. preprimers to teach beginning sight words. *The Reading Teacher, 36,* 884–891.

Cullinan, B. E. (1987). *Children's literature in the reading program.* Newark, DE: International Reading Association.

Deford, D. E. (1981). Literacy: Reading, writing, and other essentials. *Language Arts, 58,* 652–658.

Feitelson, D., Kita, B., & Goldstein, Z. (1986). Effects of listening to series stories on first graders' comprehension and use of language. *Research in the Teaching of English, 20,* 339–356.

Flood, J. (1977). Parental styles in reading episodes with young children. *The Reading Teacher, 30,* 846–867.

Holdaway, D. (1979). *The foundations of literacy.* Syndney, Australia: Ashton-Scholastic.

Joint Statement on Literacy Development in Pre-first Grade. (1986). Prepared by the Early Childhood and Literacy Development Committee of the International Reading Association. *Language Arts, 63,* 358–363.

Lauritzen, C. (1980). Oral literature and the teaching of reading. *The Reading Teacher, 34,* 787–790.

Lundsteen, S. W. (1986, October 3). *Developmental aspects of composition (or think young).* Address presented at the Meeting of Colorado Educators, Denver, CO.

Martin, B., & Brogan, P. (1971). *Teacher's guide to instant readers.* New York: Holt, Rinehart and Winston.

Martinez, M., & Roser, N. (1985). Read it again: The value of repeated readings during story time. *The Reading Teacher, 38,* 782–786.

Mason, J. (1985). Early reading from a developmental perspective. In P. D. Pearson (Ed.), *Handbook of reading research.* New York: Longman.

Morrow, L. M. (1988). Young children's responses to one-to-one story readings in school settings. *The Reading Research Quarterly, 23,* 89–107.

Pellegrini, A., & Galda, L. (1982). The effects of thematic-fantasy play training on the development of children's story comprehension. *American Education Research Journal, 19,* 443–452.

Rhodes, L. K. (1979). Comprehension and predictability: An analysis of beginning reading materials. In J. Harste & R. F. Carey (Eds.), *New perspective on comprehension* (pp. 101–131). Bloomington, IN: Indiana University School of Education.

Roser, N. (1987). Research currents: Rethinking literature and literacy. *Language Arts, 64,* 90–97.

Smith, C. B. (1991). Emergent literacy: An early reading and writing concept. *ERIC Review, 1,* 14–15.

Smith, F. (1979). *Reading without nonsense.* New York: Teachers College Press.

Sulzby, E. (1985). Children's emergent reading of favorite books: A developmental study. *Reading Research Quarterly, 20,* 458–480.

Whaley, J. (1981–1982). Readers expectation for story structures. *Reading Research Quarterly, 17,* 90–114.

Predictable Children's Books

*Aardema, V. (1975). *Why mosquitoes buzz in people's ears.* New York: Dial.

Ahlberg, J. (1978). *Each peach pear plum.* New York: Viking.

Arno, E. (1970). *The gingerbread man.* New York: Scholastic.

Barrett, J. (1970). *Animals should definitely not wear clothes.* New York: Atheneum.

Bayer, J. (1984). *A my name is Alice.* Ill. by S. Kellogg. New York: Trumpet.

Brett, J. (1985). *Annie and the wild animals.* Boston: Houghton Mifflin.

Butler, D. (1988). *My brown bear Barney.* Ill. by E. Fuller. New York: Greenwillow.

Cameron, P. (1961). *I can't said the ant.* New York: Coward-McCann.

Carle, E. (1969). *The very hungry caterpillar.* New York: Philomel.

Carlstrom, N. W. (1984). *Better not get wet, Jesse Bear.* Ill. by B. Degen. New York: Scholastic.

Cauley, L. B. (1982). *The lock, the mouse, and the little red hen.* New York: Putnam.

Charlip, R. (1964). *What good luck, what bad luck.* New York: Scholastic Press.

Charlip, R. (1971). *Fortunately.* New York: Parents Magazine Press.

de Paola, T. (1975). *Strega Nona: An old tale.* Englewood Cliffs, NJ: Prentice Hall.

Emberly, B. (1967). *Drummer Hoff.* New York: Prentice Hall.

Flander, M., & Swann, D. (1991). *The hippopotamus song.* Ill. by N. B. Westcott. Boston: Little, Brown.

Fox, M. (1990). *Hattie and the fox.* Ill. by P. Mullins. New York: Trumpet.

Fox, M. (1990). *Night noises.* Ill. by T. Denton. New York: Harcourt Brace Jovanovich.

Ginsburg, M. (1972). *The chick and the duckling.* New York: Macmillan.

Goennel, H. (1986). *Seasons.* Boston: Little, Brown.

Goodspeed, P. (1982). *A rhinoceros wakes me up in the morning.* Ill. by D. Panek. New York: Puffin.

*Greene, J. D. (1992). *What his father did.* Ill. by J. O'Brien. Boston: Houghton Mifflin.

*Grossman, V. (1991). *Ten little rabbits.* Ill. by S. Long. New York: Trumpet.

Guarino, W. (1989). *Is your mama a llama?* Ill by S. Kellogg. New York: Scholastic.

Hutchins, P. (1968). *Rosie's walk.* New York: Macmillan.

Hutchins, P. (1982). *One hunter.* New York: Mulberry.

Kasza, K. (1987). *The wolf's chicken stew.* New York: Putnam.

*Kimmel, E. A. (1988). *Anasi and the moss-covered rock.* Ill. by J. Stevens. New York: Holiday.

Langstaff, J. (1984). *Oh, a-hunting we will go.* New York: Atheneum.

Lobel, A. (1979). *A treeful of pigs.* New York: Greenwillow.

Lobel, A. (1984). *The rose in my garden.* New YOrk: Greenwillow.

Marshall, J. (1988). *Goldilocks and the three bears.* New York: Scholastic.

Martin, B. (1970). *Brown bear, brown bear, what do you see?* New York: Holt, Rinehart and Winston.

Martin, B., Jr., & Archambault, J. (1989). *Chicka, chicka boom boom.* Ill. by L. Ehlert. New York: Simon and Schuster.

McMillan, B. (1990). *One sun.* New York: Holiday House.

McMillan, B. (1991). *Play day.* New York: Holiday House.

Mollel, T. M. (1991). *Rhinos for lunch and elephants for supper.* Ill. by B. Spurll. New York: Clarion.

Nash, O. (1991). *The adventures of Isabel.* Ill. by J. Marshall. Boston: Little, Brown.

Neitzel, S. (1989). *The jacket I wear in the snow.* Ill. by N. W. Parker. New York: Greenwillow, 1989.

Nomanska, J. (1985). *Busy Monday morning.* New York: Greenwillow.

Numeroff, L. J. (1985). *If you give a mouse a cookie.* Ill. by F. Bond. New York: Harper and Row.

O'Neill, M. (1961). *Hailstones and halibut bones.* New York: Doubleday.

Peck, M. (1985). *Mary wore her red dress.* New York: Clarion.

Pizer, A. (1990). *It's a perfect day.* New York: Lippincott.

Ross, T. (1985). *Lazy Jack.* New York: Dial.

Schulevitz, U. (1967). *One Monday morning.* New York: Scribner's.

Sendak, M. (1962). *Chicken soup with rice.* New York: Scholastic Press.

Seuling, B. (1976). *Teeny-tiny woman.* New York: Viking.

Shaw, C. G. (1947). *It looked like spilt milk.* New York: Harper and Row.

Shepard, J. (1990). *The right number of elephants*. Ill. by F. Bond. New York: HarperCollins.

Slepian, J., & Seidler, A. (1967). *The hungry thing*. Ill. by R. E. Martin. Chicago: Follett.

Slobodkina, E. (1947). *Caps for sale*. Reading, MA: Addison-Wesley.

Thomas, P. (1971). *"Stand back," said the elephant, "I'm going to sneeze!"* New York: Lothrop, Lee and Shepard.

Van Allsburg, C. (1987). *The Z was zapped*. Boston: Houghton Mifflin.

Van Laan, N. (1990). *Possum come a knocking*. Ill. by G. Booth. New York: Trumpet.

Vipont, E. (1969). *The elephant and the bad baby*. New York: Coward-McCann.

Weston, M. (1992). *Bea's four bears*. New York: Clarion.

Williams, L. (1986). *The little old lady who was not afraid of anything*. Ill. by M. Lloyd. New York: Harper Trophy.

Williams, V. B. (1990). *More more more said the baby*. New York: Scholastic, 1990.

Wood, D., & Wood, A. (1984). *The napping house*. New York: Harcourt Brace Jovanovich.

Wood, D., & Wood, A. (1985). *King Bidgood's in the bathtub*. New York: Harcourt Brace Jovanovich.

Yektai, N. (1987). *What's missing?* Ill. by S. Ryan. New YOrk: Clarion.

Yektai, N. (1991). *Bears in pairs*. Ill. by D. de Groat. New York: Aladdin.

*Indicates multicultural focus.

4

Teaching Reading Comprehension

A teacher selects *Where the Red Fern Grows* (Rawls, 1961) to read to her class and one wary student asks, "Is the dog going to die in this book, too?" A father is reading the second chapter of *The Great Gilly Hopkins* (Paterson, 1978) to his daughter and she wants to know, "Why is Gilly so mean to people all of the time?" The babysitter reads *Snow White* (Heins, 1974) to her little charge and the next day the child decides that her mother is "wicked stepmothering" her when she can't wear her bathing suit to the grocery store. In each of these cases, the child involved is comprehending the printed message. Sense is being made in an ongoing process that involves the life experiences of the reader, the background information he or she has acquired, the purpose for reading, and the characteristics and quality of what is being read.

Reading Comprehension

The process of reading comprehension, at any phase, involves an active search for meaning. The reader must interact with the text on an emotional level (as we do when a particular story touches us), on an intellectual level (as when we find out more about penguins or airplanes), or on a physical level (as when we follow a recipe for chocolate cake or put together a model car). It is a process that must be continually monitored by a reader who is armed with remedies for failure at any stage. Comprehension involves the application of different kinds of knowledge—knowledge of text structure and knowledge of a certain topic or topics. Effective readers expect differences between their science textbook and a novel. They make efficient use of typographical features such as charts, graphs, illustrations, and style and size of print. A conscious knowledge of the topic being discussed by the author is applied while reading occurs.

Reading comprehension is also a strategic process. The reader can vary both the approach to the material and the rate at which it is read. We use a phone book much differently than a set of directions, and we tend to start at the beginning of a novel, the end of a financial statement, and anywhere we want with a newspaper. How we approach reading depends on our purpose for reading. Children must be made aware that what people need or want from print will dictate how they go about getting it. Readers may reread something when they are puzzled. For example, we often go back to the beginning of a sentence or phrase when we find that we are using the wrong pronunciation of *present* and it doesn't make sense. We may read ahead to see if things become clear, as we do in jokes, riddles, or mysteries.

We also vary our rate when we read, breezing through novels we read for pleasure but reading a textbook laboriously. We savor every word in a love letter but quickly scan the *TV Guide* to decide what to watch at 6:00 P.M. Readers even decide *not* to read, as is the case with most junk mail, or may make a decision to read that is completely dependent on context. For example, many of us read the back of cereal boxes for lack of anything better, and most adults have read material in airports that they would never be seen reading in any place else.

Printed words serve as a blueprint to the reader. Meaning is constructed but seldom as an exact duplicate of what the writer may have intended—a fact to which many cooks would agree when they compare their soufflé with the one pictured in the cookbook. Readers bring meaning to the page and take meaning from it. Those who have reread a childhood favorite can recall how different the book may seem the second time around. Although the words and pictures have stayed the same, the reader has not.

Teaching Reading with Children's Literature

Our primary goal when we read is to understand or comprehend. There is no purpose for reading unless we are attempting to make some sense of the words before us. Teachers of reading would agree that not only is reading comprehension the most important facet of reading but it is the area with which the students often experience difficulty (Anderson, Heibert, Scott, & Wilkinson, 1985).

The quality of reading that students do can be no better than the quality of the materials to which they are exposed. Members of the computer world refer to this philosophy as "garbage in, garbage out." Our grandmothers said it differently: "You can't make a silk purse out of a sow's ear." Regardless of which homily we prefer, in order for teachers to accomplish what they must, the world of quality children's literature has to be available to them.

Teachers today are working with students who have seen thousands of hours of television, watched hundreds of movies, and played dozens of video games. Only the world of books can match these experiences for vicarious excitement. Children come from divergent backgrounds and are part of unique family structures. No one basal reader could possibly contain stories that would interest all of the children we find in one classroom or describe characters and experiences with which they could all identify. Since the ultimate goal of reading instruction is to produce people who can read and who will read, the materials chosen for instruction must facilitate that goal. At all grade levels, children's literature can be the basis of effective instruction in reading comprehension.

Cullinan (1987) summarizes the relationship between literature and teaching reading comprehension:

1. It takes a good story to teach reading comprehension and to hold the reader's interest.

2. Students learn the language of literature by reading and hearing literature read aloud.

3. Students draw on what they read as a source of knowledge when they write.

4. Students who read a lot become fluent readers.

Reading Comprehension Instruction

Although educators would agree that reading comprehension is the most important by-product of reading, direct instruction in comprehension occupies less than 1 percent of the instructional time in the classroom (Durkin, 1978–1979). Rather than modeling strategies that enhance reading comprehension, teachers tend to mention skills and to test for their attainment (Durkin, 1981). Traditional exercises for reading comprehension seldom provide opportunities for transfer to an actual reading experience with connected text. For example, Taylor, Olson, Prenn, Rybcznski, and Zakaluk (1985) find that even though students can find the main idea on multiple choice materials, they are unable to perform at the same level on a similar task in the content area, and fail completely at generating their own main ideas for what had been read.

An overwhelming number of skills, hopefully related to understanding what has been read, are introduced during reading class, but they are seldom practiced. Reading comprehension needs to be taught directly at all levels. Through a series of teacher-led exercises, teachers should develop in their students a thorough understanding of what reading comprehension means, how it can be monitored, and what can be done when comprehension fails to occur.

It has been proposed that all learning proceeds from the social level to the individual level (Vygotsky, 1962). In other words, learning begins with an interaction with others, often through dialogue, and eventually becomes an internalized, independent process. This concept is further developed in the education setting, where it has been labeled "scaffolding" (Bruner, 1978). Scaffolding occurs when learners move from where they can function independently to their potential level of achievement if they are guided by an accomplished person. The guide may be a child teaching another child how to tie his or her shoes, a parent showing how a bed is made, or a teacher leading a child through the step-by-step process of drawing logical inferences.

The following model for comprehension instruction is reflective of the philosophy that learning is a guided process that is modeled by the teacher, that it can begin with either whole- or small-group instruction, and that it moves from cooperative experiences to independent practice and application. The following teaching model for comprehension instruction described by Taylor, Harris, and Pearson (1988) is suggested for the activities in this chapter:

1. The teacher explains to the students what will be taught.

2. The teacher tells the students why it is important.

3. The teacher models the technique, verbalizing his or her own thought processes.

4. The teacher provides experiences for either the whole class or cooperative groups.

5. The teacher provides opportunity for guided practice.

6. The teacher provides opportunity for independent practice.

The remainder of this chapter is divided into discussions of teaching reading comprehension with children's literature. Teaching ideas are given for teaching comprehension through visual literacy and during each stage of reading: before reading, during reading, and after reading.

It is recommended that picture books be used initially, even with middle grade readers. The illustrations in picture books provide concrete examples and lend support to comprehension, the stories can be completed in one setting, and the books can be enjoyed by readers of all ages.

Visual Literacy and Reading Comprehension

Children enter school adept at interpreting visual stimuli in their environment. They recognize the golden arches of McDonald's from great distances and immediately anticipate hamburgers, french fries, and milk shakes. A child who sees Mr. Yuk on a container realizes that whatever is inside will not taste good. By drawing the attention of the reader to the illustrations and format of books and/or magazines and by guiding the comprehension of nonprint information, we can lay the foundation for extracting meaning from written text. Learning to interpret illustrations can forge a vital link between visual literacy and print literacy.

The following comprehension skills can be taught through visual literacy:

1. Predicting
2. Looking at events in more than one way
3. Gathering clues to meaning
4. Finding stories within stories

Teaching Comprehension Through Visual Literacy

A logical progression for comprehension instruction is the gradual movement from a concrete experience to tasks of increasing levels of abstraction. It is easy to think of hands-on, tactile experiences for math and science, but it is more difficult when we are trying to make reading a concrete activity. Print itself is an abstraction and reading is a mental process; we can see products of reading, but we cannot see reading itself. In order to make comprehension instruction more tangible, we can begin with activities and tasks for prereading, during reading, and postreading with visual experiences.

TEACHING IDEAS FOR VISUAL LITERACY

Comprehension Skill: Predicting

- *What's Missing?* Niki Yektai. Ill. by Susannah Ryan. New York: Clarion.

1. The teacher tells the class that they will be guessing what will happen in a story by looking at pictures.
2. The teacher tells the students that it is important to make guesses before we read because then we read more carefully to find out if we were right.

3. The teacher shows students the cover of *What's Missing?* He or she verbalizes reactions to the picture: "I think the illustrator has left something out of the picture. The mother is pulling a leash but it's empty. It looks to me like a small dog would fit in the picture." The students and the teacher can check the next illustration in the book to see if the guess was correct.

4. The teacher asks the students to guess what is missing in the next picture and asks them what clues the artist has given to help us find out what has been left out of the drawing.

5. The teacher continues with the story, providing opportunities for the students to predict what has been left out of the pictures, give the reasons behind their predictions, and then reading on to see if they were right.

6. At the end of the lesson, the students can draw their own *What's Missing?* pictures for their classmates to guess.

Comprehension Skill: Looking at Things in More than One Way

- *Round Trip.* Ann Jonas. New York: Greenwillow, 1983.

1. The teacher tells the class that they are going to see pictures in stories that can be looked at in more than one way.

2. The teacher tells the students that this is an important skill in reading because authors often use words that may have more than one meaning.

3. The teacher shows the students the cover of *Round Trip* and asks the students to explain what the author may mean by the title. He or she verbalizes reactions to the cover picture: "The pictures are black and white, which are opposite colors, and the title is written right side up and upside down. If I turn the book upside down, the picture looks much different."

4. The teacher shows the students the illustrations in the story and encourages the students to notice as much detail as possible.

5. At the end of the story, the book is turned upside down and the readers read through the story from back to front to complete the journey. The book can be turned upside down so that students can look at the pictures both ways.

6. Students can make their own books with a format similar to that of Ann Jonas's or enjoy more of her books.

Comprehension Skill: Gathering Clues to Meaning

- *Gorilla.* By Anthony Browne. New York: Knopf, 1983.

1. The teacher tells the students that they will be looking at books that have clues hidden in the illustrations that help tell what is happening in the story.

2. The teacher tells the students that this is an important skill in reading because authors often give us clues in their writing that help us understand the story.

3. The teacher shows the students the cover of the book and begins reading the story. He or she can verbalize reactions to the illustrations: "It looks like Hannah is lonely; she and her father don't look at each other. Gorillas are hidden in many of the pictures. Maybe the author is giving us a hint that Hannah has an imagination."

4. After reading the page that describes Hannah going to bed after her birthday, the teacher can ask the students questions about Hannah and what she wants most for her birthday. The teacher and the students can return to the beginning of the story and look for gorillas hidden in the pictures.

5. The teacher can continue to read the story and show the students the illustrations, giving them opportunities to predict what will happen and then either confirm or reject their hypotheses.

Comprehension Skill: Finding Stories within Stories

- *Come Away from the Water, Shirley.* John Burningham. New York: Thomas Y. Crowell, 1977.

1. The teacher tells the students that they are going to look at a picture book where there are two stories going on at the same time.

2. The teacher tells the students that many authors have more than one plot in their books and that readers have to pay attention to what is happening in both situations.

3. The teacher shows the students the cover of *Come Away from the Water, Shirley* and gives the students an opportunity to discuss what is happening. As the teacher begins the story, he or she should ask the students from whose perspective the story is being told. The teacher can verbalize reactions to the pictures: "The side of the page with the parents on it has pictures that are less colorful and larger than the side of the page with Shirley's adventures. It looks to me like two stories are going on at the same time."

4. The teacher can continue to read the story and have students make two sets of predictions, one for what the parents will say and do and one for what will happen next to Shirley.

5. The teacher can read another adventure with Shirley without showing the students the illustrations and have them draw sets of pictures that reflect what the parents are doing and what Shirley is doing at the same time.

The Three Phases of Reading Comprehension

Reading comprehension occurs in three overlapping phases: before reading, during reading, and after reading (Crafton, 1982).

Comprehension Before Reading

The boy worrying about another dog dying in *Where the Red Fern Grows* (Rawls, 1961) is applying experiences with *A Dog Called Kitty* (Wallace, 1980) and *Stone Fox* (Gardiner, 1980), both stories in which the dog does indeed die, to a new situation. Before reading, readers mobilize their existing information and relate it to the experience at hand, much in the way they eagerly anticipate what will happen at a birthday party or what food they will eat at Thanksgiving dinner. Because comprehension involves the answering of questions asked and the acceptance or rejection of hypotheses made by the reader, it is a critical phase of comprehension. Lack of experience, background, or purpose can jeopardize the potential success of the reader.

Since what we already know about a topic is one of the most powerful predictors of our success with it, it is critical that teachers prepare their students sufficiently so that success will be attainable. Using prior knowledge involves calling to mind what we already know and using the text to add to and/or make changes in this store of information.

The comprehension skills given focus before reading are:

1. Reducing uncertainty
2. Predicting
3. Brainstorming
4. Relating information

Teaching Reading Comprehension Before Reading

Activities that occur before reading can serve many purposes. They may help to reduce uncertainty, particularly in the case where readers may have little background experiences with what will be read. For example, the teacher may do a Book Talk using some type of visual aid that is connected with what will be read. Listening to music or using maps and other reference materials can give children information before they begin reading. Students can sample a variety of rice dishes before reading *Everybody Cooks Rice* (Dooley, 1991) or find Japan on a world map before reading *The Boy of the Three Year Nap* (Snyder, 1988).

TEACHING IDEAS FOR TEACHING COMPREHENSION BEFORE READING

Comprehension Skill: Reducing Uncertainty (Book Talk)

- *Ira Sleeps Over.* Bernard Waber. New York: Scholastic, 1972.

    1. *Note:* Since a book talk is like an advertisement for a book or a gimmick to get kids excited about the story, the teacher does not talk about the purpose of the activity.
    2. The teacher asks students questions about their own experiences with sleepovers—for example, what kinds of things they like to do or eat when someone spends the night with a friend.
    3. The teacher shows students an overnight bag and tells them that it is packed for a sleepover. The students can guess what will be inside. (Items for inclusion: pajamas, toothbrush, hairbrush, pillow, teddy bear, and so on).
    4. The teacher can read *Ira Sleeps Over* to the students, pausing to ask them questions that relate their own experiences to the story.
    5. After hearing the story, students can make lists of what they would take with them on a sleepover.

Comprehension Skill: Reducing Uncertainty (Listening to Music)

- *Rondo in C.* Paul Fleischman. Ill. by Janet Wentworth. New York: Harper and Row, 1988.

1. The teacher tells the students that they will be thinking about how stories can mean something special to different people.

2. The teacher tells the students that it is important to think of this because our own feelings and experiences influence how much we like a story.

3. The teacher can show the students the cover of *Rondo in C* and call their attention to the picture of the child playing a piano.

4. Students who play musical instruments can talk about how often they practice, what songs they play, or what recitals they have given.

5. The teacher can play Beethoven's *Rondo in C* for the students while the students listen quietly with their eyes closed.

6. After listening to the music, the students can brainstorm and list all the things the music made them think of.

7. The teacher can read the story to the children while they listen to compare their images with those of the characters in *Rondo in C*.

8. Students may enjoy listening to classical music at other times during the day.

Prereading lessons can help readers establish a purpose for reading and provide questions that will be answered as reading progresses. When students have questions to answer or specific hypotheses to test, the reading task takes on direction that encourages comprehension. A teacher may pose specific questions that will be answered as reading occurs. In a brainstorming session, students can organize all they know about a topic before they read to add to and clarify their ideas.

Comprehension Skill: Predicting

- *How Much Is a Million?* David Schwartz. Ill. by Steven Kellogg. New York: Lothrop, Lee and Shepard, 1985.

1. The teacher tells the students that they will be guessing about how much a million of something is and then reading to find out if they were right.

2. The teacher tells the students that it is important to make guesses before reading because then we read more carefully to find out if we were right.

3. The teacher asks students if they know any cities with a population of a million or more. The teacher can read the refrain from *Millions of Cats* (Gag, 1928) and show students the pictures of the million cats.

4. The teacher can verbalize his or her guesses about what a million is: "I think it would take a long time to count to a million—maybe two days. I'll be curious to see what your guesses are."

5. Working in cooperative groups, the students complete the worksheet accompanying *How Much Is a Million?* (see Figure 4–1).

6. The students read (or listen to) the book and compare their guesses with the accurate answers.

7. The students can find references to a million in newspapers, magazines, or other books to share with the class the next day.

Figure 4–1 Worksheet to Accompany *How Much Is a Million?*

How much time would you need to count to

a million? _____

a billion? _____

a trillion? _____

How much water would you need to hold

a million goldfish? _____

a billion goldfish? _____

a trillion goldfish? _____

How many book pages would you need to draw

a million tiny stars? _____

a billion tiny stars? _____

a trillion tiny stars? _____

Comprehension Skill: Brainstorming

- *Shoes.* Elizabeth Winthrop. Ill. by William Joyce. New York: Harper and Row, 1986.

1. The teacher tells the students that they will be brainstorming, or telling everything they know about something.
2. The teacher tells the students that this is important because it helps us find out what we know about something before we read.
3. The teacher can model brainstorming by listing a topic on the board and telling all he or she knows about it.
4. The teacher divides the class into pairs or groups of threes.
5. She or he tells the students that they are going to be asked to list all the different kinds of shoes they can think of in two minutes. One student in each group will be the scribe.
6. The students are given two minutes to list shoes.
7. When the time is up, each group can total their lists and then read them to the class.
8. The teacher can read *Shoes* to the class or they can read it by themselves.
9. The students can list all the different kinds of shoes the author mentions.

The teacher may want to arouse the curiosity of the readers or help them link their own experiences with what will take place in print. Bringing in guest speakers can pique the interest of readers. Teachers can introduce a book by reading a related poem or picture book. Appropriate discussions can help readers put their own experiences in words and provide a familiar basis for a story.

Comprehension Skill: Related Information

- *What Happened to Patrick's Dinosaurs?* Carol Carrick. Ill. by Donald Carrick. New York: Clarion, 1986.

    1. The teacher tells the students that they will be reading poetry before they read the story.
    2. The teacher tells the students that this helps us look at the ideas in a book from the point of view of a poet. He or she can verbalize this relationship: "Poets have to discuss the same ideas that we read in books, only in just a few words. When I read poetry, it makes the ideas in books more obvious. Let's see how poems about dinosaurs can give us many of the same ideas that the book does." Two poems about dinosaurs that would be appropriate for this are "What If . . ." by Isabel Joshlin Glaser and "Dinosaur" by Margaret Hillert.
    3. The students can discuss the poems and their own ideas as to what happened to the dinosaurs.
    4. The students can read or listen to *What Happened to Patrick's Dinosaurs?* and see what Patrick thinks happened to them.
    5. The students can find other poems about dinosaurs.

Comprehension During Reading

Once readers are mentally prepared for the task at hand, they need to develop flexible strategies for allowing the comprehension process to move smoothly. Readers must gather clues and construct a working interpretation of the text (Crafton, 1982). They should continually refine and change their tactics while reading occurs and have at hand a variety of strategies for fixing any difficulties encountered along the way. The little girl who asks her father about Gilly's disposition in *The Great Gilly Hopkins* (Paterson, 1978) is attempting to clear up the contradiction in the negative way Gilly reacts to those who care about her and the way this girl has been taught to behave to adults. It is necessary that this difference be explained so that the reading can proceed in a logical manner.

While reading, children can develop the following comprehension skills:

1. Monitoring their comprehension
2. Perceiving information on three levels (literal, interpretive, and applied)
3. Identifying important ideas and supporting details
4. Classifying information
5. Sequencing information

Teaching Reading Comprehension During Reading

Students can be taught to monitor their own comprehension as they read. Skilled readers seem to do this automatically, but beginning and struggling readers need to develop this ability through structured activities. Teachers can reproduce sentences and paragraphs from challenging materials. Students can read silently and rate their own understanding with either a + or a − and write a brief explanation of what was causing the difficulty (Taylor et al., 1988). If the comprehension failure was caused by problems with vocabulary, teachers can instruct students in using the following strategies for repairing failure at the word level:

1. Read around the word.
2. Use context clues.
3. Use structural clues.
4. Use a dictionary.
5. Ask for help.

For comprehension failure at the idea level, the following approaches could be used:

1. Read on to clarify.
2. Reread from the beginning.
3. Look at the title, pictures, and headings.
4. Ask questions.
5. Paraphrase ideas.
6. Try to relate ideas to personal experiences.
7. Ask for help.

Authors rely on the reader to make logical inferences while reading. Students must be able to interrelate ideas from the text so that thoughts form a cohesive whole. Information in stories is given on three levels: the literal level, the interpretive level, and the applied level. Teachers can ask students specific questions from material to be read and have the students document whether the answer was directly given in the story, can be inferred from the information given, or is dependent on the ideas and experiences of the reader. For example, students can be given passages to read with a set of questions to which they will respond. Working in cooperative groups, they can answer the questions and then indicate where in the text the answer was located. A circle can be placed around answers specifically stated in the text (literal), inferential clues can be underlined, and answers that come from the experiences of the reader can be summarized.

TEACHING IDEAS FOR TEACHING COMPREHENSION DURING READING

Comprehension Skill: Perceiving Information on Three Levels

- *Amelia Bedelia.* Peggy Parrish. Ill. by Fritz Seibel. New York: Scholastic, 1970.

1. The teacher can tell the students that they will be listening to examples of figurative language (words that can have more than one meaning) and homophones (words that sound alike but have different meanings).

2. The teacher can tell students that this is important because many authors use figurative language to make their stories more interesting. He or she can verbalize interpreting figurative language: "When people say, 'That drives me up the wall,' it sounds like they are talking about cars, but what they really mean is that something frustrates them. What do people do that drive you up the wall?" The teacher can also verbalize interpreting homophones: "Some words sound the same but have more than one meaning—for example, *pair* and *pear*. We will see how Amelia Bedelia gets confused by word meanings."

3. The teacher can begin reading the story to the class and ask the class what it means to "dress a turkey" or "dust the furniture." They can compare their answers to what Amelia does.

4. The teacher can continue to read the book in this fashion, giving students an opportunity to discuss the double meanings of the words.

5. At the conclusion of the story, students may enjoy other books like this.

6. Students can draw their own interpretations of examples of figurative language literally, then write how the expression is interpreted, and then give an example.

An important comprehension skill is the ability to identify important ideas and supporting details. Students can be given an outline to follow while reading that requires them to list a key idea and important details. In the initial stages, the teacher may choose to list a main idea for the students—perhaps the theme of the story—and then have the students fill in the details as they read. This can also be done with an emphasis on story grammar (setting, point of view, characterization, plot, theme, and style) by having students write the conflict of a story and then list events that complicate the situation, the climax, and the resolution of the story (see Figure 4–2).

The ability to classify information also nurtures comprehension of text. While students read, they can sort information from a story. For example, they may list information about two characters while reading. They can sort ideas and facts from what has been read into categories, either according to the elements of story grammar or another grouping selected by the teacher.

Comprehension Skill: Classifying Information

- *The Magic School Bus at the Waterworks.* Joanna Cole. Ill. by Bruce Degen. New York: Harcourt Brace Jovanovich, 1986.

1. The teacher shows the cover of the book to the students and mentions that this is a story that contains factual information about water and water treatment and that it is also about events that could not really happen.

2. The teacher tells the students that it is important to be able to distinguish what *could* happen and what *does* happen in stories. He or she can verbalize this difference: "The cover of this book shows things that are realistic and things that are fantastic. For example, the water treatment plant is something that exists, but a school bus driving on the water could never happen. In this book, the author and the illustrator combine real and

Figure 4–2 Story Map

Title of the story:

Author/Illustrator:

Dedication:

Setting:

Characters:

What is the problem?

How is it solved?

unreal things to teach us about water. We need to be able to tell which bits of information are facts."

3. The students can fold a piece of paper in half and label one column "Fact" and the second column "Fantasy."

4. The students can fill in the information while they hear the story or read it on their own.

5. The class can discuss the clues the authors use to help us determine which information is factual (for example, facts are listed on notebook paper in the margins).

6. The students may enjoy other books in this series.

Comprehension Skill: Classifying Information

- *Heckedy Peg.* Audrey Wood. Ill. by Don Wood. New York: Harcourt Brace Jovanovich, 1987.

1. The teacher tells the students that they will be answering some questions while they read a story.

2. The teacher tells the students that this is important because we need to pay attention while we read.

3. The teacher poses the question to the students, "What is the name of the first child?" He or she then reads the first page of *Heckedy Peg* and answers the question.

4. The students read (or listen to) *Heckedy Peg* and complete the accompanying worksheet while they read (see Figure 4–3).

5. The students find other examples of traditional stories in which there were witch's spells.

Figure 4–3 Worksheet to Accompany *Heckedy Peg*

Children	Market Requests	Spell
1.		
2.		
3.		
4.		
5.		
6.		
7.		

Being able to sequence events from a story also helps students make sense of what has been read. Teachers may give students a list of events from a story that students can number while they read. Instructions can be given to the readers—for example, "List everything that happens to a character on a journey." If the story contains dates, students can fill in slots on a time line while reading.

Comprehension Skill: Sequencing

- *Alexander, Who Used to Be Rich Last Sunday.* Judith Viorst. Ill. by Ray Cruz. New York: Aladdin, 1978.

1. The teacher tells the students that they will be listening to (or reading) a story and keeping track of events as they happen.
2. The teacher tells the students that this is important because in many stories we have to remember the order in which things occur. He or she can verbalize the importance of orders: "In this story, a little boy tries to save his money but keeps spending it bit by bit. I know just how he feels!"
3. The teacher can ask the students to draw a circle and divide it into 12 segments. The top segment should be labeled $.00; the one to the right should be labeled $1.00.
4. The teacher reads the story to the students as they record all the ways Alexander spent his money and how much he spent in each venture. Each expenditure goes in one of the segments.
5. The students may enjoy writing some of their own story problems with money.

Comprehension After Reading

However valuable any of the books, magazines, or newspapers children read, it would be impossible for teachers to do more than sample the quality of work available today. Therefore, the reading task in the elementary school has to serve dual purposes. First, it gives the readers something they did not have before they read: a bit of information, new insight, a unique way of looking at something, or an emotionally satisfying experience, whether it be crying, laughing, or saying, "That happened to me once, too!" The second purpose of reading is to give the reader more information about how reading occurs. The student needs to leave the reading task with more knowledge about reading; how to monitor, control, and salvage comprehension; and the ability to apply these skills to a new situation.

After reading takes place, it is time to synthesize and clarify what has been encountered. Readers should share with one another and exchange information and opinions, encouraged by the teacher and one another to make connections between what has been read and their own lives or other reading experiences. The child who quietly listens to *Snow White* (Heins, 1974) and later on accuses her mother of "wicked stepmothering" her is not only enjoying a wonderful story but is using new information in a familiar situation.

After students have completed the reading task, their comprehension efforts can focus on:

1. Listing new information
2. Comparing and contrasting ideas
3. Determining cause and effect
4. Participating in discussions
5. Conducting research

Teaching Reading Comprehension After Reading

Comprehension after reading occurs is often overlooked. However, activities that occur at this time bring closure to the reading task. When students have completed the act of reading, it is time for them to synthesize information, making connections between what was just read and other information stored in the minds and hearts of the readers. It is also the time for readers to call to mind what has been learned about the process of reading—in other words, what is being taken away from this experience that wasn't there before. Students can write in journals and summarize the reading strategies they used during the story (perhaps a decoding skill or an inferential skill). They can evaluate and judge the story according to their own opinions. Students can also list new information they have gained from this reading experience through outlines or semantic maps.

TEACHING IDEAS FOR TEACHING COMPREHENSION AFTER READING

Comprehension Skills: Listing New Information

- *A Cache of Jewels and Other Collective Nouns.* Ruth Heller. New York: Grosset & Dunlap, 1987.

1. The teacher tells the students that they will be making lists of new things they have learned after they read something.

2. The teacher tells the students that this is important because we will remember new information better if we take the time to write it down. He or she can verbalize the importance of writing after reading: "Remembering what collective nouns are may be difficult if we don't have something to help our memories."

3. The students can read the book and make lists of several examples of collective nouns. For example, each student could choose their favorite four to illustrate on a chart:
   a BATCH of bread
   a FLEET of ships
   a MUSTER of peacocks
   a LITTER of puppies

4. As a follow-up activity, the students can find out what groups of other animals are called.

The importance of the social aspect of reading can be emphasized after reading occurs. Students can form small groups and talk about books or stories they read, much in the way adults do. Students reading the same material can prepare projects or activities that can crystalize their knowledge. Children may decide to do further reading on their own, sparked by what has just been read. A variety of activities can be used to emphasize comprehension after reading.

After reading, students can compare and contrast characters, settings, or ideas in a story. They can compare what has been read to their own lives or to other books or movies. Children may compare multiple versions of the same story or similar topics as they are dealt with in a variety of books. Using nonfiction, students can compare scientific facts as they change over time. Comparisons can also be made between books on the basis of any of the elements of story grammar or how stories are begun and concluded. The artwork in books can also be analyzed.

Comprehension Skill: Comparing and Contrasting Ideas

Giants

- *Fin M'Coul.* Tomie de Paola. New York: Holiday House, 1981.

- *Jim and the Beanstalk.* Raymond Briggs. New York: Coward-McCann, 1970.

Pigs

- *Perfect the Pig.* Susan Jeske. New York: Scholastic, 1980.

- *Small Pig.* Arnold Lobel. New York: Trumpet, 1969.

Monsters

- *Clyde Monster.* Robert Crowe. Ill. by K. Chorao. New York: E. P. Dutton, 1976.

- *I'm Coming to Get You.* Tony Ross. New York: Dial, 1984.

1. The teacher tells the students that they will be comparing and contrasting different characters from a story.

2. The teacher tells the students that this is important because it helps us understand how things can be alike and different.

3. The teacher reads two poems, "Herbert Glerbett" by Jack Prelutsky (*Random House Book of Poetry for Children,* 1983) and "Jimmy Jet and His TV Set" by Shel Silverstein (*Where the Sidewalk Ends,* 1974). The teacher then asks student to list all the ways Herbert and Jimmy are alike and the ways they are different. The teacher draws an outline of two boys that slightly overlaps. Shared qualities are written on the portion of the drawing that overlaps. Different characteristics are written on the appropriate outline (see Figure 4–4).

4. Students are separated into cooperative learning groups and each group is given two of the books and asked to read the stories and then compare and contrast either the giants, the pigs, or the monsters. Outlines are drawn on large sheets of newsprint.

5. The groups display their finished projects and explain them to each other.

6. Students can independently compare other characters from stories (see Figure 4–5).*

Recognizing cause and effect is a comprehension skill that can be a focal point after reading. Given a particular event in a story, students can list the cause or causes. They can examine the cause and effect relationships from the opposite angle by finding the effects of a particular event. Picture books can be used to examine cause and effect as it is dealt with by illustrators. Students can be asked to write their own prologues or epilogues to stories where they

Figure 4–4

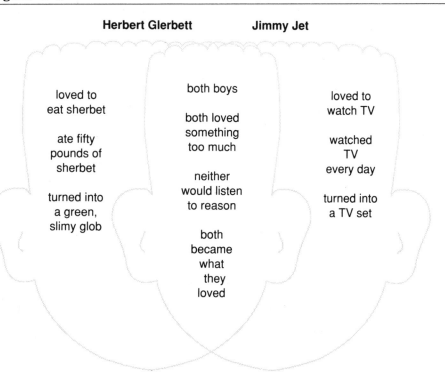

Herbert Glerbett		Jimmy Jet
loved to eat sherbet	both boys	loved to watch TV
ate fifty pounds of sherbet	both loved something too much	watched TV every day
turned into a green, slimy glob	neither would listen to reason	turned into a TV set
	both became what they loved	

*Special thanks to Dr. Karen Sweeney for this great idea.

Figure 4–5

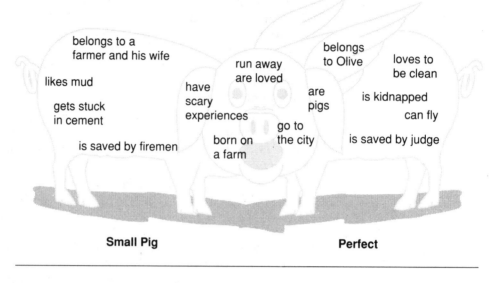

Small Pig   Perfect

either set the stage for what is happening in a story or continue with events introduced by the author.

Comprehension Skill: Determining Cause and Effect

- *If You Give a Mouse a Cookie.* Laura Joffe Numeroff. Ill. by Felicia Bond. New York: Harper and Row, 1985.

1. The teacher can show the students the cover of the book and ask them questions about the little mouse.
2. The teacher tells the students that they will be looking at events in the story that are related; everything the mouse does leads into some thing else. He or she can tell the students that cause and effect help us figure out why things happen in a story.
3. The teacher can verbalize cause and effects: "The little boy is being nice and giving the mouse a cookie, but I think that will just lead to something else. I bet he will want something to drink. That's how children usually are; they like something to drink with a snack. In this story, everything that happens leads to something else; it is a series of causes and effects."
4. As the teacher reads the book, the students can predict what will happen next.
5. After the story is finished, the teacher can ask students to relate events in the story between the little boy and the mouse and their own experiences taking care of younger children.
6. Phrases from the story can be printed on cards (for example, "He's going to ask for a glass of milk"). Students can give the resulting effect for each card.
7. The teacher can point out to the students that what is a cause in one instance becomes the effect in the next event. For example, "Because the mouse

asks for a cookie (cause), he gets thirsty (effect) and because he is thirsty (cause), he asks for a glass of water (effect).

Students can extrapolate events from a story to other situations as they examine how a particular event in history or science affected their lives. They can identify contemporary problems from a story and predict future effects.

Higher-order thinking skills require students to use cognitive processes to resolve difficulties. It may require students to infer, offer, and evaluate solutions to problems, to analyze arguments, or to identify bias and point of view. Using stories with strong themes or controversial plots, teachers can ask students to probe deeply into a story and answer open-ended questions. Working in cooperative learning groups, students may grapple with the ideas presented in a story.

Comprehension Skill: Participating in Discussion Groups

* *Fireflies!* Julie Brinckloe. New York: Macmillan, 1985.

1. The teacher tells the students that they will be talking about a book that deals with a difficult issue: keeping wild things as pets.
2. The teacher tells the students that it is important to think about a story after we read it and see how it fits in with our lives because it helps us learn from books. He or she can verbalize applying ideas from books: "In this book, the little boy wants to keep something wild as a pet. I tried to do this when I was little with a rabbit. When I read this story, I can remember having many of the same feelings as the little boy. Think about what you would have done or how you are like the boy in the story."
3. After reading (or listening to) the book, the students can be divided into cooperative learning groups to discuss the following questions:
   Have you ever tried to make a pet of something wild? How did it work out?
   Was the boy right to capture the fire flies?
   Why does he let them go?
   Why is he sad and happy at the end of the story?

The time after reading is appropriate for further study. Students may be asked to do research on some idea or fact from a story or to authenticate the information presented by discovering another source. They may choose one type of book or one factual element from a story on which they will become an expert. Written reports on topics selected by students may follow the reading of provocative material.

Comprehension Skill: Conducting Research

* *Ant Cities.* Arthur Dorros. New York: Harper and Row, 1987.

1. The teacher can tell the students that they will be reading an informational book filled with facts about ants.
2. The teacher can tell the students that they will be doing more research after this book because oftentimes one book does not tell us all we want to know.
3. The students can read *Ant Cities* independently and then answer the following questions.

Write three facts about harvester ants.

What does the queen ant do?

What does the worker ant do?

Write four things for which ants use their antennas.

Tell how to make an ant farm.

Choose one of the insects from *Bugs* by Nancy Winslow Parker (1987) for a report. Tell how this insect compares to ants. Include a labeled drawing.

4. The teacher can model doing research by choosing one of the insects from *Bugs* (Parker, 1987) and taking the students to the library to help them find additional materials.

Summary

Comprehension is the heart and soul of the process of reading. Regardless of what material we encounter—a menu, a recipe, or a newspaper—reading has not taken place until we understand the message of the author. The words on the pages of a mystery novel carry the ideas of the writer. When the personal characteristics of the reader—background, experiences, interests, and purpose—interact with those carefully chosen words so that the thoughts and ideas of the writer are revealed, then comprehension has taken place.

The following ideas summarize the information presented in this chapter:

1. Reading is an active search for meaning.

2. Reading is a strategic process.

3. Meaning is constructed while reading takes place.

4. Reading comprehension is the primary goal of reading instruction in the schools.

5. The best materials for teaching comprehension are children's books.

6. Reading comprehension is best taught through direct, teacher-led lessons.

7. Students need opportunities to apply comprehension strategies to authentic text.

8. Activities focusing on visual literacy can provide a concrete basis for instruction in reading comprehension.

9. Activities for instruction in reading comprehension should focus on all phases of reading: before reading, during reading, and after reading.

References

Anderson, R. C., Heibert, E. H., Scott, J. A., & Wilkinson, I. A. G. (1985). *Becoming a nation of readers*. Washington, DC: National Institute of Education, United States Department of Education.

Bruner, J. (1978). The role of dialogue in language acquisition. In A. Sinclair, R. J. Tarvella, & W. M. Levelt (Eds.), *The child's concept of language*. New York: Springer-Verlag.

Crafton, L. K. (1982). Comprehension before, during, and after reading. *The Reading Teacher, 36,* 293–297.

Cullinan, B. E. (1987). *Children's literature in the reading program.* Newark, DE: International Reading Association.

Durkin, D. (1978–1979). What classroom observations reveal about comprehension instruction. *Reading Research Quarterly, 14,* 481–533.

Durkin, D. (1981). Reading comprehension in five basal reader series. *Reading Research Quarterly, 16,* 515–544.

Taylor, B. M., Harris, L. A., & Pearson, P. D. (1988). *Reading difficulties: Instruction and assessment.* New York: Random House.

Taylor, B. M., Olson, B., Prenn, M., Rybcznski, M., & Zalaluk, B. (1985). A comparison of students' ability to read for main ideas in social studies and to complete main idea worksheets. *Reading World, 24,* 10–15.

Vygotsky, L. S. (1962). *Thought and language.* Cambridge, MA: MIT Press.

Children's Books

Briggs, R. (1970). *Jim and the Beanstalk.* New York: Coward-McCann.

Brinckloe, J. (1985). *Fireflies!* New York: Macmillan.

Browne, A. (1983). *Gorilla.* New York: Knopf.

Burningham, J. (1977). *Come away from the water, Shirley.* New York: Thomas Y. Crowell.

Carrick, C. (1986). *What happened to Patrick's dinosaurs?* Ill. by D. Carrick. New York: Clarion.

Cole, J. (1986). *The magic school bus at the waterworks.* Ill. by B. Degen. New York: Harcourt Brace Jovanovich.

Crowe, R. L. (1976). *Clyde Monster.* Ill. by K. Chorao. New York: E. P. Dutton.

*de Paola, T. (1981). *Fin M'Coul: The giant of Knockmanmy Hill.* New York: Holiday House.

*Dooley, N. (1991). *Everybody cooks rice.* Ill. by P. J. Thornton. Minneapolis, MN: Carolrhoda.

Dorros, A. (1987). *Ant Cities.* New York: Harper and Row.

Fleischman, P. (1988). *Rondo in C.* Ill. by J. Wentworth. New York: Harper and Row.

Gag, W. (1928). *Millions of cats.* New York: Coward-McCann.

*Gardiner, J. (1980). *Stone Fox.* Ill. by M. Sewall. New York: Harper and Row.

Heins, P. (1974). *Snow White.* Ill. by T. S. Hyman. Boston: Little, Brown.

Heller, R. (1987). *A cache of jewels.* New York: Grosset & Dunlap.

Hopkins, L. B. (1987). *Dinosaurs.* Ill. by M. Tinkleman. New York: Harcourt Brace Jovanovich.

Jeske, S. (1980). *Perfect the pig.* New York: Scholastic.

Jonas, A. (1983). *Round trip.* New York: Greenwillow.

Lobel, A. (1969). *Small pig.* New York: Trumpet.

Numeroff, L. J. (1985). *If you give a mouse a cookie.* Ill. by F. Bond. New York: Harper and Row.

Parker, N. W. (1987). *Bugs. Ill. by J. R. Wright. New York: Mulberry.*

Parrish, P. (1970). Amelia Bedelia. Ill. by F. Seibel. New York: Scholastic.

Paterson, K. (1978). *The great Gilly Hopkins.* New York: Harper Trophy.

Prelutsky, J. (1983). *The Random House book of Poetry.* Ill. by A. Lobel. New York: Random House.

Rawls, W. (1961). *Where the red fern grows.* New York: Bantam.

Ross, T. (1984). *I'm coming to get you!* New York: Dial.

Schwartz, D. M. (1985). *How much is a million?* Ill. by S. Kellogg. New York: Lothrop, Lee and Shepard.

Silverstein, S. (1974). *Where the sidewalk ends.* New York: Harper and Row.

*Snyder, D. (1988). *The boy of the three year nap.* Ill. by A. Say. Boston: Houghton Mifflin.

Viorst, J. (1978). *Alexander, who used to be rich last Sunday.* Ill. by R. Cruz. New York: Aladdin.

Waber, B. (1972). *Ira sleeps over.* New York: Scholastic.

Wallace, B. (1980). *A dog called Kitty.* New York: Archway.

Winthrop, E. (1986). *Shoes.* Ill. by W. Joyce. New York: Harper and Row.

Wood, A. (1987). *Heckedy Peg.* Ill. by D. Wood. New York: Harcourt Brace Jovanovich.

Yektai, N. (1987). *What's missing?* Ill. by S. Ryan. New York: Clarion.

*Indicates multicultural focus.

5

The Writing Process

For many years, writing has been taught with a product-oriented focus. A teacher in the past might have said, "Write a story about a witch and turn it in for a grade by the end of the period. Keep your eyes on your paper and no talking!" The emphasis in this example is on the product—a graded piece of writing—with a teacher-selected topic, a time limit given to writing, and assumptions made about students' ability to plan, edit, and revise their own writing with no time for planning or feedback from others.

The current view of writing emphasizes the process of writing. Writing is seen as a collection of individual steps or phases that overlap. Murray (1984) defines the act of writing as collecting observations, connecting them to previous experiences, writing them out, and reading them back. Graves (1983) discusses three stages of the writing process: rehearsing for writing, drafting, and revising. Calkins (1986) describes the process in this way: random drafting, refining, transitional revision, and interacting. All of these descriptions fit into the general framework of writing as prewriting, writing, revising, editing, and sharing. Each step in the writing process uniquely contributes to the final piece of writing. See Figure 5–1 for an overview of these writing components.

Prewriting

> *If you were a writer you would let ideas bounce in your brain while you watched them grow, and turned them over to see the other sides, and poked them and pushed them and pinched off parts of them, and made them go the way you wanted them to go. . . .*
>
> *If you were a writer, while you ate your cereal, and walked to school, and kicked at leaves, and jumped in puddles, and flopped on the grass, and lay in bed at night waiting for sleep, you would let the story mix and grow with the words in your mind. Together they'd zing and zap and explode into sentences you'd taste and feel and hear. Then you'd know it was time to write down the story so it would never be lost. (Nixon, 1988, unpaged)*

Murray (1984) argues that 70 percent of the time devoted to writing should be prewriting. It is here that images are collected and connections to past experiences are made.

This prewriting stage can take on many different forms. Before children begin writing, many of them practice their own prewriting strategy. Some children daydream, doodle, talk to each other, begin writing, or draw a web as an organizational pattern. The web as a means of prewriting is exemplified

Figure 5–1 Writing Process Chart

Prewriting   Collect ideas, discuss possibilities, brainstorm, think, form a tentative plan, jot down ideas, outline, web, read, dramatize, and so on.

Writing   Write first draft, discard some ideas, link others to personal experiences.

Revising   Reread, share with a friend or reader, gather ideas for improving, add to, rearrange, relate ideas, combine sentences, vary sentence length and type, gather additional facts, delete extraneous information, and rewrite.

Editing   Check the mechanics of the writing (e.g., spelling, usage, punctuation), rewrite awkward sentences, make sure tenses of verbs are consistent, check subject/verb agreement.

Sharing   Publish, reread, real orally.

Note: Not every piece of writing follows all these steps. Some ideas are abandoned or set aside before they are revised. Others are written for personal reasons only (such as a diary or a journal). The steps are also recursive. Writers often return to planning steps as they write drafts.

as an organizational pattern. The web as a means of prewriting is exemplified in the webs of 9-year-old Sheldi and 11-year-old Sarah and subsequent first draft writing (see Figures 5–2 and 5–3, respectively).

Patterned Language Books

Patterned language books can also be used for prewriting. (A complete listing of patterned language books appears at the end of the chapter.) Patterned language books model a style of writing that easily lends itself to imitation by children. There is a structure that is easily identified and repeated throughout the book (see the examples that follow). Teachers can use these books with children in the following way: (1) Read the book to the class, (2) Talk about the repetition or pattern of the writing and record it on the board, (3) Brainstorm different topics and model this pattern, and (4) Have students work alone or in groups to create their own version of the pattern.

LESSON PLAN IDEAS

An example of a patterned language book is *Some Things Go Together* (Zolotow, 1983). This book, told in poetic form, shows how a child and an adult recount things that go together: "Peace with dove, home with love. Gardens with flowers, clocks with hours. Moths with screen, grass with green. Leaves with tree and you with me" (Zolotow, 1983, unpaged).

1. Read the book to the class. Allow students to see the illustrations as well as the text.
2. Talk about the repetition or pattern of the writing. In this book, things that

Figure 5–2 Sheldi's Prewriting Web and First Draft

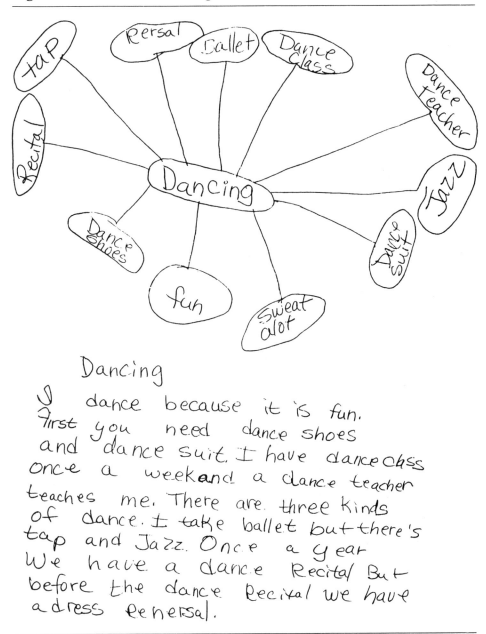

Dancing

I dance because it is fun.
First you need dance shoes
and dance suit. I have dance class
once a week and a dance teacher
teaches me. There are three kinds
of dance. I take ballet but there's
tap and Jazz. Once a year
We have a dance Recital But
before the dance Recital we have
a dress Renersal.

go together are paired and rhyme. Put this pattern on the board or on a chart for children to see:

_____ with _____, _____ with _____.

Note that the second and fourth words rhyme with each other.

3. Brainstorm for possible examples that fit this pattern and list them on the board or on a chart. For instance:

Butter with *bread, hair* with *head.*

Figure 5-3 Sarah's Prewriting Web and First Draft

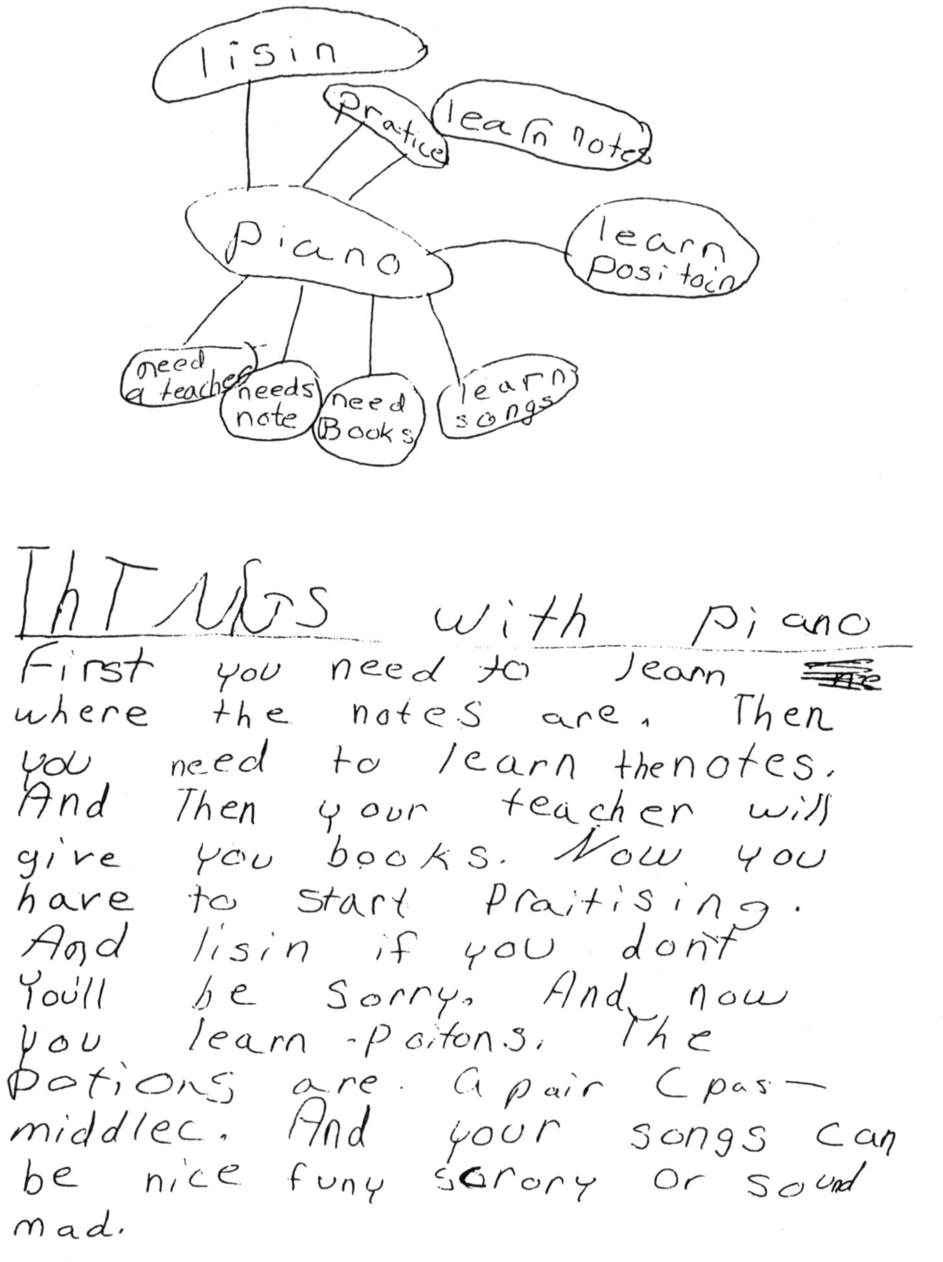

4. Have students work alone or in groups to create their own version of the pattern. Students might also want to illustrate their piece.

Figure 5-4 shows an example of this type of writing done by Elizabeth, a first-grade student. She dictated her rhymes to the teacher and the teacher wrote them down. Elizabeth then copied her poem and added illustrations.

Another patterned language book good for modeling writing is *What's*

Figure 5-4 Elizabeth's Patterned Writing Example for *Some Things Go Together*

Left? (Barrett, 1983). This question-and-answer book is very simple in its format: "What's left after you've eaten your chocolate chip cookie? Cookie crumbs. What's left after it rains? Lots of puddles" (Barrett, 1983, unpaged).

1. Read the book to the class. Allow students to see the illustrations as well as the text.

2. Talk about the repetition or pattern of the writing. In this book, the pattern is as follows:

   What's left after _____? _____.

   What's left after _____? _____.

   What's left after _____? _____.

   A question is followed by an answer.
   Put this pattern on the board or on a chart for children to see.

3. Brainstorm for possible examples that fit this pattern and list them on the board or on a chart. For instance:

   What's left after opening a present? The wrapping paper.
   What's left after a turkey dinner? The leftovers.

4. Have students work alone or in groups to create their own version of the pattern. Students might also want to illustrate their versions. The whole class could make a question-and-answer book with each child contributing several questions and answers.

Figure 5–5 shows the way a third-grade student wrote some questions and answers following this patterned language book.

Alliteration is also used in a number of books to describe a series of objects or events. In *A Snake Is Totally Tail* (Barrett, 1983), animals are described by their alliterative characteristics: "A snake is totally tail. A porcupine is piles of prickles. A skunk is oodles of odor" (Barrett, 1983, unpaged). Children could easily follow these patterns and write their own creative versions.

1. Read the book to the class. Allow students to see the illustrations as well as the text.

2. Talk about the repetition or pattern of the writing. In this book, the pattern is as follows:

   A _____ is _____ _____.

   The second and third blanks must start with the same letter. Put this pattern on the board or on a chart for children to see.

3. Brainstorm for possible examples that fit this pattern and list them on the board or on a chart. For instance:

   A dog is a hairy hound.
   A cat is a friendly feline.
   A pig is a snouting snorter.

4. Have students work alone or in groups to create their own version of the pattern. They could write about animals, food, occupations, and so on. Students might also want to illustrate their versions.

Figure 5–5 Example of Third-Grader's Questions and Answers Following the Model of *What's Left?* (Barrett, 1983)

What's left after you eat
macaroni? Chees

What's left after you break
a glass? brooken glass

What's left after you pick flowers?
the stime

What's left after you eat a cup
cake? the wopper

What's left after the leaves
fall down? brenches

What's left after ail your skin
come's off? bone's

Figure 5–6 shows the way Justin, a second-grade student, wrote about some food in this alliterative style.

Writing Folders and Journals

Organizing students' writing is an important part of the writing process because it shows students' development in writing over time. Children should be encouraged to keep a writing folder. In this folder, they can keep not only the papers they are writing but also a list of topics or writing ideas, such as the following:

What I Want to Write About

My camping trip this summer
Playing with my dog
Susie's slumber party—the scary parts
Going to Grandma's for Christmas
My favorite book

Keeping all of students' writing together helps students in a number of ways. First of all, students will not waste time looking for a draft if all of his or her writing is always left in the writing folder. Second, students get ideas for further writing based on previously written pieces. Students should periodically look through their writing folder to get ideas for other writing projects they would like to work on. Third, a folder of students' writing is important to share with parents in conferences. If the writing is kept together in one place, parents

Figure 5–6 Justin's Example of Alliterative Writing

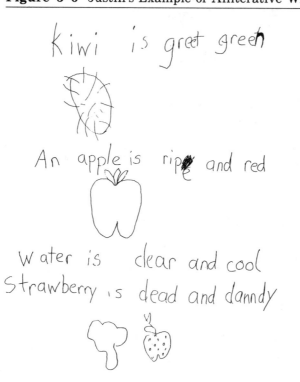

will see evidence of drafts, revisions, and final products. And finally, if the teacher has to make some evaluative measure of each student's writing, then the entire folder should be examined to show individual student's progress from draft to finished product.

Asher suggests keeping a journal of writing ideas in her book, *Where Do You Get Your Ideas?* (Asher, 1987). She offers the following seven questions to get the journal started: "1. Whom do I know? 2. What are the milestones of my life? 3. Where have I been? 4. What's wrong with my life? 5. What do I want? 6. What would happen if . . . ? 7. Why?" (Asher, 1987, p. 56).

Writing journals can assist students in making topic choices and brainstorm ideas for writing. Calkins and Harwayne (1991) suggest the use of writing notebooks for collecting impressions, noticing visual images, jotting down appealing phrases, and writing daily. Students may get ideas for writing topics from these entries.

Conferencing

Writing is an "intensely social activity" (Newman, 1986, p. 11). Writing and talking naturally seem to go together. As students talk about their own writing and the writing of other students, they become more knowledgeable about what is good writing. Conferences can be the forum for these "talking" sessions. Calkins (1983) indicates that writing conferences are intended to help writers develop specific content, reflect on the writing process, and judge their own efforts at writing.

There are a variety of conferences that can occur at different times throughout the writing process. The following descriptions have been adapted from Hoskisson and Tompkins (1987) and Graves (1983). They include on-the-spot conferences, drafting conferences, revising conferences, editing conferences, instructional conferences, peer conferences, and class conferences.

On-the-spot conferences take place when the teacher meets with each student one to one for a short time to find out what the child is writing, to ask him or her how the writing is going, and so on. The teacher might have the student read what he or she is writing or ask a question that makes the student think about the purpose or the main idea of the writing. The teacher then moves on to see what another child is doing. These types of short conferences are important in terms of record keeping. The teacher could note on a chart, like the one shown in Figure 5–7, what the child is doing that day in terms of writing.

Another type of conference is a *drafting conference*. The teacher sets up these conferences in advance and has the student bring his or her first draft. In this conference, the student and teacher might discuss a problem that the student is having and assistance is provided by talking him or her through it.

Revising conferences involve small groups and the teacher. Students read their writing and gain input from others on how to revise and improve their writing. These conferences can last as long as 30 minutes. They could possibly replace reading groups, for children are really reading and discussing their own writing. In these conferences, children discuss what they like about the writing and increasingly what they need to know more about, what is perhaps unnecessary, and what to work on further.

Editing conferences take place with small groups or individuals and the teacher. The teacher reads the students' papers that have been proofread and helps to correct the mechanics of the writing. The teacher takes special notes on each student to note what specific problems each child is having with mechanics (see Figure 5–8).

Instructional conferences are made up of students who have similar problems with mechanics. The teacher conducts a mini-lessons in which he or she teaches a certain concept and has the students use their own writing as the basis for the corrective lesson.

Peer conferences can be accomplished by dividing students into pairs and having them share their writing with each other. Students can fill out a response sheet on each other's writing or share their feedback orally with the other students.

Figure 5–7 Classroom Writing Process Progress Chart

Student	Date: 11/23/92 Working On	Date: 11/24/92 Working On
Tom	Writing first draft of "Tom Turkey"	Shared "Tom Turkey" in the Author's Chair
Cara	Brainstorming idea for Thanksgiving story	Working on first draft of story ("The Wonderful Thanksgiving")
Sarah	Editing her story "The Midnight Cat"	Editing conference with teacher, focus on sentence variety

Figure 5–8 Editing Conference Notes

Name	Date	Needs to Work On	Writing Title
Tom	11/29/90	Capitalizing proper nouns	"Tom Turkey"
Cara	11/28/90	Spelling of "a lot" (2 words, not 1)	"The Wonderful Thanksgiving"
Sarah	11/22/90	Varying sentence length and type	"My Cat, Midnight"

Class conferences with the entire class can compose together or brainstorm for ideas, messages, or moods. These whole-group meetings can be held to discuss class concerns about writing, too. Such conferences can be spontaneous or planned, depending on the students' needs.

Editing and Revising

Editing and revising can be done in small groups of children, one to one with the teacher, or with pairs of students. To edit a piece of writing, children need to reread the first draft themselves and perhaps use a self-checklist, such as that shown in Figure 5–9. Figure 5–10 provides another self-check list that the writer can use to help edit the mechanics of his or her writing.

When students share their writing with others, peers can provide them with valuable feedback. For instance, Figure 5–11 shows a peer evaluation form. As children listen to a piece of writing being read by the author, they can also

Figure 5–9 Self-Evaluation of Story Writing

Self-Evaluation of Story Writing

Put an X next to the statements that are true about your writing.

_____ This sounds good when I read it aloud to myself.

_____ I said what I wanted to say.

_____ I think the reader will be interested in it.

_____ This topic/idea is worth reading and writing about.

_____ This is written in a logical manner.

_____ There is a beginning to my story.

_____ There is a middle to my story.

_____ There is an ending to my story.

_____ When I read my story, I can picture what happened in my mind.

_____ When I read my story, I can picture what my characters look like.

_____ When I read my story, I can picture what my characters are doing.

_____ When someone else reads my story, I think they will be able to understand it.

Source: Adapted from Howie, 1984, p. 153.

Figure 5–10 Mechanics Self-Check List

Mechanics Self-Check List

Put an X next to statements that are true about your writing.

_____ I used sentences of different lengths.

_____ I put periods or other punctuation marks at the end of sentences.

_____ I used commas where necessary.

_____ I started each sentence with a capital letter.

_____ A reader could read my handwriting.

_____ I need to use a typewriter so a reader will be able to read this.

_____ I reread this story for misspelled words.

_____ I checked the spelling of the words I'm unsure about.

_____ I have a punctuation mark in every sentence.

_____ All my pronouns are clear.

Figure 5–11 Peer Critiquing Sheet

Read — Read Again — Fill in the Form

Author's name _____

Title of writing _____

Date _____

What I liked about this piece of writing (be specific) _____

_____

_____

What I need or want to know more about _____

_____

_____

_____

The part that might not be needed _____

_____

_____

_____

What I would work on if I were the writer _____

_____

(Continued)

Figure 5-11 *(Continued)*

_____

_____

Other comments _____

_____

Reader's name _____

_____

Source: Adapted from Daniels and Zemelman, 1985, p. 169.

offer ideas for omitting items, expanding certain sections, language choice, and so on.

In general, the following should be kept in mind regarding editing. It should be done by the teacher and student together if possible, with the teacher leading the sessions at the beginning and gradually giving up control to the student. Short pieces should be used at first to refine writing. A paragraph can be used with older children and a sentence with younger children. Direction should be given as to how the editing should be done. Appropriate and honest questions should be asked, such as "What other words could you use to describe your spooky setting?" or "You've started a lot of sentences with 'And then.' How can you rearrange your sentences so that each one sounds different?"

The most important element that needs improvement should be identified and focused on. Editing should not be overdone with children. One element could be worked on and then developed or studied in further sessions. Editing should also focus on the positive aspects of the writing. Teachers and other children can offer honest praise through use of the following types of comments: "I really liked the phrase 'bright glow-in-the-dark red packages,' I felt like I could see them." Or "I liked your description of your grandmother's comfortable couch. It reminded me of my grandmother's soft couch that I used to sit on."

Not every piece of writing must be edited. Some writing is personal, or students may want to set aside some pieces for a while and write about something else.

Mini-Lessons

In order to teach the skills of writing, teachers can use their knowledge of students' strengths and weaknesses as writers to teach various aspects of writing. Stephens (1989) suggests teaching students about how writers begin stories. The examples in Figure 5–12 are first paragraphs of children's books for younger students, and the examples in Figure 5–13 are first paragraphs of children's books for older students. They show different ways that authors can begin stories. The teacher can read these to students or perhaps prepare overhead transparencies of them. Together, the teacher and the students can talk about the effectiveness of each type of beginning. For instance: Does it make the reader want to read more? Does it introduce the characters or setting in an interesting manner? As students become more aware of the techniques that writers use in introducing stories, they can try to incorporate that into their own writing.

Figure 5–12 Beginning Paragraphs from Various Children's Books for Younger Students

"There was once a baby koala so soft and round that all who saw her loved her. Her name was Koala Lou" (*Koala Lou* by Mem Fox, 1988, unpaged).

"It was Christmas Eve at the Monroe's house. And Howie was scared.
'What do you mean a big fat man in a red suit is going to come down the chimney?' he said. 'What does he want?'" (*The Fright Before Christmas* by James Howe, 1988, unpaged).

"'I'm fat,' said Mrs. large.
'No you're not,' said Lester.
'You're our cuddly mommy," said Laura.
'You're just right," said Luke.
'Mommy's got wobbly bits,' said the baby.
'Exactly," said Mrs. large. 'As I was saying—I'm fat'" (*A Piece of Cake* by Jill Murphy, 1989, unpaged).

"My new friend Alex likes to brag.
Yesterday he started bragging about his dad. He told me that his dad was a fireman, and that once he rescued a little baby and a dog from a burning house.
I just had to tell Alex how great my dad is.
So I did" (*My Dad the Magnificient* by Kristy Parker, 1987, unpaged).

"When Katie came to visit her grandmother, she asked, 'Grammy, how did you ever fit on that little chair?'
'I was little, too,' her grandmother answered. 'Just as small as you'" (*Grandmother's Chair* by Ann Herbert Scott, 1990, unpaged).

"Miss Penny and Mr. Grubbs had been next-door neighbors for forty-eight years.
And for all forty-eight summers, the same thing had happened: Miss Penny's incredible garden grew enormous vegetables—mountains of them—and Mr. Grubb's garden did not" (*Miss Penny and Mr. Grubbs* by Lisa Campbell Ernst, 1991, unpaged).

"One cold night a cat walked out of the woods, up the steps, across the deck, and into the house where Elizabeth and Sarah lived" (*Charlie Anderson* by Barbara Abercrombie, 1990, unpaged).

The Author's Chair

> *If you were a writer, the stories you wrote might make people laugh, or shiver, or even cry. They'd be your stories. They'd belong to you because they'd be a part of you. . . . You could hug them to yourself like a warm secret, or you could share them with the whole world . . . if you were a writer. (Nixon, 1988, unpaged)*

The Author's Chair is a place for children to sit and read their writing to other students. It is the use of this chair that helps children to believe in themselves as authors and to gain feedback from their peers and their teacher. After observing first-grade students use the Author's Chair, Graves and Hansen (1983) hypothesized the following about the relationship between reading and writing in beginning readers and writers:

Figure 5–13 Beginning Paragraphs from Various Children's Books for Older Students

"Junior stood on top of the barn, arms outstretched, legs apart. Strapped to his thin arms were wings made out of wire, old sheets, and staples—his own design. His mouth hung open. His eyes watched a spot over the cornfield where he hoped to land. He appeared to be praying" (*The Not-Just-Anybody Family* by Betsy Byars, 1986, p. 1)

"Dear Mr. Henshaw,
    My teacher read your book about the dog to our class. It was funny. We licked it.
        Your freind,
        Leigh Botts (boy)"
(*Dear Mr. Henshaw* by Beverly Cleary, 1983, p. 1)

"In the middle of summer, Sarah and her father discover fall.
    They are in the garden, filling a baset with tomatoes and peppers. It's August, and so hot the air itself coats their skin. Everything sticks. Sarah's father's bare back gleams with sweat. Her own face, a little sunburned, shines in the heat. Every round tomato, heavy with juice, is warm with sun, warm as a baby's cheek, warm as a living thing" (*Winter Holding Spring* by Crescent Dragonwagon, 1990, p. 3).

"Like all cockroaches, Shoebag was named after his place of birth. He was snoozing there now, in the open toe of a white summer sandal. He was having his old dream of growing big enough to squash the seven-legged, black jumping spider and of moving somewhere warm and dark and filled with meats, cheeses, sweets, and starches" (*Shoebag* by Mary James, 1990, p. 1).

"Melinda Pratt rides city bus number twelve to her cello lesson, wearing her mother's jean jacket and only one sock. Hallo, world, says Minna. Minna often addresses the world, sometimes silently, sometimes out loud. Bus number twelve is her favorite place for watching, inside and out. The bus passes cars and bicycles and people walking dogs. It passes store windows, and every so often Minna sees her face reflection, two dark eyes in a face as pale as a winter dawn. There are fourteen people on the bus today. Minna stands up to count them. She likes to count people, telephone poles, hats, umbrellas, and, lately, earrings. One girl, sitting directly in front of Minna, has seven earrings, five in one ear. She has wisps of dyed green hair that lie like forsythia buds against her neck" (*The Facts and Fictions of Minna Pratt* by Patricia MacLachlan, 1988, p. 1).

"The prairie was like a giant plate, stretching all the way to the sky at the edges. And we were like two tiny peas left over from dinner, Lester and me. We couldn't even see the soddy from out there—just nothing, nothing in a big circle all around us. We still had Cap then, and he stood very still, shaking his harness now and again while we did our work, throwing cow chips into the back of the wagon, me singing all the while" (*Prairie Songs* by Pam Conrad, 1985, pp. 1–2).

"It was an April morning—a Tuesday morning, to be exact—a morning that had nothing whatsoever unusual about it. The sun was shining, the trash had been collected from the sidewalk, the breakfast toast was moderately burned but still edible, and the various clocks in the aprtment, which never agreed exactly, indicated that it was somewhere close to seven-thirty a.m.
    It was a morning just exactly like every other Tuesday morning in April on the West Side of New York City, except for one thing.
    James Priestly Tate, age twelve, had an overwhelming urge, for the first time in his life, to use deodorant" (*Your Move, J.P.!* by Lois Lowry, 1990, p. 1)

1. *Children's concept of author changes from a vague notion about some other person who writes books to the additional perception of themselves as authors to the realization that they have choices and decisions to make as authors.*
2. *Children's concept of authorship becomes more pronounced as their concepts of reading and writing become more differentiated.*
3. *Authorship concepts become more differentiated because children actively compose in both reading and writing. Composing in each of these processes consists of imitating and inventing during encoding, decoding, and the making of meaning.*
4. *Children change from imposing their own understanding so process and content upon authors, to realizing various authors can use process and content differently.*
5. *Children realize authors have options because they do the following in both the reading and writing processes: exercising topic choice, revise by choice, observe different types of composing, and become exposed to variant interpretations.*
6. *Children who learn to exercise options become more assertive in dealing with other authors. At first an author is distant, then an author is self, finally the self-author questions all authors and assertive readers emerge. (Graves & Hansen, 1983, pp. 182–183)*

Two children's books model this use of an Author's Chair and the concept of a writers' workshop in school. In *Libby on Wednesday* (Snyder, 1990), Libby is part of a writers' workshop with four other students. Together, they read, write, and share their own writing. *Write on, Rosy! A Young Author in Crisis* (Greenwald, 1988) is a story about a writer who investigates the head mistress for her report and learns a lot about how to be a good investigative reporter. Both books show the need for sharing writing with others, for improving writing, and for celebrating writing.

Students need to share their writing with each other for feedback and celebration. Teachers must provide time daily for this sharing. Students could be encouraged to sign up for Author's Chair when they have a piece of writing to share. One to two students a day could share their writing in this way.

Author's Chair can be organized in various ways. Figure 5–14 offers some suggestions for the format of an Author's Chair session. A transcript of an actual Author's Chair session in a third-grade classroom is included in Figure 5–15. Students offer feedback about what they liked and suggestions about what

Figure 5–14 Suggested Guidelines for Author's Chair

1. The author reads his or her piece of writing in the Author's Chair.
2. The author tells the audience what he or she liked best about the piece of writing.
3. The author asks the audience what they liked best about his or her piece of writing.
4. Students tell what they liked best about the writing.
5. The author tells the audience what part of the writing gave him or her trouble.
6. The author asks the audience for any suggestions on what might be improved in the writing.
7. Students tell what they feel could be improved and how.
8. The author has the option to follow the audience's advice or to revise the piece as he or she feels is needed.

Figure 5–15 Transcript of Author's Chair Session (Third-Graders)

Kourtlind: Okay, this is my story: "If You Give an Elephant Some Peanuts" by Kourtlind. If you give an elephant some peanuts he'll ask for a jelly sandwich, then he'll want some cocoa, then he'll ask for the football to throw, then he'll want some milk, then he'll want some napkins, then he'll ask for the clippers to cut his hair, then he'll want some biscuits, then he'll ask for some crackers, then he'll ask for some peanut butter, then he'll ask for some cheese, then he'll ask for some cookies, then he'll ask for some chicken, then he'll ask for some pickles, then he'll ask for some koolaid, then he'll ask for some bacon, and then he'll ask for some french fries, then he'll ask for some macaroni, then he'll ask for some grilled cheese, then he'll ask for some fish, then he'll ask for some dog bones, then he'll ask for some basketballs to shoot, then he'll ask for some black-eyed peas, then he'll ask for some turkeys, then he'll ask for some dressing, then he'll ask for some honey, then he'll ask for some chips, then he'll ask for some nuggets, then he'll ask for some candy canes, then he'll ask for some corn flakes, then he'll ask for some Jordan fruit snacks, then he'll ask for some corn meal, then he'll ask for some peas, then he'll ask for some tea, then he'll ask for some cheeseburger, then he'll ask for some cupcakes, then he'll ask for some Coke, then he'll ask for some ice cream, then he'll ask for some steaks, then he'll ask for some breakfast, then he'll ask to go to McDonald's, all if you give an elephant some peanuts.

Justin: I liked the black-eyed peas part.

Ami: I liked that he had all that food that he wanted.

Tobias: Yeah, that made me hungry.

Teacher: You used the format of the book *If You Give a Mouse a Cookie* (Numeroff, 1985), didn't you?

Kourtlind: Yeah.

Teacher: Any suggestions for Kourtlind?

Crystal: There were a lot of "thens" he said.

Teacher: Okay, so you think maybe he could try to combine some of his sentences and not use the word "then" so much?

Crystal: Yeah.

Ami: He should have said what happened at the end. He should have said he might have blew up.

Justin: Yeah—you could say he blew up at the end 'cuz he ate all that stuff.

Kourtlind: Yeah, I guess I could.

Teacher: Kourtlind, I think you have a great start there, and now you have some things to think about when you work further on your piece.

the writer might to do improve his piece of writing too. Kourtlind has written a piece modeled after *If You Give a Mouse a Cookie* (Numeroff, 1985).

Publishing

Publishing in the classroom can take on many different forms. Books can be made out of scrap materials such as wallpaper or adhesive paper covering cardboard for covers, a classroom book can be made with pages from different students, or a bulletin board can display students' writing. Writing can be shared as a gift. A class newspaper could be written as a way to display different children's writing. Art projects can be made with writing. Writing can be shared between classes, read over the school's intercom, and so on. Some pieces of writing may never reach the publication stage. Those pieces that students decide are their best should be reserved for the publishing process. See Figure 5–16 for an example of a book published by a fourth-grader, modeled after *The Giving Tree* (Silverstein, 1964).

Students may publish a variety of genres. Informational books can be made to report on a topic of interest of a child. Cookbooks could be made as class books, with each student contributing a recipe. Concept books—such as counting books, alphabet books, or books about colors—could be made by individual students or as a whole-class effort, with each student contributing a page. Students interested in a particular time period in history might try writing some historical fiction. Students interested in having animals talk or creating fanciful worlds might like to write a fantasy story. Poetry is another possibility for publishing. Students might all want to write a poem for a class anthology or write their own poetry collections or stories told in rhyme.

Retelling traditional fairy tales or folktales is another option. Other students might enjoy writing about stories occurring in the present in the form of contemporary realistic fiction. Joke or riddle books are another possibility, as are writing autobiographies. Or students might want to draw wordless picture books to tell a story without words. A list of possible writing genres with examples of quality children's books to provide examples and models for children interested in different types of writing is included at the end of this chapter.

Illustrating books to be published is another way to get students involved in the writing process. Ideas for creating pop-up illustrations are found in the books *How to Make Pop-Ups* (Irvine, 1987) and *How to Make Super Pop-Ups* (Irvine, 1992).

Already prepared blank books are available for students to use as well. Students may create their own covers for the books and then write their final draft inside the book. (Blank books may be ordered from Treetop Publishing, P.O. Box 085567, Racine, WI, 53408-5567.)

Younger students may want to make shape books relted to the topics they are writing about. For instance, students writing recipes for cookies might want to publish these recipes in a cookie-shaped book (see Figure 5–17).

Other ideas for publishing children's writing in creative ways can be found in books such as *More Book Factory* (Suid & Lincoln, 1991) *How to Make Books with Children* (Evans & Moore, 1985), and *Dora's Book* (Edwards, 1990). Students can learn a great deal about the entire writing process by reading and examining these books.

Assessment of Writing

> *When evaluation and grading are unavoidable, as they so often are, it can be made clear to the students that the "mark" is given for administrative or bureaucratic purposes that have nothing to do with "real world" writing. Grading never taught a writer anything. Writers learn by learning about writing, not be getting letters or numbers put on their efforts and abilities. (Smith, 1988, p. 30)*

Figure 5-16 Example of a Fourth-Grader's Published Book

The mysterious trees
    by levi w. molini
illustrated by levi w. molini

Dedicated to Brett

1991 by Levi W. Molini
Edited by Kimberly Molini,
Published by the Molini
Publishing Company, Inc.

There once lived a tree and he had a lot of tree friends. They lived in a forest about two miles away from a factory.

For a minute the tree thought he was going to cut all of his friends down, but all he did was trim them.

Later that year he came. He was talking to us and he said, "You know when you're really, really mad at someone and you just have to smart off. Well I did and lost my job!

One day they were playing and a man came. The man worked at the factory making canned goods.

Figure 5-16 *(Continued)*

He had a weird looking toy. It had zig zag edges and a handle.

All the trees got together that night and talked. They said, "We have to help that man because he helped us a lot."

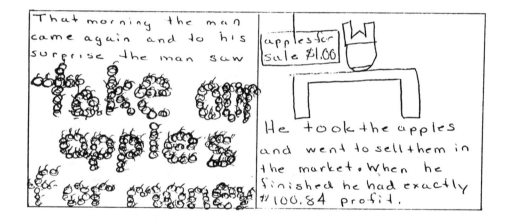

That morning the man came again and to his surprise the man saw take off apples for money

apples for sale $1.00

He took the apples and went to sell them in the market. When he finished he had exactly $100.84 profit.

The next morning he went back to the trees and said, "Trees, you really helped me. Now I have enough money until I find a job."

About a month later he became a business man, but, he still visited the trees.

Figure 5–17 Cookie-Shaped Book Directions

1. Draw a cookie shape on a piece of cardboard or oaktag paper. Cut out the shape and use it as a pattern. Trace the pattern on two pieces of sturdy construction paper or oaktag and cut the pieces out.

2. Decorate and write a title on the cover.

3. Using the pattern made in #1, trace and cut out as many sheets of paper as needed for students to write their recipes.

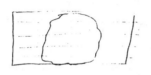

4. After students have written the recipes on the cookie-shaped paper, assemble the book. Place the recipes between the front and back oaktag or construction paper covers made in step #1. Staple the cover and the back to the papers and cover the staples with strips of tape, or punch holes through the front cover, recipes, and back cover with a paper punch and assemble with metal rings, yarn, or shoelaces.

Assigning grades to writing is very subjective and should be avoided if possible. If grades on writing are mandatory, Graves (1983) suggests that students choose their best final products for purposes of grading and that the teacher consider the content, creativity, and organization of a piece, in addition to the mechanics of writing. Grades in writing do have an effect on students' attitudes toward writing and their desire to write (Romano, 1987).

A teacher can keep careful notes about students from observations of their writing, conferences, development of writing throughout the semester, development of drafts to publishable writing, and checklists of the mechanics of writing. These pieces of information about a student's writing should also be considered in any grade determination that has to be made.

From Prewriting to Finished Product: An Example

The following provides a description of a third-grader's process of writing from reading a book, getting an idea, writing a draft, revising and editing, and finally writing a final draft.

I read my nephew Justin (age 8) the book *No Peas for Nellie* (Demarest, 1988). This book focuses on Nellie's dislike for peas and a description of other things she would rather eat than peas. Then we looked at some poetry about food, including the books *Eats* (Adoff, 1979) and *Poem Stew* (Cole, 1981). Justin decided to make a chart of the food tht he liked and disliked (prewriting). This list of "yucky" and "yummy" foods appears in Figure 5–18.

Justin then decided to write a draft of a poem about a food that he hated (liver). His first draft of a poem appears in Figure 5–19.

After Justin shared his poem with me, we talked about how I (his aunt) hated liver and he decided to put that in his next draft of the poem. We also talked about including more foods in his poem, so he added references to food in the first line, instead of the flowers. His second draft appears in Figure 5–20.

After we read his second draft. We talked about some possibilities for a better title for his poem. He suggested: "Tomatoes," "Foods I Hate," and "Tomatoes Are Red." From these, he chose "Foods I Hate" for his title. He also decided to write a second verse so the poem would truly reflect the title and be about foods that he hated.

Figure 5–18 Prewriting List of Foods

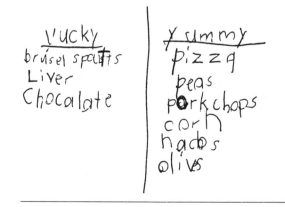

Figure 5–19 First Draft of Food Poem

Liver
Roses are red, violes are blue
I hate liver so do you!

Figure 5–20 Second Draft of Food Poem

Liver
Tomatos are red, berrys are blue
I hate liver and my aunt does too!

Figure 5–21 Draft of Second Verse

Brussul spouts
Chocolate is brown, Brussul spouts are green
If I had to eat these I'd barf all over town.

His second verse appears in Figure 5–21. As he wrote it, he thought about the word *brown* as a better rhyming word, so he reversed the order of the first line so that he could write a line that rhymed with *brown* instead of *green* (note his arrows).

After reading the revised first verse and his second verse, we went through all of the words and talked about which ones might be misspelled. He underlined the words he needed help with (*berrys* and *brussul* are examples in Figures 5–20 and 5–21). I also helped him to spell *tomatoes*. When he wrote his final draft (Figure 5–22), he added punctuation and wanted to write it like a poem with four lines.

Figure 5–22 Final Draft of Poem about Food

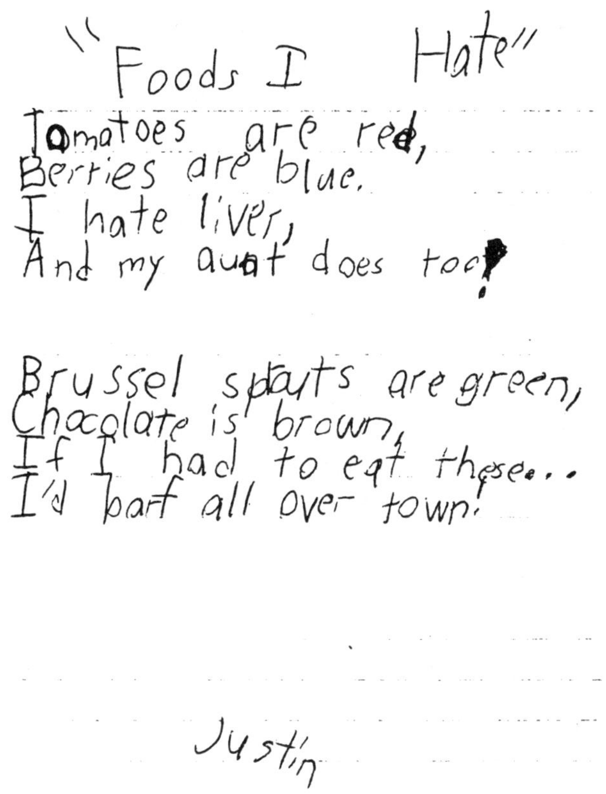

"Foods I Hate"
Tomatoes are red,
Berries are blue.
I hate liver,
And my aunt does too!

Brussel spouts are green,
Chocolate is brown,
If I had to eat these...
I'd barf all over town!

Justin

This example shows how brainstorming about a topic and reading books can give students insight into writing ideas. Justin's first draft is very different from his final draft. He needed time to think about what to do to improve on his idea. He also needed input from another person to help him think about what changes he might make.

Students can write creatively if they are given time, choice, and support for writing. Writing in such an environment can flourish and grow as students and teachers learn together about improving and enjoying writing.

Creating an Environment That Supports Writing

There are many aspects of creating a supportive environment in which students feel comfortable and creative to write. A positive atmosphere about writing must exist. Students learn to write better when their writing is praised rather than criticized (Hillerich, 1979). A classroom that focuses on students' strengths as writers, as well as one that works on the weaknesses, will enhance writing ability and desire. Students who feel they are writing for real audiences are more apt to feel some purpose to their writing as well.

ability and desire. Students who feel they are writing for real audiences are more apt to feel some purpose to their writing as well.

Teachers must model the writing process and share their writing with children. This shows students the importance of life-long writing. It also shows students that the teacher values the writing process and understands the struggles and triumphs of writing. Until teachers begin to write themselves, they do not have a true understanding or appreciation of what it takes to be a writer (Emig, 1983).

Children should be encouraged to write in a meaningful manner and they should choose their own topics for writing. Children (and teachers) need to "ache with caring" (Fox, 1988, p. 113) about their writing. This happens only when children write about topics that are meaningful to themselves–about people, places, and things that may not be meaningful to others. This diversity of topic choice should be celebrated, respected, and encouraged.

Students must have the freedom to take risks in writing. They must be reassured that their writing is private and will be made public only with their consent. As children write more and more, their willingness to share will likely increase as their self-confidence grows.

Children must also be exposed to language in a variety of forms. They should be read aloud to (even in the upper grades) so that they are exposed to the different styles and writing patterns of various authors. They must be given time to read books to themselves and others–to see words in meaningful whole pieces. They must also listen to each other's writing (as in the Author's Chair) and read it for enjoyment.

Writing should never be used as a form of punishment. Children should not be asked to copy a page from the dictionary or to write a sentence such as "I'll never talk in class" numerous times. In these instances, writing is seen as drudgery and a repetitive task. Children who have been exposed to writing as punishment will likely have difficulties enjoying writing for pleasure.

The writing process is not a system of rigid, lock-step stages. The acts of prewriting, drafting, sharing, editing, revising, and publishing may overlap and be recursive. Children should be encouraged to determine their own writing process, using the aforementioned steps as guidelines.

It is important to keep parents informed about the writing program. Teachers should explain the writing process that is in use in their classrooms, noting that students will be writing a great deal. Some of this writing will be in draft form, thus it will not be perfect in terms of mechanics. Parents need to be aware of the writing process and its use in the classroom.

Teachers need to let students choose their own topics and write about things that have special meaning and significance to them. Teachers must provide time for creative thought, to offer suggestions, and to provide a supporting, non-threatening environment in which students' writing can flourish. Finally, the following thoughts about the teacher's role in writing are given by Mem Fox (1988):

> 1) help students to care about writing by making it real; 2) give students opportunities for real responses from people they admire; 3) create situations in which students always own the investment in their writing; 4) be sensitive to the social nature of writing, and the vulnerability of writers; 5) demonstrate and encourage writing for fun and huge enjoyment and power; 6) respond after publication as well as before; and 7) help to develop powerful writing so that students can control their own lives. (p. 124)

Summary

Knowledge of the writing process has changed how writing is now taught in elementary schools. Writing is viewed as a process of rehearsing, drafting, revising, and sharing, rather than writing a final product on the first attempt. if the process of writing is respected, then children are encouraged to write.

The following ideas summarize the information presented in this chapter:

1. Writing is a process of prewriting, writing, revising, editing, and sharing.
2. Prewriting is a necessary first step of writing and takes many forms, such as talking, webbing, and keeping writing folders.
3. Patterned language books can be helpful in providing the form of writing.
4. Children should be encouraged to keep writing folders with topic choices and drafts included.
5. Conferencing about writing helps students gain feedback and improve their writing.
6. Students can be helped to self-edit their own pieces.
7. Mini-lessons can provide students with instruction in the skills of writing.
8. The Author's Chair is helpful for children to gain a sense of what it is like to be an author.
9. Publishing students' writing is a way of celebrating writing.
10. A supportive environment is necessary if children are to feel comfortable about writing.
11. Children should be encouraged to determine their own successful writing processes.
12. Teachers need to write too.

References

Calkins, L. M. (1983). *Lessons from a child.* Portsmouth, NH: Heinemann.

Calkins, L. M. (1986). *The art of teaching writing.* Portsmouth, NH: Heinemann.

Calkins, L. M., & Harwayne, S. (1991). *Living between the lines.* Portsmouth, NH: Heinemann.

Daniels, H., & Zemelman, S. (1985). *A writing project: Training teachers of composition from kindergarten to college.* Portsmouth, NH: Heinemann.

Emig, J. (1983). *The web of meaning: Essays on writing, thinking, learning, and teaching.* Montclair, NJ: Boynton/Cook.

Evans, J., & Moore, J. E. (1985). *How to make books with children.* Monterey, CA: Evan-Moor.

Evans, J., Morgan, K., & Moore, J. E. (1989). *Making big books with children.* Monterey, CA: Evan-Moor.

Fox, M. (1988). Notes from the battlefield: Toward a theory of why people write. *Language Arts, 65,* 112–125.

Frank, M. (1979). *If you're trying to teach kids how to write, you've gotta have this book.* Nashville: Incentive Publications.

Graves, D. (1983). *Writing: Teachers and children at work.* Portsmouth, NH: Heinemann.

Graves, D., & Hansen, J. (1983). The author's chair. *Language Arts, 60,* 176–183.

Hall, J. K. (1988). *Evaluating and improving written expression: A practical guide for teachers* (2nd ed.). Boston: Allyn and Bacon.

Hillerich, R. (1979). Developing written expression: How to raise — not raze — writers. *Language Arts, 56,* 769–777.

Hoskisson, K., & Tompkins, G. (1987). *Language arts content and teaching strategies.* Columbus, OH: Merrill.

Howie, S. H. (1984). *A guidebook for teaching writing in content areas.* Boston: Allyn and Bacon.

Murray, D. (1984). *Write to learn.* New York: Holt, Rinehart and Winston.

Newman, J. M. (1986). Conferencing: Writing as a collaborative activity. *Educational Perspectives, 24,* 11–15.

Nixon, J. L. (1988). *If you were a writer.* Ill. by Bruce Degen. New York: Four Winds Press.

Romano, T. (1987). *Clearing the way: Working with teenage writers.* Portsmouth, NH: Heinemann.

Smith, F. (1988). *Joining the literacy club.* Portsmouth, NH: Heinemann.

Stephens, D. (1989). First graders taking the lead: Building bridges between literature and writing. *The New Advocate, 2,* 249–258.

Suid, M., & Lincoln, W. (1991). *More book factory.* Palo Alto, CA: Monday Morning Books.

Tompkins, G. E. (1990). *Teaching writing: Balancing process and product.* Columbus: Merrill.

Children's Books

Abercrombie, B. (1990). *Charlie Anderson.* Ill. by M. Graham. New York: McElderry.

Adoff, A. (1979). *Eats.* New York: Morrow.

Aliki. (1986). *How a book is made.* New York: Crowell.

Asher, S. (1987). *Where do you get your ideas?* Ill. by S. Hellard. New York: Walker and Company.

Barrett, J. (1983). *A snake is totally tail.* Ill. by L. S. Johnson. New York: Atheneum.

Barrett, J. (1983). *What's left?* New York: Atheneum.

Byars, B. (1986). *The not-just-anybody-family.* New York: Delacorte.

Cleary, B. (1983). *Dear Mr. Henshaw.* New York: Morrow.

Cole, W. (1981). *Poem stew.* New York: Lippincott.

Conrad, P. (1985). *Prairie songs.* New York: Harper & Row.

Demarest, C. L. (1988). *No peas for Nellie.* New York: Macmillan.

Dragonwagon, C. (1990). *Winter holding spring.* New York: Macmillan.

Dubrovin, V. (1984). *Write your own story.* New York: Watts.

Edwards, M. (1990). *Dora's book.* Minneapolis: Carolrhoda.

Ernst, L. C. (1991). *Miss Penny and Mr. Grubbs.* New York: Bradbury.

*Fox, M. (1988). *Koala Lou.* Ill. by P. Lofts. San Diego: Harcourt Brace Jovanovich.

Greenwald, S. (1988). *Write on, Rosy! A young author in crisis.* Boston: Little, Brown.

Howe, J. (1988). *The fright before Christmas.* Ill. by L. Morrill. New York: Morrow.

Irvine, J. (1987). *How to make pop-ups.* New York: Morrow.

Irvine, J. (1992). *How to make super pop-ups.* New York: Morrow.

James, M. (1990). *Shoebag.* New York: Scholastic.

Lowry, L. (1990). *Your move, J.P.!* Boston: Houghton Mifflin.

MacLachlan, P. (1988). *The facts and fictions of Minna Pratt.* New York: Harper & Row.

Martin, R. (1989). *The making of a picture book.* Milwaukee, WI: Gareth Stevens.

Murphy, J. (1989). *A piece of cake.* New York: Putnam.

Nixon, J. L. (1988). *If you were a writer.* Ill. by Bruce Degen. New York: Four Winds Press.

Numeroff, L. J. (1985). *If you give a mouse a cookie.* New York: Harper & Row.

Parker, K. (1987). *My dad the magnificient.* Ill. by L. Hoban. New York: Dutton.

Scott, A. H. (1990). *Grandmother's chair.* Ill. by M. K. Aubrey. New York: Clarion.

Silverstein, S. (1964). *The giving tree.* New York: Harper & Row.

Snyder, Z. K. (1990). *Libby on Wednesday.* New York: Delacorte.

Something about the author. Detroit: Gale Publications.

Tchudi, S. J., & Tchudi. S. (1984). *The young writer's handbook.* New York: Scribners.

Zolotow, C. (1983). *Some things go together.* Ill. by K. Gundersheimer. New York: Harper & Row.

Patterned Language Books

Barrett, J. (1977). *Animals should definitely not wear clothing.* New York: Atheneum.

Barrett, J. (1980). *Animals should definitely not act like people.* New York: Atheneum.

Barrett, J. (1983). *A snake is totally tail.* New York: Atheneum.

Barrett, J. (1983). *What's left?* New York: Atheneum.

Barrett, J. (1986). *Pickles have pimples.* New York: Atheneum.

Base, G. (1987). *Animalia.* New York: Abrams.

Bauer, C. F. (1985). *My mom travels a lot.* New York: Viking Penguin.

Bauman, A. F. (1989). *Guess where you're going, guess what you'll do.* Boston: Houghton Mifflin.

Bayer. J. (1984). *A my name is Alice.* New York: Dial.

Brown, M. (1949). *The important book.* New York: Harper & Row.

Butler, D. (1989). *My brown bear, Barney.* New York: Greenwillow.

Charlip, R. (1964). *Fortunately.* New York: Four Winds.

Cuyler, M. (1991). *That's good! That's bad!* New York: Holt.

Demarest, C. L. (1988). *No peas for Nellie.* New York: Macmillan.

Dragonwagon, C. (1987). *Alligator arrived with apples: A potluck alphabet feast.* New York: Macmillan.

Elting, M., & Folsom, M. (1980). *Q is for duck.* New York: Clarion.

Goennel, H. (1987). *When I grow up.* Boston: Little, Brown.

Goennel, H. (1988). *My day.* Boston: Little, Brown.

Goennel, H. (1989). *If I were a penguin.* Boston: Little, Brown.

Goennel, H. (1989). *My dog.* New York: Orchard.

Goennel, H. (1989). *Sometimes I like to be alone.* Boston: Little, Brown.

Goennel, H. (1990). *Colors.* Boston: Little, Brown.

Grejniec, M. (1992). *What do you like?* New York: North-South.

Hartman, G. (1990). *For sand castles or seashells.* New York: Bradbury.

Hoberman, M. A. (1978). *A house is a house for me.* New York: Viking.

*Joose, B. M. (1991). *Mama, do you love me?* New York: Scholastic.

Lester, A. (1989). *Rosie sips spiders*. Boston: Houghton Mifflin.

Lobel, A. (1990). *Alison's zinnia*. New York: Greenwillow.

Martin, B. (1983). *Brown bear, brown bear, what do you see?* New York: Holt.

Martin, B. (1991). *Polar bear, polar bear, what do you hear?* New York: Holt.

McMillan, B. (1990). *One sun*. New York: Holiday House.

McMillan, B. (1991). *Play day*. New York: Holiday House.

Neitzel, S. (1989). *The jacket I wear in the snow*. New York: Greenwillow.

Neitzel, S. (1992). *The dress I'll wear to the party*. New York: Greenwillow.

Numeroff, L. J. (1985). *If you give a mouse a cookie*. New York: Harper & Row.

Numeroff, L. J. (1991). *If you give a moose a muffin*. New York: Harper & Row.

Omerod, J. (1984). *101 things to do with a baby*. New York: Viking.

Omerod, J. (1986). *Our Ollie*. New York: Lothrop.

Peek, M. (1985). *Mary wore her red dress*. New York: Clarion.

Rockwell, A. (1992). *What we like*. New York: Macmillan.

Roe, E. (1990). *All I Am*. New York: Macmillan.

Rylant, C. (1982). *When I was young in the mountains*. New York: Dutton.

Van Allsburg, C. (1987). *The Z was zapped*. Boston: Houghton Mifflin.

Viorst, J. (1972). *Alexander and the terrible, horrible, no good very bad day*. New York: Atheneum.

Walton, S. (1989). *Books are for eating*. New York: Dutton.

Williams, S. (1989). *I went walking*. Ill. by J. Vivas. San Diego: Harcourt Brace Jovanovich.

Zolotow, C. (1983). *Some things go together*. New York: Harper & Row.

Zolotow, C. (1988). *Sleepy book*. New York: Harper & Row.

Writing Genres and Examples of Children's Books

Informational Books

Definition: Nonfiction Books Written about a Variety of Topics

Aliki. (1988). *Dinosaur bones*. New York: Crowell.

Carter, P. (1992). *The bridge book*. New York: Simon and Schuster.

Gibbons, G. (1991). *The puffins are back!* New York: HarperCollins.

Parker, N. W. (1992). *Working frog*. New York: Greenwillow.

Patent, D. H. (1988). *Babies*. New York: Holiday House.

Simon, S. (1992). *Our solar system*. New York: Morrow.

Cookbooks

Definition: A Collection of Recipes

*Bjork, C. (1990). *Elliot's extraordinary cookbook*. New York: Farrar, Straus, Giroux.

Colgan, D. R. (1992). *Pizza all around*. New YOrk: Parachute Press.

Coyle, R. (1988). *My first baking book*. New York: Workman.

Krementz, J. (1985). *The fun of cooking*. New York: Knopf.

Walker. B. M. (1979). *The little house cookbook*. New York: Harper.

Watson, N. C. (1987). *The little pigs' first cookbook*. Boston: Little, Brown.

Concept Books:

Definition: Books Written about Ordinal Numbers, Counting, the Alphabet, or Colors

Counting Books
*Grossman, V. (1991). *Ten little rabbits.* San Francisco: Chronicle Books.
Kitchen, B. (1987). *Animal numbers.* New York: Dial.
Serfozo, M. (1989). *Who wants one?* New York: McElderry.
Walsh, E. S. (1991). *Mouse count.* San Diego: Harcourt Brace Jovanovich.

Alphabet Books
Gretz, S. (1986). *Teddy bears ABC.* New York: Macmillan.
Kellogg, S. (1987). *Aster Aardvark's alphabet adventures.* New York: Morrow.
Leedy, L. (1986). *The dragon ABC hunt.* New York: Holiday House.

Color Books
Ehlert, L. (1988). *Planting a rainbow.* San Diego: Harcourt Brace Jovanovich.
Kunhardt, E. (1992). *Red day, green day.* New York: Greenwillow.
Serfozo, M. (1988). *Who said red?* New York: McElderry.

Historical Fiction

Definition: Stories Set in the Past
Conrad, P. (1992). *Pedro's journal.* New York: Scholastic. (novel).
*Hesse, K. (1992). *Letters from Rifka.* New York: Henry Holt. (novel).
Kimmel, E. A. (1989). *Charlie drives the stage.* New York: Holiday House. (picture book)
Mills, L. (1991). *The rag coat.* Boston: Little, Brown. (picture book)
*Rappaport, D. (1991). *Escape from slavery.* New York: HarperCollins. (novel)
Turner, A. (1992). *Kate's trunk.* New York: Macmillan. (picture book)

Fantasy

Definition: Stories with Animal Personification or Taking Place in Make-Believe Kingdoms
Alphin, E. M. (1991). *The ghost cadet.* New York: Henry Holt. (novel)
Conrad, P. (1990). *Stonewords.* New York: HarperCollins. (novel).
Ernst, L. C. (1989). *When Bluebell sang.* New York: Bradbury. (picture book)
Heide, F. P. (1982). *The problem with Pulcifer.* New York: Lippincott. (novel)
Lester, H. (1988). *Tacky the penguin.* Boston: Houghton Mifflin. (picture book)
Murphy, J. (1989). *A piece of cake.* New York: Putnam. (picture book)

Poetry

Definition: Anthologies of Poems with a Related Theme or Stories Told in Rhyme

Anthologies
Carle, E. (1989). *Animals animals.* New York: Putnam. (poems about animals)
Cole, W. (1981). *Poem stew.* New York: Lippincott. (poems about food)

Hopkins, L. B. (1991). *Happy birthday.* New York: Simon and Schuster. (poems about birthdays)

Livingston, M. C. (1990). *If the owl calls again.* New York: McElderry. (poems about owls)

O'Neill, M. (1989). *Hailstones and halibut bones.* New York: Bantam. (poems about colors)

Stories Told in Rhyme

Aylesworth, J. (1992). *The cat and the fiddle and more.* New York: Atheneum.

Gerrard, R. (1989). *Rosie and the rustlers.* New York: Farrar Strauss Giroux.

Lindbergh, R. (1990). *Benjamin's barn.* New York: Dial.

Nerlove, M. (1989). *Just one tooth.* New York: McElderry.

Traditional Stories

Definition: Fables, Myths, Fairy Tales, and Other Stories Passed Down from Generation to Generation

Kellogg, S. (1991). *Jack and the beanstalk.* New York: Morrow.

Marshall, J. (1990). *Hansel and Gretel.* New York: Dial.

Stevens, J. (1986). *Goldilocks and the three bears.* New York: Holiday House.

Contemporary Realistic Fiction

Definition: Stories Set in Present Times That Could Really Happen

Bunting, E. (1991). *Night tree.* San Diego: Harcourt Brace Jovanovich. (picture book)

*Havill, J. (1989). *Jamaica tag-along.* Boston: Houghton Mifflin. (picture book)

Kline, S. (1990). *Orp and the chop suey burgers.* New York: Putnam. (novel)

Ruckman, I. (1989). *Who invited the undertaker?* New York: Crowell. (novel)

Sachar, L. (1987). *There's a boy in the girls' bathroom.* New York: Knopf. (novel)

Wilhelm, H. (1985). *I'll always love you.* New York: Crown. (picture book)

Wood, A. (1990). *Weird parents.* New York: Dial. (picture book)

Joke or Riddle Books

Definition: Riddles or Jokes Related to a Particular Theme

Adler, D. A. (1987). *Remember Betsy Floss and other colonial American riddles.* New York: Holiday House.

Adler, D. A. (1989). *A teacher on roller skates and other school riddles.* New York: Holiday House.

Berger, M. (1990). *101 president jokes.* New York: Scholastic.

Eisenberg, L., & Hall, K. (1987). *101 school jokes.* New York: Scholastic.

Stine, J. B. (1990). *101 school cafeteria jokes.* New York: Scholastic.

Terban, M. (1992). *Funny you should ask: How to make up jokes and riddles with wordplay.* New York: Clarion.

Autobiographies

Definition: A Story of One's Own Life or Experiences

Byars, B. (1991). *The moon and I.* Englewood Cliffs, NJ: Julian Messner. (novel)

Little, J. (1989). *Little by little.* New York: Viking. (novel)

Naylor, P. R. (1987). *How I came to be a writer.* New York: Macmillan. (novel)
Peet, B. (1989). *Bill Peet: An autobiography.* Boston: Houghton Mifflin. (novelette)
Stevenson, J. (1986). *When I was nine.* New York: Greenwillow. (picture book)
Stevenson, J. (1992). *Don't you know there's a war on?* New York: Greenwillow.
    (picture book)
Stevenson, J. (1987). *Higher on the door.* New York: Greenwillow. (picture book)
Stevenson, J. (1990). *July.* New York: Greenwillow. (picture book)

Worldless Picture Books

Definition: Stories Told in Pictures Only with No Words

Schubert, D. (1987). *Where's my monkey?* New York: Dial.
Wiesner, D. (1988). *Free fall.* New York: Lothrop, Lee & Shepard.
Winter, P. (1976). *The bear and the fly.* New York: Crown.

*Indicates multicultural focus.

6

Writing in Response to Literature

"What is an adam's apple and where did it come from?"
"It was funny when Maggie said, "Vernnnnn.""

These entries were written in fifth-graders' literature logs while they were reading *The Not-Just-Anybody Family* (Byars, 1986). As they read the book, the wrote questions and comments about the book so that they could talk about the book later in discussion groups.

Response to literature is a transactional process (Rosenblatt, 1978). The reader responds to what is read in a personal manner, drawing from prior experiences, engagement with the topic, or previous stories read.

Writing about literature has been advocated as a way to link the reading and writing processes and to encourage rich response: "I suspected kids' written responses to books would go deeper than their talk; that writing would give them time to consider their thinking and that thoughts captured would spark new insights" (Atwell, 1987, p. 165).

The more students are exposed to writing about what they have read, the better their chance of improving both reading and writing: "The more opportunities that students have to read and to write about books, the deeper their responses to literature will be, and the likelier the chance that we will become partners in learning" (Pierpont, 1990, p. 105).

There are many opportunities for students to write in response to literature. Journals, dialogue journals, literature logs, letters, postcards, and other forms of writing extend the reading process. Writing about a book can help the student to further understand the book and become more critical readers and writers.

Perhaps most significant, literature has the power to help develop students as critical readers, writers, and thinkers. As adults, these are the people who read with questions in mind, substantiate their opinions, take an intelligent stand on an issue, read the newspoaper analytically, question politicians' jargon, and act as thoughtful citizens. If we are to educate students thoughtfully for the future, literature can be the vehicle for thinking on the most critical levels. (Routman, 1991, p. 133)

Journals

Many children's books model journal writing (see the list at the end of the chapter). These books can also serve as models and encourage students to write in journals. Time can be set aside every day to allow students to write in a personal journal about what they have done during the day, what bothered them, what made them happy, and so on. Journal writing is a way for students to practice reflective writing and informal writing. It helps students of all ages to practice writing in a functional and meaningful manner. The following guidelines will help facilitate journal writing in the classroom:

1. Distribute notebooks to students at the beginning of the year and allow them to decorate the cover the the notebook.
2. Set aside 10 to 15 minutes every day for students to write in their own personal journals.
3. Generate a list of possible topics to write about in journals and display this list in chart form in the classroom. Invite students to add to this list whenever they get an idea (see Figure 6–1).
4. Invite students to share their journal entries with each other if they wish.
5. The teacher writes in his or her journal every day too.
6. Students are encouraged to continue their personal journal writing during the summer or holiday vacations at home.

Dialogue Journals

Dialogue journals are conversations in writing. This type of writing is meant to be functional, purposeful, and interactive. Students write an entry in a journal or notebook and then teachers or others respond to that entry with an entry of their own, encouraging, modeling, and extending what students have written. Dialogue journals have been used successfully in a variety of contexts to encourage practical language use for communication with a real audience. ESL (English as a second language) students, students who are profoundly deaf, and very young and older students have all benefitted from this "real" context for writing (Staton, 1980, 1988; Kreeft, 1984; Kreeft, Shuy, Staton, Reed, & Morroy, 1984; Bailes, Searls, Slobedzian, & Staton, 1986; Danielson, 1988).

Figure 6–2 shows a dialogue journal between a fifth-grade student and her

Figure 6–1 Ideas for Writing in Personal Journals

1. My favorite TV show.
2. What I did over the weekend.
3. My family.
4. My pet.
5. What I saw today that was funny.
6. What I saw today that was unusual.
7. My dreams.
8. Funny jokes I've heard or told.
9. My favorite smells.
10. My favorite sights.

Figure 6–2 Dialogue Journal Entries about *The Quilt Story* (Johnston, 1985)

I would like to have a quilt like that. It
would probably be warm, since it's gone
through so much. I thought it was a
neat story.
  Our family has moved alot, and we are
finishing our house right now! My mom
and dad say we are never going to
move again

    Martha,
        That quilt was beautiful!
    Where have you lived?
        Is the house that you are finishing
in the country? Why are your parents tired
of moving? (actually, I think I know
the answer to that)
        I have lived in Nebraska all my
life, but in different cities. I also
lived in Yellowstone National Park,
for 3 summers. Moving is _not_ fun!
        Thanks—
            Mrs. Danielson
    I've lived in Cheyenne, Wyoming, then my
sister, my mom, and me moved to my
aunts house, while my brother, my other
sister, and my dad stayed at Cheyenne.
Then we all moved to a house
near Hickman. Then we moved into
a trailer, then we moved into our
house. Our house is in the
country.
    My parents are tired of moving because
they think it is too much of a hassle.

teacher about the book *The Quilt Story* (Johnston, 1985). This type of written interaction about books allows students to extend stories to their own lives and to create and maintain a discussion of the book with their teacher. It is also a way that the teacher can assess students' comprehension of the books they are reading.

Dialogue journals can be used for other purposes besides writing about books. The teacher models appropriate language and extends and expands what students have written in their entries. This is also an excellent way for teachers to communicate personally with every student in the class. Dialogue journals are not meant to be a forum for strictly question-answer sessions; rather, they serve as a natural conversation in writing that is meaningful practice of interactional writing.

> *Dialogue writing allows writers to use the full range of available language functions of "speech actions." Complaints, questions, promises, challenges, directives, are all part of dialogue writing. The direct, functional nature of this writing sets it apart from the usual modes of written discourse we are familiar with. Language uses not commonly allowed to students in classrooms such as personal opinions, direct evaluations of lessons and negative as well as positive feelings, are freely expressed in the journal. (Staton, 1988, p. 4)*

Literature Logs

There are many varied uses for literature logs. Students can write about a variety of themes or ideas with a book. They can make predictions about what will happen next in a book or they can write about their own experiences. Figure 6–3 shows many different types of comments and questions used by a groups of fifth-grade students reading *The Not-Just-Anybody Family* (Byars, 1986).

Literature logs allow students to write about what they read in a manner that is meaningful to them. They provide for rich, deep, and diverse response to literature in a way that both enhances and enriches the transactional act of reading. Literature logs can also give structure to discussion groups about books being read by students. The logs allow students to monitor their own comprehension of the book and provide a forum for asking questions about the book.

Notes about a character could be made in a literature log and then students might want to make puppets based on these character sketches. For instance, Figures 6–4 and 6–5 show how a 14-year-old and a 9-year-old prepared sketches and then puppets related to characters in the book *Matilda* (Dahl, 1988).

Figure 6–3 Literature Log Examples from Fifth-Graders

"Is there going to be another story about Maggie and Ralphie getting married?"

"Did Mud look the same in your mind (like on page 119)?"

"Why did Maggie paint her fingernails green?"

"I think Ralphie is pretty smart. He knows almost everything, but he is a little annoying."

"I know what Junior means when he said stiff and clean sheets (p. 25). When I was in the hospital I had stiff and clean sheets too."

"I'm happy that they're all together again."

"I cried a little this chapter."

Figure 6–4 Character Sketches by 9- and 14-Year-Olds about Characters in *Matilda* (Dahl, 1988)

I think Miss Agatha Trunchbull
is really fat and she is a slob. She might
look like a ~~baseball~~ and she might have ~~fatty~~
hair. I also think she is a teacher
    I think Bruce Bogtrotter looks like
a baseball bat and he likes trotting on a
~~to~~ horse.
                        Laurie
                        9 years old

Miss Honey ~~sweet~~ kind, caring – helpful
Kind of tall, slim, smiles, ~~with~~ with curly ~~soft~~ hair!
Matilda, shy & timid. Short ~~At~~ with
short brown, strait hair.
                        Stacey
                        14 years old

Figure 6–5 Puppets Made for the Book *Matilda* (Dahl, 1988)

LESSON PLAN: LITERATURE LOG PROMPTS

1. Students are asked to write in their literature log after the reading of the whole book (picture book) or several chapters (novel).

2. Students may be guided by the following prompts or questions that encourage response to literature (Kelly, 1990; Bleich, 1978):
   a. What did you notice about the book?
   b. How did the book make you feel?
   c. What experiences have you had that relate to the book?

3. Answers to these questions may be discussed in small groups or in whole-class discussions about similar books read.

Other Forms of Writing

Letters and Postcards

Letters and postcards are natural forms of writing that emphasize the social aspect of language. Before students write letters or postcards, the format of various letters can be discussed using the book *Messages in the Mailbox* (Leedy, 1991), which models various types of letters. Other books that model letter and postcard writing are listed at the end of this chapter.

Letters can be written to characters simulating the characters' response to extend students' comprehension of a story and to allow for critical and creative thinking. For instance, Figure 6–6 shows the dialogue that occurred between a college student impersonating Arthur of the Marc Brown series and a class of second-graders.

Children may want to write to other characters of books they are reading. Older students can serve as character impersonators and write back to younger children as the character. Teachers or preservice teachers may also act as the character impersonators.

Students also often want to write to the author of a book. Students should never be assigned to write to authors; however, if they individually decide that they would like to write to an author, then teachers can help students mail the letter to the appropriate place. Letters can be sent to the publisher in care of the author's name and should include a self-addressed, stamped envelope. Students can then display letters received from authors in a prominent place in the classroom or school. Figure 6–7 shows a heartfelt letter from an ardent 10-year-old fan of the *Sweet Valley Twins* books to their author, Suzanne Pascal.

Other forms of writing may seem appropriate for the particular book. For instance, after reading *The Jolly Postman* (Ahlberg & Ahlberg, 1986), it would be only natural to write postcards to other fairy tale characters. Figure 6–8 shows a postcard written by a 9-year-old to the wolf, asking about the three little pigs after the reading of *The True Story of the Three Little Pigs* (Scieszka, 1989) and *The Jolly Postman* (Ahlberg & Ahlberg, 1986). And Figure 6–9 shows a postcard written to Mr. Troll from The Three Billy Goats. Other books that model letter and postcard writing are listed at the end of this chapter.

Figure 6–6 Letters Between Arthur and Second-Graders

Hello Everybody!!!!!

 My name is Arthur. I have a problem. I am not happy with my nose. When I have a cold my nose turns red and it looks funny. It is a nuisance at school. It is a problem when I play Hide and Seek. I went to a rhinologist to see if she could help me with my problem. Do you know what a rhinologist is? If you don't, read my story "Arthur's Nose" to find out. Also read my story to find out how I solved my problem. If you didn't like your nose, what would you do? Please tell me what you would do if you were in my situation.
Please help!
Arthur

P.S. What kind of animal am I?

Dear Arthur,

 We got your letter. We know that you are an aardvark. Somebody in our class knew a few things about you. We liked your story. Your nose is not too big. We think your nose looks good the way it is. We also think Francine is mean. Maybe you shouldn't be friends with her if she's going to make fun of you. We are going to do some studying about aardvarks because we don't know much about you. We have 13 people in our class, 4 boys and 9 girls. We go to school at Scribner, NE. Tomorrow we will write a partner letter to you.
Love,
The Second Graders

Dear Arthur,

 Do you have any pets? Please tell us their names. We learned about you today in school. How fast do you burrow? Where do you live? Do you go to school? Do you have a mother? Are you out in the winter? Do you have a wife? Do you think Francine is a brat? Did you think Francine was mean to you? Did you really want to change your nose? Your glasses are very cute. We saw them in one of your other books. We will read that story tomorrow. What school do you go to? Did you ever get over your cold?
Love,
Ashley and Kim Settles

Dear Arthur,

 What state do you live in? How old are you? We like your nose! Why don't you like your nose? What town do you live in? How many people are in your class? Happy St. Patrick's Day 5 days early. How are you? We are fine. We think your books are good. What is your teacher's name? Have the teacher move Francine. Francine is rude. Are you over your cold? We like you. We are glad we are writing to your.
Your friends,
Andrea and Angela

Dear Arthur,

 Why don't you like your nose? How are you? We are fine. How many more days of school do you have? We have 51 days of school left. We read your books. We liked your books. Your nose is fine the way it is. We are glad that you didn't change your nose. What do you do in school? We do a lot of stuff in school. What is the name of your school? Did you like any of the noses? We did. If we were you we would have picked one of the noses. Why didn't you pick a nose? We have 13 people in our class. How old are you? How old are your mom and day? Do you have math? Nate is the tallest in our class. Amberly and Heather are the shortest.
Your friends,
Jeff and Katie

(Continued)

Figure 6-6 *(Continued)*

Dear Arthur,

How old are you? We both are eight. Why do you hate your nose? We think it looks fine. I wish I had a nose like yours. Where do you live in Africa? Do you live in the zoo? We do not live in the zoo. Do you live in a hole? We live in a house. We think Francine is a smarty-pants. That rhinologist was no help to you. Do you have a pet? We like you. Is your cold better? Do you really have glasses?

Your friends,

Nate and Kim M.

Dear Arthur,

You should tell your teacher that the kids are teasing you. If kids tease you just ignore them. When is your birthday? How old are you? We are both eight. Joseph read your story about glasses. He likes your glasses. They are neat. Do you have a crush on Francine? Where do you live? What is the name of your school?

Your friends,

Joseph and Bryan

Dear Arthur,

We like your nose! We think you are nice! How old are you? We are both eight. When is your birthday? Heather's is Dec. 13th and Amberly's is Nov. 7th. Why did you want to change your nose? You should not play with Francine!!!!! Heather has had a big bully pick on her after school. What is your sister's name?

Your pals,

Heather and Amberly

Dear Ashley and Kim,

I do have a pet, and it is a puppy. He is very cute. I got him because I took care of his mother, Perky. That was my reward for taking such good care of her. You can read more about this in my book called "Arthur's Pet Business." I have not named him yet. Do you have any suggestions? I really do not burrow. I am more like a human than an aardvark. I live in a house, and I go to school. My teacher's name is Mr. Ratburn. You can read all about him in "Arthur's Teacher Trouble." I have a mother and a father. I had one sister, D.W., but in my book "Arthur's Baby" I get a brand new baby sister named Eliza. Francine is my friend, but sometimes she is mean, but not always. She is very nice to me in my book "Arthur's Valentine." Yes, at first I really wanted to change my nose, but after I thought about it, I decided that I would keep it because that is what makes me unique. Everybody has to have something unique about themselves. What things are unique about you? I am glad that you liked my glasses. Yes, I did get over my cold finally, and my nose is not red anymore. Some other books that you might want to read are "Arthur's April Fool," "Arthur's Thanksgiving," and "Arthur's Birthday." Hope you like them. In all of my books except one there are the names "Tolon" and "Tucker" hidden somewhere in the book. In the later books the name "Eliza" is also hidden with "Tolon" and "Tucker." Can you find them? It was nice to get a letter from you.

Arthur

Dear Andrea and Angela,

I am glad that you like my book. At first I did not like my nose because I thought it was too big. But after I tried on all those other noses (they just weren't me), I decided that I liked my nose the best. That is what makes me unique. What things make you unique? I live in Chicago, Illinois. I am eight yeas old. My birthday is May 25. You can read more about my birthday in my book "Arthur's Birthday." I have a mom, a dad, and for a long time only one sister—D.W.—who sometimes is not very nice. Later on my mom and dad had another baby—Eliza. Another sister. Do you have any brothers or sisters? My teacher's name is Mr. Ratburn. You can read more about him in my book "Arthur's Teacher

Trouble." Yes, I am over my cold. Some of my other books to read are "Arthur's Thanksgiving," "Arthur's April Fool," and "Arthur's Pet Business"—where I get my puppy. Do you have any pets? I am glad that I am writing to you also—it is fun. Happy St. Patrick's Day to you also. Well, I have to go because I have homework to do.

Arthur

P.S. The names Tolon and Tucker are hidden somewhere in all of my books except one. Also the name Eliza is also hidden in some. Can you find them? Happy hunting!

LESSON IDEA: POSTCARDS TO FAIRY TALE CHARACTERS

1. Read *The Jolly Postman* (Ahlberg & Ahlberg, 1986) and *The Jolly Christmas Postman* (Ahlberg & Ahlberg, 1991).
2. Have students brainstorm different fairy tale characters and list these names on the board.
3. Model for students a possible postcard that might be sent to a fairy tale character, such as an advertisement for hair products for Rapunzel (shown in Figure 6–10).
4. Go over the format of a postcard with students, using *Stringbean's Trip to the Shining Sea* (Williams & Williams, 1988) and *Messages in the Mailbox* (Leedy, 1991) as resources.
5. Invite students to write postcards to fairy tale characters.
6. Display the postcards on a bulletin board and respond to each postcard as the fairy tale character, or invite other students to respond as the fairy tale characters.

Series Stories

Writing a new story for a familiar character allows students to participate in another form of response to literature. It enhances their comprehension of the story and permits them to make real predictions about what may happen in a story. New adventures for familiar characters can be written or alternative endings to stories could be written. This allows students to use their imaginations as they reflect on a book's plot or characters. It allows them some interaction with a book they are reading.

Figure 6–11 shows how a 9-year-old wrote a new adventure for Miss Viola Swamp from the books about Miss Nelson and Viola Swamp by Harry Allard and James Marshall.

Series books such as *George and Martha* by James Marshall, *Arthur* by Marc Brown, and *Henry and Mudge* by Cynthia Rylant are good ways to encourage sequel writing with younger students. Older students might want to write another adventure of *Bingo Brown* by Betsy Byars or *Anastasia* by Lois Lowry. A list of series books is included at the end of this chapter.

Figure 6–7 Letter to an Author

November 29
10535 Izard St.
Omaha, Nebraska
68114

Dear Ms. Suzzanne,

I am _10_ years old and my name is Chrystal Hopkins. I am writing to you to tell you. I love your Sweet Valley Twins Books. They're terrific! I am your number _1_ fan! I have read 43 out of 46 books. I really want to read <u>Carnival Ghost</u>.

But, I was thinking about your books they are great but... well how about this: Elizabeth will want to go out with Todd Wilkins, but her parents won't let her and she sneaks out. And their brother sees her and thinks its Jessica. And he tells on Jessica. Jessica knows she didn't do it. But she can't prove it. Elizabeth won't tell. Jessica tries to tell her parents, but they won't listen... The rest is up to you. We could call it <u>The Case of the Stolen Idenity</u>. How does it sound? I just think that Jessica is the one who always get in trouble. Some people say your too predictable. I don't think so. I hope you will give some consideration. Your a genious! So I know you will. I hope you will wright back. My address is up there.

Sinserly Yours,
Chrystal Hopkins
10 years old

P.S. Sorry for the spelling!

Figure 6–8 Postcard to Mr. Wolf

Dear Mr. Wolf,
   I would like to know if you were
truthful about your side of the three little pigs?
I also want to know if you did eat the pigs when
you xposeably sneazed on their houses and
knocked it down? If you did eat the pigs did they
taste good? Well wright back to me when
you can. By Bye.
                    Sincerly,
                    Becky Riley

Transactional/Research Writing

Elementary students should also be encouraged to write in nonfiction formats. Instead of copying the encyclopedia, students can be exposed to a variety of alternative forms for writing expository text.

LESSON IDEA: FACTS AND FABLES

1. Read the book *Animal Fact, Animal Fable* (Simon, 1979). Each section of the book poses a statement that is either proven true or false on the following pages.
2. Students can brainstorm statements they have heard to be generally true or false regarding nature, animals, and so on.
3. Students can then investigate the validity of the statements and write a paragraph about why a statement is true or false.

LESSON IDEA: FIVE FACTS ABOUT A FAMOUS PERSON

1. Have students draw a name of a classmate from a hat and write five facts about that classmate.

Figure 6–9 Postcard to Mr. Troll

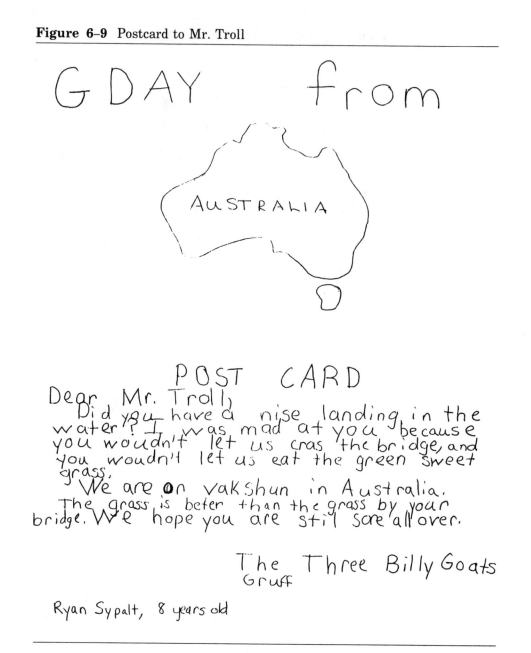

G DAY   from

AUSTRALIA

POST CARD

Dear Mr. Troll,
Did you have a nise landing in the water? I was mad at you because you woudn't let us cras the bridge, and you woudn't let us eat the green sweet grass.
We are on vakshun in Australia. The grass is beter than the grass by your bridge. We hope you are stil sore all over.

The Three Billy Goats
Gruff

Ryan Sypalt, 8 years old

---

2. Then model riddle writing about a famous person. List five facts about a mystery person and have students guess the identity. See Figure 6–12 for an example.

3. Encourage students to find five facts about a famous person of their choice. A good collection of picture book biographies is given at the end of this chapter. These books could be used with younger students or as models for older students on how to look for important information on famous people.

4. Share the clues with the whole class and encourage students to guess the identities of the mystery persons.

Figure 6–10 Rapunzel Postcard Example

Dear Rapunzel —

We are having a sale on all of our shampoo and conditioner products. If you would like to receive a 25% discount, please come to Hair Unlimited before December 5th and bring this postcard!

Sincerely,
Harry Harrison
Manager, Hair Unlimited

Hair Unlimited

Career Webs

Another possibility is to allow students choices in the types of writing they do about a particular topic. Figure 6–13 shows a web of ideas related to careers. Students may chose from the activities listed or develop their own activities and expository writing ideas.

Figure 6–11 New Story of Viola Swamp

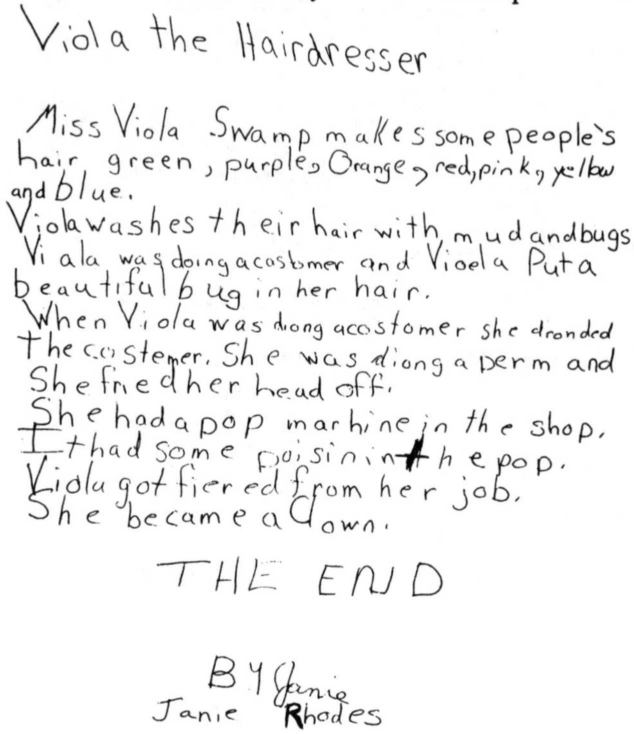

Viola the Hairdresser

Miss Viola Swamp makes some people's
hair green, purple, Orange, red, pink, yellow
and blue.
Viola washes their hair with mud and bugs
Viala was doing acostomer and Vioela Put a
beautiful bug in her hair.
When Viola was diong acostomer she dranded
the costemer. She was diong a perm and
She fried her head off.
She had a pop marhine in the shop,
It had some poisin in the pop.
Viola got fiered from her job,
She became a Clown.

THE END

BY Janie
Janie Rhodes

LESSON IDEA: CAREER WEB

Language

1. Match the term with the meaning in Figures 6–14 and 6–15.
2. Study the language of a particular occupational group.
3. Interview a person of the career of your choice.
4. Make a lingo dictionary for the career of your choice.

Resources
    Frank and Ernest
    Frank and Ernest Play Ball
    Slanguage

Special Clothing: Shoes

1. Examine different shoes needed for different occupations.
2. Make a picture dictionary of the different types of shoes needed for various occupations (e.g., ballet slippers, clown shoes, ice skates, etc.).

Figure 6–12 Clues about Martin Luther King Jr.

1. He was born on January 15, 1929 in Atlanta, Georgia.
2. In 1953 he married Coretta Scott.
3. In 1954 he was a minister in Montgomery, Alabama.
4. In 1963 he led a protest march in Washington, D.C.
5. In 1964 he was awarded the Nobel Peace Prize.

Resources
   Shoes
   Whose Shoes Are These?
   Whose Shoe?

Special Clothing: Hats

1. Examine different hats needed for different occupations.
2. Role-play situations using different hats.
3. Write a description of a hat that would be suitable for a career you would like to have.

Resources
   Ho for a Hat
   Hats, Hats, Hats
   Whose Hat?
   Whose Hat Is That?

Nontraditional Roles

1. Brainstorm nontraditional careers for men and women.
2. Interview a male or female in a nontraditional role (e.g., a male kindergarten teacher or a female farmer).

Resources
   My Mom Travels a Lot
   Mommies at Work
   Daddies at Work
   What Can She Be? A Farmer
   What Can She Be? A Film Producer
   What Can She Be? A Lawyer
   What Can She Be? A Musician
   What Can She Be? A Scientist
   What Can She Be? A Veterinarian
   What Can She Be? An Architect

Alphabet Books

1. Read one of the following books and create your own alphabet book of an occupation of your choice.

Resources
   Teachers from A to Z
   Firefighters from A to Z
   Police Officers from A to Z
   Sanitation Workers from A to Z
   Librarians from A to Z

Figure 6–13 Career Web

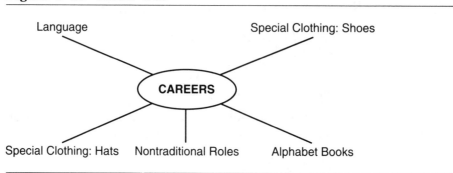

Figure 6–14 Lunch Counter Lingo from *Frank and Ernest* (Day, 1988)

Match the lunch counter lingo with its real meaning:

1. Adam's ale	a.	Swiss cheese sandwich
2. Baled hay	b.	Spinach
3. Black cow	c.	Lettuce
4. Chokies	d.	Mustard
5. Georgie pie	e.	Water
6. Hen fruit	f.	Chocolate milk
7. Life preservers	g.	Artichokes
8. One from the Alps	h.	Peach pie
9. Popeye	i.	Shredded wheat
10. Rabbit food	j.	Egg
11. Raft	k.	Orange juice
12. Sneeze	l.	Slice of toast
13. Sun kiss	m.	Donuts
14. Vermont	n.	Pepper
15. Yellow paint	o.	Maple syrup

Answers: 1-e, 2-i, 3-f, 4-g, 5-h, 6-j, 7-m, 8-a, 9-b, 10-c, 11-l, 12-n, 13-k, 14-o, 15-d

Figure 6–15 Baseball Lingo from *Frank and Ernest Play Ball* (Day, 1990)

Match the baseball lingo with its real meaning:

1. Dinger		a.	A ball hit between two outfielders
2. Dish		b.	A bat
3. Ducks on the pond		c.	A ball pitched at a fast speed
4. Fat pitch		d.	Strikeout
5. K		e.	Rack of bats
6. Lumber		f.	A noisy argument between players on opposing team
7. Tweener		g.	A home run
8. Woodpile		h.	A pitch that is easy to hit
9. Rhubarb		i.	Home plate
10. Heat		j.	Runners on base waiting to be driven home

Answers: 1-g, 2-i, 3-j, 4-h, 5-d, 6-b, 7-a, 8-e, 9-f, 10-c

Summary

Students must be provided with a variety of options for writing about literture. Journal writing, dialogue journals, literature logs, letters, postcards, new story endings, and research writing are just some of the ways to extend literature through writing.

References

Atwell, N. (1987). *In the middle: Writing, reading and learning with adolescents.* Portsmouth, NH: Heinemann.

Bailes, C., Searls, S., Slobodzian, J., & Staton, J. (1986). *It's your turn now: Dialogue journal communication with deaf students.* Washington DC: Gallaudet College Outreach Program.

Bleich, D. (1978). *Subjective criticism.* Baltimore: John Hopkins University Press.

Danielson, K. E. (1988). *Dialogue journals: Writing as conversation.* Bloomington, IN: Phi Delta Kappa.

Kelly, P. R. (1990). Guiding young students' response to literature. *The Reading Teacher, 43,* 464–470.

Kreeft, J. (1984). *Dialogue journal writing and the acquisition of grammatical morphology in English as a second language.* Unpublished doctoral dissertation. Washington, DC: Georgetown University.

Kreeft, J., Shuy, R., Staton, J., Reed, L., & Morroy, R. (1984). *Dialogue writing: Analysis of student-teacher interactive writing in the learning of English as a second language.* Final Report to the National Institute of Education, NIE-G-83-0030. Washington, DC: Center for Applied Linguistics.

Pierpont, J. (1990). Writing informally about reading. In N. Atwell (Ed.), *Coming to know: Writing to learn in the intermediate grades* (pp. 97–106). Portsmouth, NH: Heinemann.

Rosenblatt, L. (1978). *The reader, the text, the poem: The transactional theory of literary work.* Carbondale, IL: Southern Illinois University Press.

Routman, R. (1991). *Invitations: Changing as teachers and learners K–12.* Portsmouth, NH: Heinemann.

Staton, J. (1980). Writing and counseling: Using a dialogue journal. *Language Arts, 57,* 514–518.

Staton, J. (1988). An introduction to dialogue journal communication. In J. Staton, R. Shuy, J. K, Peyton, & L. Reed (Eds.), *Dialogue journal communication: Classroom, linguistic, social and cognitive views* (pp. 1–32). Norwood, NJ: Ablex.

Children's Books

Ahlberg, J., & Ahlberg, A. (1986). *The jolly postman and other people's letters.* Boston: Little, Brown.

Ahlberg, J., & Ahlberg, A. (1991). *The jolly Christmas postman.* Boston: Little, Brown.

Bauer, C. F. (1981). *My mom travels a lot.* New York: Warne.

Byars, B. (1986). *The not-just-anybody family.* New York: Delacorte.

Carothers, G., & Lacey, J. (1979). *Slanguage: America's second language.* New York: Sterling.

Dahl, R. (1988). *Matilda.* New York: Viking.

Day, A. (1988). *Frank and Ernest.* New York: Scholastic.

Day, A. (1990). *Frank and Ernest play ball.* New York: Scholastic.

Goldreich, G. (1972). *What can she be? A veterinarian.* New York: Lothrop.

Goldreich, G. (1973). *What can she be? A lawyer.* New York: Lothrop.

Goldreich, G. (1974). *What can she be? An architect.* New York: Lothrop.

Goldreich, G. (1975). *What can she be? A musician.* New York: Lothrop.

Goldreich, G. (1976). *What can she be? A farmer.* New York: Lothrop.

Goldreich, G. (1977). *What can she be? A film producer.* New York: Lothrop.

Goldreich, G. (1981). *What can she be? A scientist.* New York: Lothrop.

Johnson, J. (1985). *Firefighters from A to Z.* New York: Walker.

Johnson, J. (1986). *Police officers from A to Z.* New York: Walker.

Johnson, J. (1987). *Teachers from A to Z.* New York: Walker.

Johnson, J. (1988). *Librarians from A to Z.* New York: Walker.

Johnston, T. (1985). *The quilt story.* New York: Putnams.

Leedy, L. (1991). *Messages in the mailbox.* New York: Holiday House.

Merriam, E. (1989). *Daddies at work.* New York: Little Simon.

Merriam, E. (1989). *Mommies at work.* New York: Little Simon.

Miller, M. (1988). *Whose hat?* New York: Greenwillow.

Miller, M. (1991). *Whose shoe?* New York: Greenwillow.

*Morris, A. (1989). *Hats, hats, hats.* New York: Lothrop.

Roy, R. (1987). *Whose hat is that?* New York: Clarion.

Roy, R. (1988). *Whose shoes are these?* New York: Clarion.

Scieszka, J. (1989). *The true story of the three little pigs.* New York: Viking.

Simon, S. (1979). *Animal fact, animal fable.* New York: Crown.

Smith, W. J. (1989). *Ho for a hat.* Boston: Little, Brown.

Williams, V. B., & Williams, J. (1988). *Stringbean's trip to the shining sea.* New York: Greenwillow.

Winthrop, E. (1988). *Shoes.* New York: Harper Trophy.

Books with Journal Writing

Anderson, J. (1987). *Joshua's westward journal.* New York: Morrow. (nonfiction picture book)

Byars, B. (1988). *The burning questions of Bingo Brown.* New York: Viking. (novel)

Cleary, B. (1983). *Dear Mr. Henshaw.* New York: Morrow. (novel)

Cleary, B. (1991). *Strider.* New York: Morrow. (novel)

Cummings, P. (1992). *Petey Moroni's Camp Runamok diary.* New York: Bradbury. (picture book)

Dahlstrom, L. M. (1990). *Writing down the days: 365 creative journaling ideas for young people.* Minneapolis: Free Spirit. (teacher resource book)

Hamm, D. J. (1990). *Bunkhouse journal.* New York: Scribners. (novel)

McPhail, D. (1992). *Farm boy's year.* New York: Atheneum. (picture book)

Rocklin, J. (1988). *Dear baby.* New York: Macmillan. (novel)

Smith, R. K. (1987). *Mostly Michael.* New York: Delacorte. (novel)

Thaxter, C. (1992). *Celia's island journal.* Boston: Little, Brown. (picture book)

Wilder, L. I. (1962). *On the way home.* New York: Harper & Row. (novel)

Books with Letter Writing and Postcards

Ahlberg, J., & Ahlberg, A. (1986). *The jolly postman and other people's letters.* Boston: Little, Brown. (picture book)

Ahlberg, J., & Ahlberg, A. (1991). *The jolly Christmas postman.* Boston: Little, Brown. (picture book)

Brighton, C. (1991). *Dearest Grandmama.* New York: Doubleday. (picture book)

Brisson, P. (1989). *Your best friend, Kate.* New York: Bradbury. (picture book)

Brisson, P. (1990). *Kate heads west.* New York: Bradbury. (picture book)

Brisson, P. (1992). *Kate on the coast.* New York: Bradbury. (picture book)

Caseley, J. (1991). *Dear Annie.* New York: Greenwillow. (picture book)

Dragonwagon, C. (1986). *Dear Miss Moshki.* New York: Macmillan. (novel)

Free Stuff Editors. (1990). *Free stuff for kids.* New York: Meadowbrook. (teacher resource)

Giff, P. R. (1991). *The war began at supper: Letters to Miss Loria.* New York: Delacorte. (novel)

James, S. (1991). *Dear Mr. Blueberry.* New York: McElderry. (picture book)

Leedy, L. (1991). *Messages in the mailbox.* New York: Holiday House. (picture book)

Lowry, L. (1991). *Anastasia at this address.* Boston: Houghton Mifflin. (novel)

MacLachlan, P. (1985). *Sarah, plain and tall.* New York: Harper & Row. (novel)

Selway, M. (1992). *Don't forget to write.* Nashville: Ideals. (picture book)

*Stewart, M. (1986). *Dear Emily.* New York: Viking Penguin. (novel)

Stowe, C. (1992). *Dear Mom, in Ohio for a year.* New York: Scholastic. (novel)

*Wild, M. (1992). *Thank you, Santa.* New York: Scholastic. (picture book)

Williams, V. B., & Williams, J. (1988). *Stringbean's trip to the shining sea.* New York: Greenwillow. (picture book)

Series Books

Picture Books

About Miss Nelson/Viola Swamp

Allard, H., & Marshall, G. (1977). *Miss Nelson is missing.* Boston: Houghton Mifflin.

Allard, H., & Marshall, G. (1982). *Miss Nelson is back.* Boston: Houghton Mifflin.

Allard, H., & Marshall, G. (1985). *Miss Nelson has a field day.* Boston: Houghton Mifflin.

About the Stupids

Allard, H., & Marshall, G. (1974). *The Stupids step out.* Boston: Houghton Mifflin.

Allard, H., & Marshall, G. (1978). *The Stupids have a ball.* Boston: Houghton Mifflin.

Allard, H., & Marshall, G. (1981). *The Stupids die.* Boston: Houghton Mifflin.

Allard, H., & Marshall, G. (1989). *The Stupids take off.* Boston: Houghton Mifflin.

About Arthur

Brown, M. (1976). *Arthur's nose.* Boston: Little Brown.

Brown, M. (1979). *Arthur's eyes.* Boston: Little Brown.

Brown, M. (1980). *Arthur's valentine.* Boston: Little Brown.

Brown, M. (1981). *The true Francine.* Boston: Little Brown.

Brown, M. (1982). *Arthur's Halloween.* Boston: Little Brown.

Brown, M. (1983). *Arthur's April Fool.* Boston: Little Brown.

Brown, M. (1983). *Arthur's Thanksgiving.* Boston: Little Brown.

Brown, M. (1984). *Arthur's Christmas.* Boston: Little Brown.

Brown, M. (1985). *Arthur's goes to camp.* Boston: Little Brown.

Brown, M. (1986). *Arthur's teacher trouble.* Boston: Little Brown.

Brown, M. (1987). *Arthur's baby.* Boston: Little Brown.

Brown, M. (1987). *D.W. flips.* Boston: Little Brown.

Brown, M. (1988). *D.W. all wet.* Boston: Little Brown.

Brown, M. (1989). *Arthur's birthday.* Boston: Little Brown.

Brown, M. (1990). *Arthur's pet business.* Boston: Little Brown.

Brown, M. (1991). *Arthur meets the president.* Boston: Little Brown.

Brown, M. (1992). *Arthur babysits.* Boston: Little Brown.

About Willy

Browne, A. (1984). *Willy the wimp.* New York: Knopf.

Browne, A. (1985). *Willy the champ.* New York: Knopf.

Browne, A. (1991). *Willy and Hugh.* New York: Knopf.

About George and Martha

Marshall, J. (1972). *George and Martha.* Boston: Houghton Mifflin.

Marshall, J. (1972). *George and Martha tons of fun.* Boston: Houghton Mifflin.

Marshall, J. (1973). *George and Martha encore.* Boston: Houghton Mifflin.

Marshall, J. (1976). *George and Martha rise and shine.* Boston: Houghton Mifflin.

Marshall, J. (1978). *George and Martha one fine day.* Boston: Houghton Mifflin.

Marshall, J. (1984). *George and Martha back in town.* Boston: Houghton Mifflin.

Marshall, J. (1988). *George and Martha round and round.* Boston: Houghton Mifflin.

About Emily and Eugene

Marshall, J. (1973). *Yummers.* Boston: Houghton Mifflin.

Marshall, J. (1986). *Yummers too.* Boston: Houghton Mifflin.

About Henry and Mudge

Rylant, C. (1987). *Henry and Mudge.* New York: Bradbury.
Rylant, C. (1987). *Henry and Mudge in the green time.* New York: Bradbury.
Rylant, C. (1987). *Henry and Mudge in puddle trouble.* New York: Bradbury.
Rylant, C. (1987). *Henry and Mudge under the yellow moon.* New York: Bradbury.
Rylant, C. (1988). *Henry and Mudge in the sparkle days.* New York: Bradbury.
Rylant, C. (1989). *Henry and Mudge and the forever sea.* New York: Bradbury.
Rylant, C. (1989). *Henry and Mudge get the cold shivers.* New York: Bradbury.
Rylant, C. (1990). *Henry and Mudge and the happy cat.* New York: Bradbury.
Rylant, C. (1991). *Henry and Mudge and the bedtime thumps.* New York: Bradbury.
Rylant, C. (1991). *Henry and Mudge take the big test.* New York: Bradbury.

Novelettes

About Adam Joshua

Smith, J. L. (1981). *The monster in the third dresser drawer.* New York: Harper.
Smith, J. L. (1984). *The kid next door and other headaches.* New York: Harper.
Smith, J. L. (1988). *The show-and-tell war.* New York: Harper.
Smith, J. L. (1989). *It's not easy being George.* New York: Harper.
Smith, J. L. (1990). *The turkey's side of it.* New York: Harper.

Novels

About Bingo Brown

Byars, B. (1988). *The burning questions of Bingo Brown.* New York: Viking.
Byars, B. (1989). *Bingo Brown and the language of love.* New York: Viking.
Byars, B. (1990). *Bingo Brown, gypsy love.* New York: Viking.
Byars, B. (1992). *Bingo Brown's guide to romance.* New York: Viking.

About the Blossom Family

Byars, B. (1986). *The Blossoms meet the vulture lady.* New York: Delacorte.
Byars, B. (1986). *The not-just-anybody family.* New York: Delacorte.
Byars, B. (1987). *The Blossoms and the green phantom.* New York: Delacorte.
Byars, B. (1987). *The Blossom promise.* New York: Delacorte.
Byars, B. (1991). *Wanted: Mud blossom.* New York: Delacorte.

About Jenny Archer

Conforde, E. (1988). *A case for Jenny Archer.* Boston: Little Brown.
Conford, E. (1988). *A job for Jenny Archer.* Boston: Little Brown.
Conford, E. (1989). *Jenny Archer: Author.* Boston: Little Brown.
Conford, E. (1989). *What's cooking Jenny Archer?* Boston: Little Brown.
Conford, E. (1990). *Jenny Archer to the rescue.* Boston: Little Brown.
Conford, E. (1991). *Can do, Jenny Archer.* Boston: Little Brown.

About Rosy and Hermione

Greenwald, S. (1981). *Give us a great big smile, Rosy Cole.* Boston: Little Brown.
Greenwald, S. (1984). *Valentine Rosy.* Boston: Little Brown.
Greenwald, S. (1985). *Rosy Cole's great American guilt club.* Boston: Little Brown.
Greenwald, S. (1988). *Write on, Rosy.* Boston: Little Brown.

Greenwald, S. (1989). *Rosy's romance.* Boston: Little Brown.
Greenwald, S. (1991). *Here's Hermione.* Boston: Little Brown.

About Anastasia and Sam
Lowry, L. (1979). *Anastasia Krupnik.* Boston: Houghton Mifflin.
Lowry, L. (1981). *Anastasia again.* Boston: Houghton Mifflin.
Lowry, L. (1982). *Anastasia at your service.* Boston: Houghton Mifflin.
Lowry, L. (1984). *Anastasia ask your analyst.* Boston: Houghton Mifflin.
Lowry, L. (1985). *Anastasia on her own.* Boston: Houghton Mifflin.
Lowry, L. (1986). *Anastasia has the answers.* Boston: Houghton Mifflin.
Lowry, L. (1987). *Anastasia's chosen career.* Boston: Houghton Mifflin.
Lowry, L. (1988). *All about Sam.* Boston: Houghton Mifflin.
Lowry, L. (1991). *Anastasia at this address.* Boston: Houghton Mifflin.
Lowry, L. (1992). *Attaboy, Sam.* Boston: Houghton Mifflin.

About Alice
Naylor, P. R. (1985). *The agony of Alice.* New York: Atheneum.
Naylor, P. R. (1989). *Alice in rapture, sort of.* New York: Atheneum.
Naylor, P. R. (1991). *Reluctantly Alice.* New York: Atheneum.
Naylor, P. R. (1992). *All but Alice.* New York: Atheneum.
Naylor, P. R. (1993). *Alice in April.* New York: Atheneum.

Easy-to-Read Biographies

Adler, D. A. (1989). *A picture book of Abraham Lincoln.* New York: Holiday House.
Adler, D. A. (1989). *A picture book of George Washington.* New York: Holiday House.
*Adler, D. A. (1989). *A picture book of Martin Luther King Jr.* New York: Holiday House.
Adler, D. A. (1990). *A picture book of Benjamin Franklin.* New York: Holiday House.
Adler, D. A. (1990). *A picture book of Helen Keller.* New York: Holiday House.
Adler, D. A. (1990). *A picture book of Thomas Jefferson.* New York: Holiday House.
Adler, D. A. (1991). *A picture book of Christopher Columbus.* New York: Holiday House.
Adler, D. A. (1991). *A picture book of Eleanor Roosevelt.* New York: Holiday House.
Adler, D. A. (1991). *A picture book of John F. Kennedy.* New York: Holiday House.
*Adler, D. A. (1992). *A picture book of Simon Bolivar.* New York: Holiday House.

*Indicates multicultural focus.

7

Poetry

A quick inventory of the shelves of any bookstore reveals the endless variety available: We see books on gardening and football, exposés of famous people, self-help books for every shortcoming, spy thrillers, and classics from another time. A glance through the Children's Choice books in the October issues of *The Reading Teacher* makes us wonder if our preferences in literature were so diverse, even at young ages, that no one type of writing could please us all.

Fortunately, there *is* one genre of literature to which we all are inexplicably drawn. A brief recollection of childhood experiences will help us recall that the one type of writing that has universal appeal, from birth, is poetry. Only poetry contains all the lyrical elements that immediately catch the ear of the very youngest listeners. It is almost as though a need for rhyme and rhythm was in our soul. The earliest poetry that we love is "baby talk," also called "motherese," or more inclusively, "parentese."

When listening to a parent talk to an infant in parentese, we notice obvious changes in manners of speech. The voice of the parent becomes more lilting, there are longer pauses between words, some words are clearly given more stress, the parent repeats what is said, and occasionally the parent makes up nonsense words. The affectionate, intimate tone in the voice is obvious. This might be a typical monologue: "Well, *hi* there cutie-pie. Are you momma's little sweetie? Yes, you are. Look at those little feetie-weeties. Let's put on your ducky sockies. Hm?"

The baby responds to all this jabber with smiles, arm waving, and possibly some nonsense of his or her own. We know that even within the first three months of life, babies prefer to hear baby talk. Infants will suck on a blind nipple connected to a mechanism that plays recorded speech to hear parentese, but not to hear regular adult talk (Reich, 1986). It isn't long before children outgrow parentese and enjoy some of the poetry written for the very youngest listeners: Mother Goose. Many Mother Goose rhymes are acted out as they are spoken, further adding to their inclusive charm:

> *Pat-a-cake,*
> *Pat-a-cake,*
> *Baker's man,*
> *Bake me a cake as fast as you can.*
> *Roll it, and roll it,*
> *And mark it with a "B,"*
> *Toss it in the oven for Baby and me.*

Even though some Mother Goose rhymes have little meaning, their rhyme and rhythm appeal to young children:

Peter, Peter Pumpkin Eater
Had a wife and couldn't keep her.
Put her in a pumpkin shell
And there he kept her very well.

Children further demonstrate this preference for rhyme by inventing poetry when they first learn to talk. The following excerpt is from the monologue of two-year-old Elizabeth as she played with her toys:

Pinky Pong
Suffy
Beepa and Boppa
Pinky Pong
Suffy
Beepa and Boppa!

The taunting behavior of toddlers becomes poetic in a typical sing-song threat:

Nyah, nyah, nyah, nyah, nyah.
I'm gonna tell.
Nyah, nyah, nyah, nyah, nyah.
You can't get me.

We need only to observe recess at an elementary school to notice the many organized games for school-aged children that are accompanied with their own special chorus of words. Playgrounds are filled with children playing games such as Red Rover, each with its own rhythmic narration:

Red Rover,
Red Rover,
Send Sally right over!

Games of Hide and Seek depend on this brief rhyme to keep things in tact:

One, two, three, four, five,
six, seven, eight, nine, ten!
Ready or not, here I come!

Jumping rope requires a particular set of rhymes. The jumper chooses his or her favorite, and everyone chants:

Not last night but the night before,
Twenty-four robbers came knocking at my door,
I ran out and they ran in,
This is how the story did begin:
Spanish Dancer, turn around,
Spanish Dancer, touch the ground,
Spanish Dancer, do the splits,
Spanish Dancer, give a kick!
One . . . two . . . three . . . four . . .

When children first begin to play baseball, their enthusiastic coaches train them in infield chatter that is more of a chant:

Hey batter,
Hey batter,
Hey batter,
Swing!

Surely every adult recalls being tormented by the following ditty that was used to tease boyfriends and girlfriends:

Jamie and Kelly,
Up in a tree
K-I-S-S-I-N-G!

So, we know that children are born with an ear for poetry, even a preference for it, and that their own games and rituals are filled with it. Unfortunately, over time, many children learn to dislike poetry and soon avoid it like the plague. The mere mention of the word *poetry* elicits a chorus of groans and moans from entire classes. College students often indicate that they would rather take any other class than a poetry class. Most do not like to read it, talk about it, or write it.

How did this behavior develop? How did students come to abandon the poetry of their early years and view the entire genre with disdain? There are numerous causes of the disaffection of poetry lovers:

- *The traditional curriculum does not include enough emphasis on merely enjoying poetry. An early love of rhyme and rhythm becomes extinct.*

In many cases, poetry is completely absent from the curriculum. Perhaps it appears occasionally in a language arts textbook or is included in a basal reader, but usually poetry is only part of a lesson and its reading is often followed by a series of scrutinizing questions. Poetry must be savored. Sometimes we just need to hear the words and appreciate their sounds in silence. Enjoying a poem can simply mean listening to it, having a private moment to absorb it all, and then getting on with other business, carefully leaving the spell unbroken. For example, Lilian Moore's haunting verse, "Foghorns" brings forth a melancholy mood that is best left undisturbed.

- *There is an emphasis on reading archaic poetry that has little appeal.*

In our desire to expose children to the classics, we oftentimes overlook the inability of very young children to deal with abstract, sophisticated concepts and to understand cultures that are very different from their own. Surely, classic poetry has a place in modern education, but taste is something that develops gradually. For instance, most children are familiar with Halloween and they easily associate this favorite day with goblins, magic spells, and spooky creatures. With this background, reading Shakespeare's timeless tale of witch's brews is an easy step to take. Halloween is an ideal time to expose children to classic poetry relevant to experiences they can appreciate:

Song of the Witches

Double, double toil and trouble;
Fire burn and caldron bubble.
Fillet of a fenny snake,

> *In the caldron boil and bake;*
> *Eye of newt and toe of frog,*
> *Wool of bat and tongue of dog,*
> *Adder's fork and blind-worm's sting,*
> *Lizard's leg and howlet's wing,*
> *For a charm of powerful trouble,*
> *Like a hell-broth boil and bubble.*
>
> *Double, double toil and trouble;*
> *Fire burn and caldron bubble.*
> *Cool it with a baboon's blood,*
> *Then the charm is firm and good.*

Macbeth IV. i. 10–19; 35–38
   William Shakespeare
   Macbeth, act 4, sc. 1, lines 10–19, 35–38

- *There is an emphasis on overanalyzing and discussing poetry.*

Forcing children to analyze and discuss poetry can ruin the experience. Even Robert Frost became annoyed with people who insisted he explain the deeper meaning of his wonderful poem, "Stopping by Woods on a Snowy Evening." (Hopkins, 1987). Jean Little has summarized the frustration of every student who has ever had to dissect a poem to death in "After English Class."

Children will naturally want to repeat the words of a poem they like and will always ask questions if they are confused. We certainly don't need to have a clear definition of each word for the entire verse to please us. The quality of the words chosen by poets provides a rich, supportive context for unfamiliar vocabulary. In the poem "The Pig" (Roland Young), the word *tranquil* may be unfamiliar to children, but the overall humor in this poem about pigs does not escape them.

The novelty of many of the words in "Cave Beast Greets a Visitor" by Jack Prelutsky just adds to the mystery and spookiness of the poem. The refined behavior of a host with such a superior vocabulary sets forth a contrast that makes it a perfect monster. Readers are invited to relax in a "humble domicile" while they "sip some liquid from a flask," and to ignore teeth, talons, and a knife sharpener.

- *Children are not exposed to poetry that they like.*

It is essential that we look at what children like when we choose poetry for them. They have their preferences and our curriculum can be sprinkled with more abstract poetry and still have room for children's favorites. The more they listen to poetry and read it, the more of it they will want and the more willing they will be to explore all types of poetry. Even a simple poem about spaghetti ("Oodles of Noodles" by Lucia and James L. Hymes, Jr.) can charm young listeners and lead them to more sophisticated fare.

When children's love of poetry is intact, they will be patient enough to appreciate some of the more difficult classic poetry that we treasure. For example, history is given a haunting perspective in Carl Sandburg's poem about vanishing buffaloes, entitled "Buffalo Dusk."

- *We overemphasize reading poetry silently rather than listening to it.*

Poetry was meant to be read aloud. Although we can certainly read it to ourselves and enjoy it, young children are sometimes limited by their reading skills and cannot read for themselves much of the poetry they love. By hearing poetry orally first, children can savor the wonderful variety of poetry long before they can read it independently. Surely, McDonald's advertising campaign for their Big Macs was based on this understanding that many of their customers who couldn't read, "Two all beef patties special sauce lettuce cheese pickles onions on a sesame seed bun," would still hear it, remember it, and order it.

Understanding Poetry for Children

Although there is an infinite variety of poetry for children, it all shares certain features that differentiate it from prose. Poetry involves the parsimonious selection of words that evoke emotions and give clarity and fresh originality to experiences. A harmonious blend of rhyme, rhythm, and words enables poets to create a mood, conjure up a sensory experience, suggest a different perspective, intrigue us, perhaps surprise us, and help to satisfy our need for beauty in words. Tennyson celebrated the majesty of the eagle in this timeless classic. Careful selection of words helps us envision the cliff, the water, the blazing sun, and the power of this bird of prey:

The Eagle

He clasps the crag with crooked hands;
Close to the sun in lonely lands,
Ringed with the azure world, he stands.

The wrinkled sea beneath him crawls;
He watches from his mountain walls,
And like a thunderbolt he falls.

Alfred Lord Tennyson

Poets use all the features of written language as vehicles for their thoughts and ideas. We see infinite varieties in how the words and lines are arranged, how punctuation and capitalization are used, even in the selection of typeset. Poets are free to defy the conventions of written communication in order to deliver their messages. Every word and space in a poem carries its message to the audience. Arnold Adoff uses spaces and a careful arrangement of lines and words to give motion to his no-frills sports poetry book, *Sports Pages*.

A use of capital letters dramatizes Eve Merriam's staccato poetry about the fast pace of modern lives and our dependence on gimmicks and machines in "A Charm for Our Time."

Poetry is simultaneously reductive and expansive. For example, a poet can take an extremely difficult concept, such as death, and give us a sense of it in one touching verse. Poets also take ideas with which we are quite familiar and stretch our understanding of them.

Even though children are limited in their abilities to discern abstract concepts, they can enjoy the imagery created by poets. Rosetti's poem about the effects of the wind, "Who Has Seen the Wind?", will be easily understood by children who have carefully observed dry leaves chasing down the street.

Poets express their ideas in challenging patterns that further the meaning of the poem. Paul Fleischman's collection of insect poetry is meant to be read aloud by two voices (just like the title tells us) and the information about the insects is carefully imbedded in the patterns of the poem. Completely opposite, but parallel, perspectives on the interdependent lives of bees are conveyed both visually and aurally by his poem, "Honeybees."

Choosing Quality Poetry for Children

Naturally, we want to choose good poetry for our students. If we value them as listeners, then we are careful in our selections. The music of poetry, the words selected by the poet, and the content of the poem play critical roles in judging its quality (Sutherland & Arbuthnot, 1986).

The Music of Poetry

An important characteristic of poetry for children is the musical or lyrical quality of the work. Good poetry has melody and the mood of the poem is carried forth by the elements of movement.

The Words of Poetry

The selection of words in poetry is critical. The poet chooses each word carefully; there are no wasted words or commonplace, humdrum words. Each word contributes to the overall quality of the poem. By this careful selection of a few precise words, the poet can create a mood and stir emotions.

The Content of Poetry

The content of the poem also plays a critical role in its selection. Poetry may be about common, everyday experiences or the unique and bizarre, but the poem gives us an alternative perspective or invigorating outlook. Poetry makes us feel and think.

Selecting Poetry Children Prefer

Research with children has given us an understanding of what type of poetry appeals to them (Sutherland & Arbuthnot, 1986). Children in the primary grades like limericks, narrative and rhymed verse, and rhyming story poems. They also enjoy nonsense and humor and like poems about animals, fantasy, children, and familiar experiences. Children in the upper elementary grades do not like sentimental poetry but instead prefer humorous poems, narrative poetry, and poems with everyday language and content.

Limericks

Limericks appeal to the sense of humor favored by young children. These poems are brief and represent the slapstick comedy branch of children's poetry:

A Young Farmer of Leeds

There was a young farmer of Leeds
who swallowed six packets of seeds.
*   It soon came to pass*
*   He was covered with grass*
And he couldn't sit down for the weeds.

Unknown

Narrative Poetry

Narrative poetry, or poetry that tells a story, is a special favorite of children. Since this kind of poetry has many of the same characteristics as good stories—plot, characters, setting, style, and theme—children find it familiar. "Casey at the Bat," which was written over 100 years ago, will still captivate audiences:

Casey at the Bat

The outlook wasn't brilliant for the Mudville nine that day:
The score stood four to two, with but one inning more to play,
And so when Cooney died at first, and Barrows did the same,
A deadly silence fell upon the patrons of the game.

A straggling few got up to go in deep despair. The rest
Clung to the hope which springs eternal in the human breast;
They thought, "If only Casey could but get a whack at that—
We'd put up even money with Casey at the bat . . .

Ernest Lawrence Thayer

Children seem to have a limitless capacity for nonsense in poetry. They can be delighted with the sounds of words that are just fun to hear and say.

Humorous Poetry

Poetry that tickles the funny bone and elicits a chuckle will always be popular with young audiences. Especially appreciated by children, as well as adults, are the many selections in Shel Silverstein's *Where the Sidewalk Ends* and *A Light in The Attic.*

Familiar Topics

Children also like poetry that deals with topics with which they are familiar. Russell Hoban's poem, "Homework" never fails to draw an appreciative audience. Because children's lives are filled with bosses, structure, and rules that may seem quite arbitrary, Karla Kuskin's poem "Rules" reflects the frustration of the rule-bound child. Jean Little writes of the difficulties in always trying to live up to the expectations of others in her poem about dropping out for a time, "Today." Shel Silverstein is a perennial favorite with children. His delightful humor is irresistible and he also chooses subjects of concern for every child: parents, siblings, school, chores, friends.

The poem written by an unknown poet will draw a chuckle from every child who ever had trouble with spelling:

The Ptarmigan

The ptarmigan is strange,
As strange as he can be;
Never sits on ptelephone poles
Or roosts upon a ptree.
And the way he ptakes pto spelling
Is the strangest thing pto me.

Anonymous

Sharing Poetry with Children

Since simply surrounding children with poetry will ignite an interest in it, the primary responsibility of the teacher will be to make a variety of poetry available to his or her students and to share it with them whenever possible throughout the day. Instilling a love for rhyme can be enhanced by the following suggestions:

1. *Have a variety of collections on hand.* The teacher will want to keep a section of poetry books in the classroom library. Many of the anthologies can remain all year, and poetry books dealing with specific subjects or times of year can be brought in as they become appropriate. The teacher may want to feature a new book of poems each week and display the book in a prominent place.

2. *Have poems on tape.* Since poetry was meant to be read out loud, having poems on cassette tapes allows children to hear their favorites again and again. Listening to a preferred poem and following along in a book reinforces reading skills and introduces children to wonderful words beyond their independent decoding ability.

3. *Invite visiting readers to class.* People from the community, parents, students from other classes, and school personnel make ideal readers of poetry. The teacher can set aside a specific time each week when guests come and read poetry they have chosen or something recommended by the teacher.

4. *Share poetry throughout the day.* Because of its brevity, poetry can be integrated into the school day. Each day can begin and end with a poem. Poetry may also be used during the transition between subjects and included in study in the content areas.

5. *Keep poetry on flip charts.* The teacher can copy a poem each day on a flip chart. This allows children to reread poetry at their leisure and to enjoy the accumulated poetry the teacher has shared with the class. Hearing these works read out loud first provides a secure base for independent reading.

6. *Focus on specific poets.* As children come to enjoy poetry, they become curious about the poets. The teacher can select a poet whose work will be displayed and read during a certain period of time. While students learn more about the life of this person, they can begin to appreciate the individual sense of style each poet has. Children can also choose favorite poets and, working alone or in cooperative groups, present information about their poet to the class.

7. *Share poetry with one another.* As children become comfortable with poetry, they will want to read it to each other. A certain time each week can be set aside for these poetry-sharing sessions. Children can bring their favorite poems to read to one another, and they may want to present some of the works as choral readings or duets. On a rotating basis, children may read a favorite poem as part of the opening exercises each morning, after lunch, or to close the day.

8. *Collect poetry.* Although we would never want to force children to copy poetry, many of them like their own copy of favorite poems. Children can be given notebooks in which they can periodically select poems they want to have on hand. By the end of the year, each child will have his or her own anthology. From time to time, children can take their poetry books home to read or can read them to other classes. These poetry collections can become part of the portfolios discussed in Chapter 9.

9. *Encourage children to write poetry.* Not long after children have rekindled an appreciation for listening to poetry, they will want to try a hand at writing their own. The wise teacher makes poetry writing an important facet of the writing workshop.

Helping Children Write Poetry

Once we free them from a requirement that their works rhyme, children become quite skilled at composing poetry. The following types of poems will help children develop confidence in their own ability to write poetry.

"I Used to Be . . . But Now . . ."

This pair of contrasting thoughts creates a framework for young writers:

I used to be _____
But now I'm _____.

I used to be a word
But now I'm an entire mystery novel.

Similes

Using *like* or *as* to enhance description will help children take a second look at things:

The snow was like _____.
The snow was like glittering mounds of ice cream.

As quiet as _____.
As quiet as a class right before a test.

Haiku

Haiku is a type of Japanese poetry in which a single episode of nature is described. These three-line poems have a 5-7-5 syllable count:

Rumbling thunderclouds
The sullen sky turns angry
A storm is waiting.

Hink-Pinks

Hink-pinks, also called *terse verse,* are two-word poems that either answer riddles or are descriptive. Each word contains only one syllable:

Sledding

Glide
ride

Football

Ball
brawl

Alphabet Pyramids

Alphabet Pyramids are composed of words that all begin with the same letter. These poems are cumulative and contain specific parts of speech:

Line 1: the letter
Line 2: a noun
Line 3: an adjective and the noun
Line 4: an adjective, the noun, and a verb
Line 5: an adjective, the noun, a verb, and an adverb

A
ant
awkward ant
awkward ant answers
awkward ant answers afterwards

Terquains

Terquains are descriptive three-line poems:

Line 1: one word, the subject
Line 2: two or three words about the subject
Line 3: one word, a feeling about the subject or a synonm

Kitten
Silky, frisky
Treasure

Cinquains

Cinquains are descriptive five-line poems. The poem is composed of approximately 22 syllables in a 2-4-6-8-2 pattern:

Line 1: a word for the subject
Line 2: four syllables describing the subject
Line 3: six syllables showing action
Line 4: eight syllables expressing a feeling or observation about the subject
Line 5: two syllables describing or renaming the subject

Piggy
Pink and portly
Grunting, yumming, smacking
He is getting fatter daily
Porkchop

Diamantes

Diamantes are also descriptive poetry. These seven-line poems compare a set of antonyms using specific parts of speech:

Line 1: one noun as the subject
Line 2: two adjectives describing the subject
Line 3: three participles telling about the subject
Line 4: four nouns—the first two about the first noun, the second two about the antonym
Line 6: two adjectives describing the antonym
Line 7: the antonym

City
tall noisy
honking yelling growing
crowds cars spaces nature
strolling hiking breathing
calm open
Country

Parodies

Parodies are poems that borrow structure and rhythm from the poetry that has been written by someone else.

A Young Lady of Lynn

There was a young lady of Lynn,
Who was so uncommonly thin
That when she essayed
To drink lemonade,
She slipped through the straw and fell in.

Anonymous

Pattern:
There was a _____ _____ of _____.
Who was so _____ _____
That when he/she _____
To _____ _____.
He/she _____ _____ _____ _____ _____ _____ _____.

Example:

The Tall Man of St. Cloud

There was a tall man of St. Cloud
Who was so horribly loud
That when he hollered, "Hello!"
To a quiet shy fellow,
He startled the rest of the crowd.

The Benefits of Sharing Poetry with Children

- *Poetry transmits our literary heritage.*

Knowing the literary heritage that is uniquely ours is the privilege of all children; it is their right to the contents of this literary storehouse. There is a body of poetry that ties us with our past and without which we would be impoverished. We have all walked alone on a dark, windy night and can appreciate Stevenson's poem that likens the night wind to a galloping horse.

Windy Nights

Whenever the moon and stars are set,
Whenever the wind is high,
All night long in the dark and wet,
*   A man goes riding by,*
Late in the night when the fires are out,
Why does he gallop and gallop about?

Whenever the trees are crying aloud,
*   And ships are tossed at sea,*
By, on the highway, low and loud,
*   By at the gallop goes he;*
By at the gallop he goes, and then
By he comes back at the gallop again.

Robert Louis Stevenson

* *Poetry transmits our cultural heritage.*

The United States is a country composed of wonderfully unique cultural groups. Sharing poetry from every culture helps expose children to the values and ideas of backgrounds other than their own and can be an initial step in respecting and appreciating differences:

"Twinkle Twinkle Little Star" can precede a discussion of bedtime poems and songs from every culture:

Twinkle Twinkle Little Star

Twinkle, twinkle little star,
*   How I wonder what you are.*
Up above the world so high,
*   Like a diamond in the sky.*

When the blazing sun is gone,
*   When he nothing shines upon.*
Then you show your little light.
*   Twinkle twinkle all the night.*

Unknown

* *Reading and hearing poetry enhances oral reading skills and improves listening skills.*

Because poetry is meant to be read aloud, it puts pressure on poets to choose words that will be a pleasure to hear. Because of its rhythmic nature and the use of the elements of literary style (onomotopeia, consonance, etc.), reading poletry will help children develop good oral reading and listening skills.

* *Readers of all levels can share the same written text.*

Because understanding poetry is dependent more on the subject of the poem than the vocabulary, children of a variety of reading abilities can enjoy the same poem. The brevity of poetry and the structure, rhyme, and rhythm of the poem make it easier to read than prose. The child who has difficulty with reading can experience and appreciate poetry with the rest of the class.

- *Poetry can be integrated into any content area.*

Poems have been written about every topic and can be used to give children a refreshing slant on every subject.

- *Poetry exposes children to rich vocabulary words that they can make a part of their own writing and that they will encounter in independent reading.*

Poets select the words of their work carefully and poetry can play a key role in stretching a child's vocabulary.

- *Poetry improves with repetition.*

Rereading written text is a valuable component of reading instruction. Rereading improves comprehension and oral reading skills and establishes a secure basis for instruction. The lyrical nature of poetry makes it ideal for reading again and again.

- *Poetry can be selected for any occasion.*

Since poetry has been written for every possible topic and touches on a myriad of feelings, ideas, and situations, it can be shared with students whenever the need arises. Sharing these poems helps instill a sense of community in the classroom:

- *Poetry is ideal written material for beginning readers.*

The text of poetry makes it perfect for teaching children how to read. Certain elements of poetry—the rhyme, rhythm, and repetition—make it easy for children to predict what words will come next, thereby providing security for beginners and reducing uncertainty:

I'm Glad the Sky Is Painted Blue

I'm glad the sky is painted blue,
*   And the earth is painted green,*
With such a lot of nice fresh air
*   All sandwiched in between.*

Anonymous

Summary

From birth, humans are attracted to rhyme, rhythm, and repetition. Our preference for lyrical language carries over to a natural love of poetry. Because of its brevity and the wide range of topics, poetry can be an integral part of the curriculum. From kindergarten on, students can begin to develop an understanding of poetry, refine their own preferences for particular types of verse, become active members in a community of poetry lovers, and attempt some poetry writing of their own.

The following ideas summarize the information presented in this chapter:

1. In the past, methods of sharing poetry with children were flawed: The presence of poetry in the curriculum was often sparse, the instructional focus was on analyzing and discussing poems, much of the poetry children read was antiquated, and there was little focus on sharing poetry that children preferred.

2. When choosing poetry to share with students, we should base our judgments on three aspects of the poem: the linguistic music of the poem, the quality of the words selected by the poet, and the content of the poem.

3. Children have definite preferences in poetry: They like humorous poetry and poetry that tells a story. They also enjoy limericks and poems about everyday experiences.

4. Teachers can employ a variety of methods of making poetry come alive in their classrooms: Making sure a diverse collection of poetry is on hand in the classroom, having poems on tapes and on flip charts, encouraging children to share poetry with one another, inviting guests to read poetry to the class, and involving students in writing poetry of their own.

5. Teachers can provide opportunities for children to write poetry of their own that focuses on rhythm and pattern rather than rhyme. The variety of verses that children can write includes similes, haiku, hink-pinks, alphabet pyramids, terquains, cinquains, diamantes, and parodies.

6. The benefits of sharing poetry with children are numerous: Poetry transmits our literary and cultural heritage, it refines both oral reading and listening skills, readers of all levels can enjoy the same material, poetry is easily integrated into the content areas, and it complements any topic or occasion.

References

Hopkins, L. J. (1987). *Pass the poetry, please!* New York: Harper and Row.

Reich, P. A. (1986). *Language development.* Englewood Cliffs, NJ: Prentice Hall.

Sutherland, Z., & Arbuthnot, M. H. (1986). *Children and books* (7th ed.). Glenview, IL: Scott Foresman.

Poetry Cited in Chapter

*Adoff, A. (1986). *Sports Pages.* New York: Lippincott.
  "Afternoons: Two" (Adoff)

Fleischman, P. (1988). *Joyful noise.* New York: Harper and Row.
  "Honeybees" (Fleischman)

Little, J. (1986). *Hey world, here I am.* New York: Harper.
  "After English Class" (Little)
  "Today" (Little)

Poems children will sit still for. (1969). New York: Scholastic.
   A Young Farmer of Leeds" (Unknown)

Prelutsky, J. (1983). *The Random House book of poetry for children.* Ill. by A. Lobel. New York: Random House.

   "The Eagle" (Tennyson)
   "Song of the Witches" (Shakespeare)
   "Windy Nights" (Stevenson)

Prelutsky, J. (1984). *The new kid on the block.* Ill. by J. Stevenson. New York: Greenwillow.
   "The Cave Beast Greets a Visitor" (Prelutsky)

The real Mother Goose. (1977). (67th ed.). Chicago: Rand McNally
   "Pat-a-cake"

Thayer, E. L. "Casey at the Bat"

Recommended Poetry Anthologies

*Adoff, A. (1986). *Sports pages.* New York: Lippincott.
 Adoff, A. (1989). *Chocolate dreams.* New York: Lothrop.
*Adoff, A. (1991). *Hard to be six.* New York: Lothrop.
*Adoff, A. (1991). *In for winter, out for spring.* San Diego: Harcourt Brace Jovanovich.
 Bennett, J. (1989). *Spooky poems.* Boston: Little, Brown.
 Brent, I. (1992). *Cameo cats.* Boston: Little, Brown.
 Brown, M. (1985). *Hand rhymes.* New York: Dutton.
 Brown, M. (1987). *Play rhymes.* New York: Dutton.
 Carle, E. (1991). *Animals, animals.* New York: Scholastic.
 Choroa, K. (1990). *The baby's good morning book.* New York: Dutton.
 Ciardi, J. (1990). *Mummy took cooking lessons.* Boston: Houghton Mifflin.
 Cole, W. (1981). *Poem stew.* New York: Harper & Row.
 Dakos, K. (1990). *If you're not here, please raise your hand.* New York: Four Winds Press.
 de Regniers, B., et al. (1988). *Sing a song of popcorn.* New York: Scholastic.
 Duncan, L. (1989). *Songs from dreamland.* New York: Knopf.
 Fleischman, P. (1985). *I am Phoenix.* New York: Harper & Row.
 Fleischman, P. (1988). *Joyful noise.* New York: Harper & Row.
 Goldstein, B. (1990). *Bear in mind.* New York: Trumpet Club.
 Goode, D. (1990). *Diane Goode's American Christmas.* New York: Dutton.
 Hague, K. (1989). *Bear hugs.* New York: Holt.
 Hayes, S. (1988). *Stamp your feet: Action rhymes.* New York: Greenwillow.
 Heide, F. P. (1992). *Grim and ghastly goings on.* New York: Lothrop.
 Higginson, W. (1991). *Wind in the long grass.* New York: Simon and Schuster.
*Hoberman, M. A. (1991). *Fathers, mothers, sisters, brothers.* Boston: Little, Brown.
 Hopkins, L. B. (1982). *Rainbows are made: Poems by Carl Sandburg.* San Diego: Harcourt Brace Jovanovich.
 Hopkins, L. B. (1984). *Surprises.* New York: Harper.
 Hopkins, L. B. (1988). *Side by side.* New York: Simon and Schuster.
 Hopkins, L. B. (1989). *Still as a star.* Boston: Little, Brown.
 Hopkins, L. B. (1990). *Good books, good times.* New York: Harper.

Hopkins, L. B. (1991). *Happy birthday.* New York: Simon and Schuster.

Hopkins, L. B. (1991). *On the farm.* Boston: Little, Brown.

Hopkins, L. B. (1992). *Through our eye.* Boston: Little, Brown.

Hubbell, P. (1990). *A grass green gallop.* New York: Atheneum.

Jabar, C. (1992). *Shimmy shake earth quake: Don't forget to dance poems.* Boston: Little, Brown.

Kennedy, X. J. (1989). *Ghastlies, goops, and pincushions.* New York: McElderry.

Kennedy, X. J. (1992). *The beasts of Bethlehem.* New York: McElderry.

Lear, E. (1980). *A book of nonsense.* New York: Viking.

Lewis, C. (1987). *Long ago in Oregon.* New York: Harper & Row.

Lewis, C. (1991). *Up in the mountains.* New York: Harper.

Lewis, J. P. (1991). *Earth verse and water rhymes.* New York: Atheneum.

Lewis, J. P. (1991). *A hippopotamusn't.* New York: Trumpet Club.

Lewis, J. P. (1991). *Two-legged, four-legged, no-legged rhymes.* New York: Knopf.

Little, J. (1986). *Hey world, here I am.* New York: Harper.

Livingston, M. C. (1985). *Celebrations.* New York: Holiday House.

Livingston. M. C. (1987). *I like you, if you like me.* New York: Holiday House.

Livingston, M. C. (1987). *New Year's poems.* New York: Holiday House.

Livingston, M. C. (1989). *Halloween poems.* New York: Holiday House.

Livingston, M. C. (1990). *If the owl calls again.* New York: Holiday House.

Livingston, M. C. (1990). *My head is red.* New York: Holiday House.

Livingston, M. C. (1991). *Lots of limericks.* New York: Holiday House.

Livingston, M. C. (1992). *Let freedom ring.* New York: Holiday House.

Lobel, A. (1988). *The book of pigericks.* New York: Harper.

Merriam, E. (1985). *Blackberry ink.* New York: Morrow.

Merriam, E. (1986). *Fresh paint.* New York: Macmillan.

Merriam, E. (1987). *Halloween ABC.* New York: Macmillan.

Merriam, E. (1988). *You be good and I'll be night.* New York: Morrow.

Merriam, E. (1989). *Chortles.* New York: Morrow.

Merriam, E. (1992). *The singing green.* New York: Morrow.

Metopolitan Museum of Art. (1991). *Songs of the wild west.* New York: Simon and Schuster.

*Milnes, G. (1991). *Granny will your dog bite.* New York: Knopf.

Moore, L. (1992). *Adam Mouse's book of poems.* New York: Atheneum.

National Gallery of Art. (1991). *An illustrated treasury of songs.* New York: Rizzoli.

O'Neill, M. (1989). *Hailstone and halibut bones.* New York: Trumpet Club.

Prelutsky, J. (1983). *The Random House book of poetry for children.* New York: Random House.

Prelutsky, J. (1984). *The new kid on the block.* New York: Greenwillow.

Prelutsky, J. (1986). *Read-aloud rhymes for the very young.* New York: Knopf.

Prelutsky, J. (1986). *Ride a purple pelican.* New York: Greenwillow.

Prelutsky, J. (1988). *Tyrannosaurus was a beast.* New York: Greenwillow.

Prelutsky, J. (1989). *Poems of A. Nonny Mouse.* New York: Knopf.

Prelutsky, J. (1990). *Something big has been here.* New York: Greenwillow.

Silverstein, S. (1974). *Where the sidewalk ends.* New York: Harper.

*Sneve, V. D. H. (1989). *Dancing teepees.* New York: Holiday House.

Steele, M. Q. (1989). *Anna's garden songs.* New York: Scholastic.

Recommended Stories Told in Rhyme

Ackerman, K. (1992). *This old house.* New York: Atheneum.

Archambault, J. (1989). *Counting sheep.* New York: Holt.

Aylesworth, J. (1990). *The complete Hickory Dickory Dock.* New York: Atheneum.

Aylesworth, J. (1992). *The cat and the fiddle and me.* New York: Atheneum.

*Baer, E. (1990). *This is the way we go to school.* New York: Scholastic.

Bunting, E. (1986). *Scary, scary Halloween.* New York: Scholastic.

Carlstrom, N. W. (1990). *It's about time, Jesse bear.* New York: Macmillan.

Carlstrom, N. W. (1992). *Better not get wet, Jesse bear.* New York: Macmillan.

Carlstrom, N. W. (1992). *How do you say it today, Jesse bear?* New York: Macmillan.

Charles, D. (1989). *Paddy Pig's poems.* New York: Simon and Schuster.

Cherry, L. (1988). *Whose sick today?* New York: Dutton.

Collins, J. (1989). *My father.* Boston: Little, Brown.

Dabcovich, L. (1992). *The keys to my kingdom.* New York: Lothrop.

Dominguez, A. (1991). *Diary of a Victorian mouse.* New York: Arcade.

Dragonwagon, c. (1989). *This is the bread I baked for Ned.* New York: Macmillan.

Edens, C. (1991). *Santa Cows.* New York: Simon and Schuster.

Field, R. (1988). *General store.* Boston: Little, Brown.

Gerrard, R. (1990). *Mik's mammoth.* New York: Farrar, Straus, Giroux.

Gerrard, R. (1991). *A pocket full of posies.* New York: Farrar, Straus, Giroux.

Gerrard, R. (1991). *Rosie and the rustlers.* New York: Sunburst.

Gerrard, R. (1992). *Jocasta Carr.* New York: Farrar, Straus, Giroux.

Gross, T. (1990). *Everyone asked about you.* New York: Philomel.

Hennessey, B. G. (1989). *The missing tarts.* New York: Viking.

Hennessey, B. G. (1990). *School days.* New York: Viking.

Hoopes, L. L. (1990). *Wing-a-ding.* Boston: Little, Brown.

King, L. (1988). *Because of Lozo Brown.* New York: Viking.

*Lenski, L. (1987). *Sing a song of people.* Boston: Little, Brown.

Lindbergh, R. (1987). *The midnight farm.* New York: Dial.

Lindbergh, R. (1990). *Benjamin's barn.* New York: Dial.

Lindbergh, R. (1990). *The day the goose got loose.* New York: Dial.

Lindbergh, R. (1990). *Johnny Appleseed.* Boston: Little, Brown.

Livingston, M. C. (1989). *Up in the air!* New York: Holiday House.

McMillan, B. (1990). *One sun.* New York: Holiday House.

McMillan, B. (1991). *Play day.* New York: Holiday House.

Nerlove, M. (1989). *Just one tooth.* New York: McElderry.

Pelham, D. (1992). *Sam's surprise.* New York: Dutton.

Pelham, D. (1990). *Sam's sandwich.* New York: Dutton.

Pilkey, D. (1990). *'Twas the night before Thanksgiving.* New York: Orchard.

Provensen, A. (1990). *The buck stops here.* New York: Harper.

Shaw, N. (1991). *Sheep in a shop.* Boston: Houghton Mifflin.

Shaw, N. (1992). *Sheep out to eat.* Boston: Houghton Mifflin.

Siebert, D. (1989). *Heartland.* New York: Crowell.

Siebert, D. (1991). *Sierra.* New York: Harper.

Smith, W. J. (1989). *Ho for a hat.* Boston: Little, Brown.

Winthrop, E. (1986). *Shoes.* New York: Harper.

Winthrop, E. (1989). *Sledding.* New York: Harper.

*Indicates multicultural focus.

8

Teaching the Skills

André was in the fourth grade when punctuation seemed to be given serious emphasis in language arts class. On a regular basis he would bring home papers that required him to choose the appropriate end marks for a series of sentences. His grades on these assignments were inconsistent and somewhat puzzling; they ranged from a high of 87 percent to a low of 60 percent. So, his mother asked him how he was deciding when to use what punctuation. "It's really easy," was his reply, "First of all, you don't even need to read anything (I'm sure that delighted his teacher). You just look at the first word of the sentence, if it's 'who, what, when, where, why, or how,' you end it with a question mark. If the sentence is really short, I put in an exclamation mark. And I use periods for everything else that's left over. It works good enough for me."

This story typifies many of the follies of traditional methods of teaching the skills. Too often this work is done with worksheets for which children quickly determine a pattern and complete with as little expenditure of mental energy as possible. Like adults, children are cognitive misers—they never do more thinking than they need to. Certainly more than one first-grader has announced proudly that he or she could do an entire worksheet on phonics, get a 100, and "never have to read a thing." Since seatwork is often done individually, it is impossible for the teacher to know if a child got the beginning sound of *spaceship* wrong because he or she didn't know what letters made up the beginning sound or because the student mistook the picture of a spaceship for that of a rocket.

Since phonics concepts are often taught as absolutes, children form rather bizarre conclusions about the graphophonic connection. One child explained her spelling of *have* as *haev* this way, "You need an *e* next to the *a* to make the *v* long." In spite of the considerable emphasis given to skill work during reading class, many children leave grade school lacking the tools that would make them strategic, effective readers.

The faults of traditional methods of teaching reading skills are numerous:

1. Worksheets that accompany many basal texts have no actual connection to the text itself. It is not unusual for the seatwork to be totally unrelated to what the children are reading.
2. Several skills are taught on one page. Oftentimes, children will do three, or as many as four, different tasks on one page.
3. The writing samples on worksheets are contrived. Sentences and even paragraphs are made up to teach the skill selected. These artificial examples of writing are void of the typical clues to meaning that are woven into the writing of real authors.

157

4. The skillwork is completed individually and silently. Since reading skills are complex and abstract, students need to be guided through their written work with numerous opportunities for discussion and questions.

5. Children seldom apply the concepts from worksheets to actual reading and writing situations.

6. Children do little writing or thinking while completing their seatwork. Responses often require that they only circle or underline correct answers or give the briefest written responses.

The teaching of specific skills is not ignored in a literature-based reading program. Indeed, one of the primary goals of such programs is that students become strategic readers who use every possible tool available to them to make sense of what is being read. But how these skills are taught is quite different.

1. The skills are taught in connection with the material being read. Written work is tied to a reading task so that students are learning skills in the process of comprehending what is being read, in a manner very similar to what readers do in everyday situations.

2. Teachers focus on only one or two skills at a time so that children have more opportunities for practice and application.

3. The writing is taken from children's literature and poetry. Quality material is the basis for skillwork. Two purposes are served simultaneously: Children are being exposed to wonderful writing that will captivate them and they are learning skills that will make them mature, independent readers who can read and who know what wonders books have to offer.

4. Much of the skillwork is completed orally in teacher-directed lessons. This allows the teacher to guide and monitor the lesson and provides a solid basis from which children can generalize.

5. Children immediately use what is learned from the lesson in actual reading situations.

6. Once the oral portion of the lesson is completed, the students are often required to write. Since these activities are taken from genuine text, the students also need to make sense of what they read. Meaning is not separated from the task at hand.

Designing seatwork that teaches skills is a demanding task for classroom teachers. It can be most efficiently approached by teams or groups of teachers who pool their ideas and divide the work. To begin, teachers need to examine the reading and writing skills that their district emphasizes at each grade level. The next step is to peruse the reading materials available and select one or two skills appropriate to each. For example, poetry provides an excellent opportunity to focus on elements of style, parts of speech, or morphology. The use of informational books is ideal for emphasis on facility with reference tools. Modern fiction is an effective vehicle for teaching the elements of story grammar. Any sample of quality writing yields limitless opportunities for focus on the use of decoding skills.

The direct teaching method is recommended for use the majority of the time. The teacher leads the instruction by identifying what will be taught and why it is important. He or she provides opportunities for guided practice and concludes with a chance for students to apply the information in an actual reading situation. The lessons begin as concretely as possible and move to levels of increasing abstractness with a heavy emphasis on oral activities. Children need several opportunities to apply the concepts from a skill lesson.

Our primary goal is to help children gather an arsenal of tools—a variety of strategies—that they can use in reading situations. The more strategies a reader has, the more efficient that person is. However, teachers must recognize that children are unique individuals and have different strengths and weaknesses. For some children, using phonetic clues is an easily understood and efficiently applied strategy. These children can sound out just about any word, providing they have the word in their oral vocabulary. For other children, phonics will remain an elusive skill they never quite master. Children who fall into this category must be adept at determining clues from context, and like all readers, they need an extensive sight vocabulary.

An easily understood analogy to this situation is driving. Certainly, the driver who can angle park and parallel park, and who is unafraid of dark parking garages has an advantage. But those of us who can only parallel park when given an acre on a deserted street and who question the structural stability of parking garages are not sentenced to a life of confinement within our houses. We merely look more carefully for opportunities to angle park or to park in open lots. And in the end, all varieties of drivers meet their objectives: They get where they are going so they can do what they need or want to do. In most cases, driving is only a means, it is not an end. Skill work in reading is similar: All readers need to make sense of the text at hand. The strategies they employ are a means to the end, but they are not the purpose of reading.

The remainder of this chapter gives examples of ways to use literature and poetry to teach reading skills to children. Since the skills that pertain to reading comprehension and writing are discussed in other chapters, the following areas are given emphasis in this chapter:

1. Vocabulary development
2. Decoding
   a. Gathering a sight vocabulary
   b. Using context clues
   c. Using phonetic clues
3. Literary skills
4. Study skills

Vocabulary Development

Without much direct instruction, most children enter school with impressive vocabularies just by being surrounded by and participating in oral language (Norton, 1985). The intricacies of this linguistic phenomenon have piqued the curiosity of educators and researchers for years. A realization that better readers have bigger vocabularies has fueled extensive research with school-aged children in an attempt to explain such a relationship (Stahl & Fairbanks, 1986).

It is indisputable that vocabulary is positively correlated with reading comprehension (Davis, 1968). We know that the more words a child knows, the better his or her chances are for success with a particular piece of writing. Vocabulary is related to the major ideas in a text (Anders & Vos, 1986) and affects sentence comprehension and reading speed (MacGinitie, 1976).

Children need repeated exposure to a word in a variety of situations (Beck, McKeown, McCaslin, & Burkes, 1982) and need to be able to relate the new word to their own background experiences (Eeds & Cockrum, 1985). The persistent attention to detail that stimulates vocabulary development is most productive when stories contain novelty, humor, conflict, suspense, incongruity, and/or vividness (Berlyne, 1960)—qualities found in children's literature but not necessarily in basal readers or traditional worksheets (Morrow, 1988).

Vocabulary development can take three paths: teaching students techniques for deriving meaning of unfamiliar words from context, designing direct activities when specific or technical vocabulary words must be mastered, and teaching the basic morphology of our language. For each of the three approaches the teacher uses children's books and poetry, plans significant time for oral discussion, and requires writing activities.

Using Context Clues

Students can be taught skills that help them infer word meaning from context. Deriving word meaning from context accounts for a significant proportion of vocabulary growth that occurs during the elementary years. However, learning vocabulary words through context is a considerable accomplishment (Konopak, 1988) and gradually develops with age, general knowledge, and reasoning ability (Werner & Kaplan, 1952). Context clues can be semantic when the meaning is ascertained from surrounding words, and/or syntactic when the meaning is derived from the grammar of a sentence. Elley (1989) concluded that intense involvement with what is being read stimulates deeper comprehension, and when this happens, then children will maintain enough attention to learn word meanings readily from context.

Children's books and poems are ideal tools for helping students enhance their vocabularies through context. Unlike traditional textbooks, they are not accompanied with a teaching manual or teacher who helps students figure out what they are reading. Authors and poets know that their work will often be read completely independent of any adult help (or interference, as the case may be). The writing and the artwork (if a book is illustrated) must be rich enough that children can read comfortably and still satisfy their needs to continually gather new words. The story or poem employs language that carries the ideas of the writer and in the process does not become a stumbling block. Only tradebooks have the quality of writing necessary for children to infer meaning from the context.

Authors and poets use five basic strategies in their writing that make it possible for children to infer word meaning from the context in which it appears:

1. *Definition.* The meaning of the word is given directly: "The water came out of the *spigot,* or faucet."

2. *Comparison/Contrast.* Similar and different examples help the reader identify meaning: "Unlike *carnivores* that eat meat, *vegetarians* prefer a diet of plants and insects."

3. *Summary.* The unfamiliar word summarizes the words or ideas that surround it: "The woman was the first person to help a neighbor in need; she took time out to do things for others with no thought of a reward or thanks. She was a true *Samaritan.*"

4. *Synonym/Antonym.* A word meaning the same or opposite provides the clue: "There was no hope; he was filled with *despair.*"
5. *Textual clues.* Pictures, charts, graphs, diagrams, quotation marks, parentheses, and footnotes serve as clues.

Instruction can take a direct approach when the teacher uses these guidelines:

1. The teacher selects material with context that supports unfamiliar words.
2. The teacher teaches students specific strategies for deriving word meaning from context.
3. The teacher provides opportunities for oral practice and discussion.
4. The teacher uses a variety of activities that reinforce the strategies.
5. The teacher provides opportunities for independent application of the skills.

Introducing Context Strategies

Using an introductory activity to help children realize how important context is in defining words can be helpful. In the following example, children have a chance to find clues within a poem that helps define a word that may be unfamiliar. The teacher can begin by reading the entire poem, "Casey at the Bat," to the class and then they can be given the reprint of the first two verses of the poem. After reading on their own, children can underline the phrases and words that gave them clues to the meaning of the target word *despair.*

- *Casey at the Bat.* Ernest Lawrence Thayer.

   The outlook wasn't brilliant for the Mudville Nine that day:
   The score stood four to two, with but one inning more to play,
   And then when Cooney died at first, and Barrows did the same,
   A pall-like silence fell upon the patrons of the game.

   A straggling few got up to go in deep despair. *The rest*
   Clung to the hope which springs eternal in the human breast;
   they thought, "If only Casey could but get a whack at that—
   We'd put up even money now, with Casey at the bat."

Analogies

Since effective vocabulary instruction helps students make connections between new words and words they already know well, activities that require students to complete analogous word pairs will help refine their skills at deriving meaning from the context. The following analogies are taken from "Giant's Delight," by Steven Kroll (in Wallace, 1978). The teacher could begin by reading the poem to the class and explaining what analogies are. He or she could remind the class that in this activity they will be using their own vocabularies to make connections with unfamiliar words.

ACTIVITY

1. Complete the following analogies for the words from the poem, "Giants' Delight" (Example: yellow : banana :: purple : grapes).

> vessel : ship :: *vat* :
> fore : front :: *haunch* :
> stallion : horse :: *mammoth* :
> vixen : fox :: *ewe* :
> feline : cat :: *snake* :
> bison : buffalo :: *boar* :

2. Textual clues: What clues are found in the pictures for the meanings of *haunch* and *score*?

3. Why did the poet enclose *(Giants have such Piggy habits)* in parentheses?

4. Write a set of word analogies for the class to solve.

Finding Definitions Within a Story

The following activity requires that children read carefully and attend to the both the artwork and the text within a book. *A Medieval Feast* (Aliki, 1983) contains many unusual words. The richness of the text and the detailed illustrations given considerable support to the reader.

ACTIVITY

- *A Medieval Feast.* Aliki. New York: Harper & Row, 1983.

This story takes place hundreds of years ago in England. The king and queen have announced that they will be visiting a certain manor. The news throws the entire place into days of frenzied preparation. Read the book carefully and study the artwork and you will be able to figure out the meaning of the following words.

1. Draw pictures of the following animals found around the manor:

boar	quail
stag	lamprey
hare	partridge
quail	curlew

2. Use the information within the story and the pictures to tell what the following words are. Tell how you figured out each one. What clues did you use?

   a. *Trenchers*
   Clues:

   b. *Ale*
   Clues:

   c. *Scullion boy*
   Clues:

   d. *Cockentrice*
   Clues:

e. *Ewerer*
   Clues:

f. *Egerdouce*
   Clues:

g. Bukkenade
   Clues:

h. *Subtletey*
   Clues:

3. What do you use at your house instead of a trencher?
4. What do you eat that is like Bukkenade?

Teaching Specific Vocabulary

In certain circumstances, the teacher will preselect certain words that he or she believes children must become familiar with before a story is read. In these cases, specific vocabulary instruction is necessary. Unfortunately, trying to improve children's vocabulary through methods of direct instruction using traditional methods have been frustratingly inefficient (Nagy, Herman, & Anderson, 1985). Too often, target words are given in isolation and out of context and methods of instruction are limited to rote drill and memorization (Durkin, 1979).

The teacher will want to use a variety of creative strategies that help children master the meaning of these unfamiliar words that are necessary for reading success. Students will need to use these words in both oral and written exercises before they are added to their vocabularies.

Teaching Technical Vocabulary

The following technique will help children visualize new words and will give them an opportunity to link an unfamiliar vocabulary word with a label they know quite well.

ACTIVITY

Bugs. Nancy Winslow Parker and Joan Richards Wright. Ill. by Nancy Winslow Parker. New York: Mulberry, 1987.

1. Use this book to help you learn new words about insects. Draw and label the parts of the cricket. Use page 37 in your book to help you. Beside each word, write what you think that body part does for the cricket.
cercus

    jumping leg

    wings

    antennae

    simple eye

    compound eye

    palpi

    ear

2. Use your book to find the scientific name for these terms:
    a. waist (p. 9)

    b. nose (p. 21)

    c. sharp foot (p. 31)

    d. feelers (p. 11)

3. Why do you think people consider most insects to be pests and nuisances?

Predicting Word Meaning
Having students guess what they think a word might mean before they read helps them mobilize their existing knowledge, recall connected experiences, and develop a curious mindset before reading takes place. The teacher would choose words essential to understanding the reading and then ask children to guess the meanings. After a discussion of these guesses, students can find the meanings in the story.

ACTIVITY

- *Firefighters*. Robert Maass. New York: Scholastic, 1989.

1. The following words are essential to understanding what firefighters do and what tools they use. Read the following words and write what you think each word means. Then use your book to find the exact meaning.
    a. *pumper hydrant*
       My guess:

       Exact meaning:

    b. *lines*
       My guess:

       Exact meaning:

    c. *Jaws of life*
       My Guess:

       Exact meaning:

    d. *Resuce unit*
       My guess:

       Exact meaning:

    e. *Tiller*
       My guess:

       Exact meaning:

2. What typographical aids does Robert Maass use to help you recognize new vocabulary words?
3. Why is an ax so important to a fireman?
4. What three things do you do if you are caught in a fire?

Possible Sentences

Another strategy for introducing new words to students is to ask them to write possible sentences for unfamiliar words, using the context clues available. Walter de la Mare's (in Prelutsky, 1983) superb poem about the moon ("Silver") is an ideal combination of visual imagery and novel vocabulary. The teacher can read the poem to the class and then ask the children to write a detailed sentence that lends meaning to certain words. Students can discuss their guesses and explain their reasoning. The actual word meanings can be checked with a dictionary.

ACTIVITY

1. Read the following words and write what you think each word means. Then write a sentence using each word.
   a. *shoon*
      Possible meaning:

      Sentence:

   b. *casements*
      possible meaning:

      Sentence:

   c. *thatch*
      Possible meaning:

      Sentence:

   d. *cote*
      Possible meaning:

      Sentence:

2. Check the actual word meanings in the dictionary.

Note Cards
Students can also keep note cards of vital words for each content area or unit of study. The cards can contain the word, a dictionary definition, the word in a sentence, and a clue for remembering what it means. This becomes essential in the middle and upper grades where social studies and science texts are so overloaded with new vocabulary for students. The following is an example of a note card:

M Metamorphosis

> *Definition:* The process of physical change of some animals, including insects.
>
> *Sentence:* Insects go through a series of changes, or metamorphosis, as they develop from eggs to full-grown adult insects.
>
> *Clue:* meta*mor*phosis: There is *more* than one change in an insect's life.

Understanding Morphology

Student's vocabulary development can also be aided by helping them recognize morphemes, or meaning-bearing units that affect word meaning. A study of structural analysis—the recognition of affixes and root words—is a helpful tool for readers (Lapp & Flood, 1992). Examples of affixes and discussions of how they modify what words mean can be the focus of brief, direct lessons. Children must be cautioned that certain letter formations are not always morphemes. For example, in the word *unhappy, un-* is a bound morpheme that means "not" and consequently completely changes that meaning of the word *happy.* However, in the word *under, un-* is merely a syllable; it has no precise meaning.

Focusing on Affixes

The poem "Leopard" by Gretchen Kreps (in Prelutsky, 1983) contains words with the prefix *un-*. The teacher can introduce the activity by reading the poem to the class. The text of the poem can either be written on a chalkboard or a transparency and students can underline the examples and discuss how the prefix changes word meaning.

ACTIVITY

1. Write three other examples of words that begin with the prefix *un-*.

2. Find an *un-* word in a book or poem. Write the word and the sentence or phrase in which it was included.

Morpheme Maps

Studying the etymology of our language also helps students take words apart to determine their meanings. Focusing on common root words, prefixes, and suffixes helps students refine their understanding of the morphology of our language. Cooperative learning groups can be assigned a morpheme, required to develop a schematic map that explains the meaning of the morpheme, and asked to give a variety of examples. Groups of students can teach each other these morphemes and develop writing exercises that help assure mastery (see Figure 8–1).

Decoding

Decoding refers to recognition of the words of our language. For mature readers, decoding becomes an automatic byproduct—the reader gives his or her entire

Figure 8–1 Morpheme Map

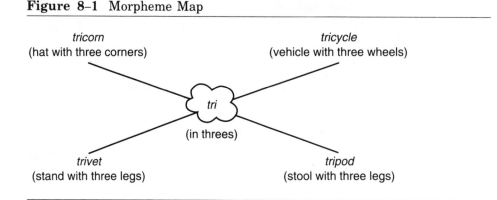

attention to the meaning of what is being read and samples only enough clues from the print to facilitate the process. It is inefficient to focus more time on words that they need; indeed, it is even unnecessary, since words are only vehicles for meaning. Just as we only need to see a bit of our own coat in a crowded cloakroom to know it is ours, we often need only a bit of a word to know what it is. The more unfamiliar we are with the message, the more attention we give to the written vehicle. Those of us who have spent fretful moments trying to identify the unisex drawings on bathroom doors in airports can recall what it means to need to attend to detail extensively.

Obviously, children need a variety of decoding strategies in their reading arsenal. Since students will not always have an adult in the room to tell them what a particular word is, they must have the means for unlocking the code on their own. But we must remember that children are unique individuals; they do not all learn in one way. Some are musically superior, other are artistically talented, and still others are physically adept. They vary in length of attention span, memory capacity, and dozens of other characteristics that influence success in school.

There are children who have the sufficient auditory/analytic expertise to learn to employ phonics as a strategy for unlocking the pronunciation of unrecognizable words. They can distinguish subtle differences in phonemes, make the connections between sounds and letters, blend letter sounds, and can learn in discrete, sequential, rule-driven units.

Other children have sufficient visual and global strengths to amass large sight vocabularies and develop an intuitive grasp of word patterns and letter clusters. These children need only to see a word and hear it pronounced and it is theirs. Still other students are tactile/kinesthetic/global learners who need a hands-on holistic approach to reading. These children are the ones who are assembling model cars while the rest of us are sorting the pieces and trying to read the directions.

Studies where individual learning styles were matched with instructional techniques showed better-than-average gains in reading, even in the cases of readers previously described as "learning disabled" or "emotionally disturbed" (Carbo, 1987).

Three decoding strategies that can be effectively taught to students are: gathering a sight vocabulary, using context clues, and using phonetic clues.

Gathering a Sight Vocabulary

A *sight vocabulary* refers to all the words automatically recognized by a reader. For each of us, our sight vocabularies reflect our own unique lives. Beyond the common words often seen in print, we have mastered huge numbers of personal words: names of people, places, food, and technical words.

Traditional reading programs spend considerable time with lessons aimed at teaching common English sight words to children. Words such as *in, of, to, from,* and *once* make up a sizable number of the words we encounter in our day-to-day reading. Although these words look very simple to adults, we must remember that they can be very difficult for children. In isolation, many of them have no meaning. We would be unable to conjure up a picture of *so* in our minds; the word takes its meaning from context. Furthermore, many words look very similar, such as *on* and *no, from, of,* and *for* are also remarkably similar. It is the sentence in which these words appear that makes their meaning clear.

Two methods have proven effective for helping children amass large sight vocabularies: extensive reading and extensive writing. The more children read, the more they encounter the same words over and over again. We know that less than 100 words make up over half of all written communication. The more often children see *was* and *saw* within the context of a story, the more easily the word becomes their own. Exhaustive research comparing methods of learning sight words is conclusive: Children amass larger sight vocabularies from reading tradebooks than from basal lessons and stories specifically designed to teach those same words (Bridge, Winograd, & Haley, 1983).

Writing is also a powerful tool for adding to one's sight vocabulary. As children write, they undoubtedly use the same words over and over and thereby master their own particular sight words: their names, the names of their family members and pets, names of favorite television characters, and the town and state in which they live.

The Daily News

Teachers can use opportunities from group writing experiences, such as the Daily News, to point out common words within what children dictate:

The Daily News

Today is Election Day in the United States. Our parents *will* be voting for who they like the best. Our state *will* get a new governor. We voted in our class. Clinton and Gore won.

Today is Amy's birthday; she is seven. She wants to get lots of presents.

Rod's cat had kittens last night. There were five of them. They *will* be ready to give away in six weeks. Rod's mom said, "No more pets!"

The teacher can underline the word *will* in the story dictated by the class. Students can copy the word and the sentence in which it is contained to help them add *will* to their reading vocabulary. They can also write their own sentences containing *will* and find examples of this word in the stories and poems they read during the day.

Teaching Targeted Sight Words

Teachers can also make specific plans to teach sight words to students. Poetry makes an excellent vehicle for these lessons. The following strategy may be used:

1. The teacher introduces the word and tells students that its a good idea to commit it to memory because they will encounter often in their reading.
2. The teacher can show students the text of a poem containing the word and read it to the class.
3. Students can dictate their own sentences containing the target word.
4. As a follow-up activity, students can be challenged to find the word in something they read during the day. The examples can be added to a class list.

In the following example, the target sight word to be given focus is *got.*

I've Got a Dog

I've got *a dog as thin as a rail,*
He's got *fleas all over his tail.*
Every time his tail goes flop,
The fleas on the bottom all hop to the top.

Unknown

In this case, the poem is written about a favorite pet. Children can bring pictures of their own pets or cut some out of a magazine. Using the same pattern, children can write their own verse that will give them numerous opportunities to read and write the target sight word.

Using Context Clues

Children can also use context clues to help them decode words they encounter in print. Teachers will want to encourage children to look at pictures, diagrams, or illustrations for hints for particular words. In a story about a zoo accompanied by photographs of a family of giraffes, the text on the opposite page is supported by full-color pictures:

It is impossible to confuse the long-legged, long-necked giraffe *with any other mammal. Giraffes are the tallest animals on earth. Adult males, called bulls, grow to a height of nearly 19 feet (6 m). Their legs are about 6 feet (183 cm) long. And their necks can be even longer than that!"* (National Geographic Book of Mammals, *1981, p. 226)*

Children can also be taught to use semantic, syntactic, and phonemic clues to decode words. Unlike using context clues to determine word meanings, the use of context in this case assumes that the child knows the definition of a particular word but he or she does not recognize it in print. The word is part of the student's oral vocabulary; he or she just needs more practice for the word to become a permanent fixture in an individual sight vocabulary.

The child who reads *was* for *saw* and says, "I *was* a dog on the way home from school," is only looking at the letters of a word; he or she is not given necessary attention to the meaning. There is a considerable difference between seeing a German shepherd while walking home from school and being one!

The following activity can serve to remind children that making sense is always the primary purpose of reading and that the words they say must be consistent with the meaning of a piece. Children can read this next poem and fill in the blanks so that the meaning remains intact. They can discuss their particular choices and list their justifications for selecting each word and the clues they used. To bring closure to the activity, children can compare their choices with those of the author.

The Codfish

The codfish lays _____ _____ eggs,
The _____ hen lays one.
The codfish never cackles
To tell you what she's _____.
And so we _____ the codfish
While the humble hen we _____.
Which only goes to show you
That it pays to advertise.

The Codfish

The codfish lays ten thousand eggs,
The homely hen lays one.
The codfish never cackles
To tell you what she's done.
And so we scorn the codfish
While the humble hen we prize.
Which only goes to show you
That it pays to advertise.

Unknown

Using Phonetic Clues

Phonics is one of the strategies that students can use when they encounter an unrecognizable word during reading. Phonics instruction concerns the teaching of letter-sound relationships as they pertain to reading. In order for phonics skills to be effective, the reader must come close enough to the puzzling word so that he or she can guess it. The word must be part of the child's oral vocabulary so that a match can be made. Adults may recall their first encounter with the word *hor d'oeuvre* in print; there was probably some type of "So-that's-how-it's-spelled" reaction.

Phonics is of little use if the unrecognizable word is also unknown to the reader. For example, nature readers could sound out the word *omoksee* fairly accurately, even though they may be unsure of the intricacies of accenting it. But few people are aware that an omoksee is a Plains Indian rodeo involving contests on horseback.

Because of the inconsistencies in the spelling of English words, letter-sound correspondence can be very tricky. The /oo/ in food can be spelled with a variety of letter combinations: r*ui*n, t*u*ne, or thr*ough*. We also have words in which sounds are heard but not seen, as the /w/ in *once,* or cases in which letters are seen but the corresponding is not heard, as the *b* in *lamb.*

Phonics, as a word attack skill, cannot function in isolation. The context of surrounding print and syntax will determine how many words are pronounced:

lead, read, present, and *bow,* for example. Learning phonics labels probably has limited value. Just as a child learned to talk without knowing a label from a fricative, he or she can learn to read without knowing a dipthong from a digraph.

The visual and auditory acuity stressed in traditional phonics instruction is less critical than one would imagine, since people who are blind or deaf learn to read quite well. Furthermore, people who speak English as a second language can always read and understand it much better than they can pronounce it. The subtle nuances involved in matching sounds to letters are illusive.

In order for phonics instruction to be effective, it must be predominantly oral. The teacher must be sure that the child is making the correct connections between letters and sounds. Our purpose in teaching phonics is to give children concepts about letters and sounds that they can apply in actual reading situations. When children are encouraged to sound out a word, we ask that they start with the beginning of the word for clues, then look at the ending of a word, and finally give attention to the letters in the middle. Once children have received direct instruction concerning letter/sound relationships, they must be encouraged to apply these connections as they read. Direct instruction can follow these steps:

1. The teacher introduces the phonetic concept that will be the focus of the lesson.
2. Children will verbalize the sound/symbol connection.
3. The teacher will provide opportunities for children to apply the phonetic concept to actual text.
4. Children will generalize rules for applying the sound/symbol connection.
5. Children will find examples in other texts that are consistent with the sound/symbol connection.
6. Children will note exceptions to the generalization.

Teaching Vowel Sounds

The following lesson emphasizes the connection between the letter *u* and the /ŭ/. The teacher would begin the lesson by telling children they will be studying the /ŭ/ so that they can have a good guess for how words sound that contain that particular letter. He or she should alert the students that they will be trying to form a generalization about when to use the /ŭ/ in words they read from a poem in *The Three Bears' Rhyme Book* (Yolen, 1987).

After hearing the poem, children can read their own copy of it and look for words that contain the /ŭ/. The teacher can write the words on the board:

bubbles	*cub*
tub	*scrub*
rubber	*plug*
duck	*pull*

The teacher can help the children label the letters surrounding the /ŭ/:

check /u/ and put in accents

bubbles	*cub*
cvcc	cvc
tub	*scrub*
cvc	cccvc
rubber	*plug*
cvcc	ccvc
duck	*pull*
cvcc	cvcc

A word containing the letter *u* in the poem that does not have the /ŭ/ also be noted:

sure
cvcv

The teacher can help the children make the following generalization: When the letter *u* is surrounded by single or double consonants, the best guess would be that it has the /ŭ/. If the letter *u* is next to a vowel or a consonant and a vowel, the /ŭ/ is not the best guess. A chart for /ŭ/ words can be displayed in the room so that children can add words that fit the generalization and those that are exceptions.

As a follow-up activity, children can sort the underlined words in this poem, "Sulk" byu Felice Hilman (in Prelutsky, 1983) into *u* categories.

/u/	*exceptions*
sulk	slurps
scuff	
puff	
huff	

When this activity is completed, the teacher should discuss with the children why, even though *pout* and *about* contain the letter *u* and it is not a /ŭ/, they are not exceptions.

Teaching Phonics Labels
In some instances, the teacher may determine that children need to know specific labels. It is beneficial for them to try to form their own conclusions about these terms. For instance, if the teacher intends for children to know what blends and digraphs are, the following approach will be appropriate:

1. The teacher introduces the labels to the children.
2. Appropriate examples are read to the class.
3. Students are given list of words from the Mother Goose Rhyme, "Sleep, Baby, Sleep" and asked to come up with a generalization about the phonics labels for the underlined words.

Sleep, Baby, <u>Sleep</u>

<u>Sleep</u>, Baby, <u>Sleep</u>
Our cottage vale is deep:
The little lamb is on the <u>green</u>,
With woolly <u>fleece</u> so soft and <u>clean</u>—
<u>Sleep</u>, baby, <u>sleep</u>,
<u>Sleep</u>, baby, <u>sleep</u>,
Down where the woodbines <u>creep</u>;
Be always like the lamb so mild,
A kind, and <u>sweet</u>, and gentle child.
<u>Sleep</u>, baby, <u>sleep</u>,

Beginning Blends

   sleep
   green
   fleece
   clean
   creep
   sweet

To conclude the activity, students can find other examples of blends and digraphs in stories and poems to add to a wall chart. Teachers can emphasize the generalization that consonant blends, such as *br*, retain a bit of the sound of each of the letters, whereas diagraphs, such as *sh* are two consonants that produce a new sound not associated with either letter by itself.

Literary Skills

Teaching specific information about stories, authors, poems, and poets is vital. Within their classrooms, children are members of a community of readers and can be bonded by shared literary information. We also know that readers' expectations concerning literature are formed by early reading experiences (Meek, 1982). The children in our schools who enjoy reading are those who have become intimately involved with a story at some time in their lives (Mason & Au, 1986). Within the pages of a book, they left the confines of their real existence and became a part of other places and times.

As children become friends with characters in books, they develop a passion for certain subjects, specific authors, and favorite illustrators (Cullinan, 1989). We can easily remember those students who became hooked on certain types of books. For example, a group of third-grade girls formed a horse club, complete with horse names for each other and typical dramatic horse adventures that they enacted during recess. Each club meeting convened with the reading of a chapter from their latest horse book favorite.

The values of reading books and poetry during the elementary years are of inestimable importance (Norton, 1991):

1. Literature transmits our heritage from one generation to the next. Without books, many characters from our past, such as Johnny Appleseed or Pecos Bill, would have been lost in antiquity.

2. Through literature, we learn to value our cultural heritage and that of others. Reading about early pioneers in *Prairie Songs* (Conrad, 1985) helps foster a feeling of respect for those who had the courage to try for a better life. As we read of the struggles of early immigrants, we appreciate the tenacity of people who fought both the elements and human prejudice in order to survive.

3. Literature provides opportunity for vicarious experiences. We are born into one family, live in one community, experience one life. Through literature, we get a firsthand glimpse of ancient Egypt in *Pyramid* (Macaulay, 1977), and experience life in the future in *This Place Has No Atmosphere* (Danziger, 1986). We can identify with characters from every station in life. Children with no brothers or sisters can become a part of a large family with the Blossoms in *The Not-Just-Anybody Family* (Byars, 1986), and children with numerous siblings can take time for solitude when stranded on an island in *Island of the Blue Dolphins* (O'Dell, 1960).

4. Literature stimulates vocabulary development. Figurative language in *Charlie Drives the Stage* (Kimmel, 1989) enriches the story of a daring stagecoach driver through colorful language: "Jumping Jerusalem! That puts a new face on things, don't it?"

5. Literature lengthens attention span and nurtures curiosity. As a book captures our attention, minutes become hours and time passes without notice. The plight of the innocent children in the evil clutches of Miss Slighcarp in *The Wolves of Willoughby Chase* (Aiken, 1963) keeps us glued to this adventure-filled story.

6. Literature gives us insight into understand ourselves and others. Two interpretations of the same events by a brother and a sister in *The Pain and the Great One* (Blume, 1974) remind us that who is telling his or her side is everything when sibling rivalry is involved.

7. Literature improves reading and writing skills. A map of the area surrounding Loon Lake not only helps us get an understanding of the setting for this mystery but it gives young readers a technique they can use in their own stories: the use of a map (*Mystery at Loon Lake* [Cross, 1986]).

The following literary information is an important part of the reading curriculum:

1. Understanding artistic style
2. Identifying the aspects of story grammar:
   a. Characters
   b. Perspective
   c. Conflict
   d. Setting
   e. Theme
   f. Style
3. Learning about authors and illustrators
4. Identifying the genres of literature:

a. ABC, Concept, and Counting Books
b. Wordless Books
c. Traditional Literature
d. Modern Fiction
e. Modern Fantasy
f. Science Fiction
g. Historical Fiction
h. Poetry

Understanding Artistic Style

Young children are often attracted to a particular book because of the illustrations (Norton, 1991). The comic illustrations in *The Trouble with Mom* (Cole, 1983) tell them that they will be in for a good time when they open that book. In *The Napping House* (Wood, 1984), the brightening of the colors in the illustrations parallel the coming of day. The slightly grainy, faded illustrations in *In Coal Country* (Hendershot, 1987) are perfect recollections for a childhood that took place during the Depression. The illustrations appear to be mounted in an old photograph album. A photograph of children behind barbed wire in *Smoke and Ashes* (Rogasky, 1988) sets the somber tone for this grim informational book about the Holocaust.

Many illustrators also give clues to the text of the story. Little Bush Deer is hidden in all the illustrations in *Anansi and the Moss-Covered Rock* (Kimmel, 1988) and she and the reader are the only ones who know what Anansi is up to. This partnership with a story character creates a comaraderie that enhances understanding. In *Rosie's Walk* (Hutchins, 1968), only the reader is aware that Rosie is in danger from the fox who, unbeknownst to her, plans to have her for dinner. Soft pencil illustrations on a pink background on the cover of *Sarah, Plain and Tall* (MacLachlan, 1985) reflect the nurturing warmth of the story. By contrast, a dark brown cover and penciled illustrations are a suitable background for a slightly macabre tale of witches and superstitions in *The Widow's Broom* (Van Allsburg, 1992).

As children become more aware of the intricacies of the illustrations of children's books, they become more skilled in receiving the messages of the writers. They become fine-tuned to any nuance that provides a hint about the story or the characters. The reader who is oblivious to the illustrations in a picture book is missing half the story. Children also learn tricks from professional artists that they can incorporate into their own writing. One only need notice the explosion of Waldo-like books (*Where's Waldo?* [Handford, 1987]) on the market to realize how much we use the ideas of others.

Helping children learn about artistic style can follow these steps:

1. The teacher identifies the element of style that will be the focal point of the lesson.

2. The teacher helps the children recognize the aspect of artistic style.

3. Children have opportunities to look in additional books for other examples.

Teaching Page Arrangement   Illustrators use the arrangement of objects on the page of the story to help convey what is happening and to give subtle clues to the reader about the relationships of many characters. The teacher can remind the students that the positioning of the pictures on the page has meaning. In a casual discussion, children can discuss how the pages in the following books tell us about the story:

Stringbean's Trip to the Shining Sea (Williams)
Piggy Book (Browne)
Night Noises (Fox)
The Wolf's Chicken Stew (Kasza)

Teaching Style   Various authors prefer certain styles and media of artwork to carry forth their messages. The choices must be consistent with the text of the story and the particular genre. For example, biography is usually illustrated with photographs, folk art is often seen in traditional literature. The teacher can discuss numerous examples of picture books with children. The following will serve as good examples that connect style and media:

The Third Story Cat (Baker)
Loudmouth George and the Sixth-Grade Bully (Carlson)
The Last Puppy (Asch)
A Williamsburg Household (Anderson)
Millions of Cats (Gag)

Understanding Story Grammar

The more children learn about the elements of story grammar, the better they understand literature and the better they write. Learning about the structures of stories positively influences how well children understand and remember what they read (Hoskisson & Tompkins, 1987). As children refine their understanding of characters, perspective, setting, plot, theme, and style, they grow increasingly sophisticated in their ability to comprehend what they read on a sophisticated level.

Characters   Characters that stay with us long after we close the books are those who are as complex as people in real life. Oftentimes, these characters become real friends to us and we miss them once the story has ended. Children's fondness for sequels and series books is a testimony to their predilection for sticking with characters they know and like. Regardless of the literary genre, characterization is one of the most powerful elements of story grammar (Bond, Tinker, & Wasson, 1984). As skillful authors reveal their characters through description, dialogue, and action, these people (or animals, objects, and creatures) become real. Their fears are our fears, their triumphs are our triumphs, and their tragedies are our tragedies. *Beat the Turtle Drum* (Greene, 1976), *Bridge to Terabithia* (Paterson, 1977) and *Sadako and the Thousand Paper Cranes* (Coerr, 1977) leave no dry eyes as we grieve over the loss of people we have grown to love.

None of us likes Gilly very well when we begin *The Great Gilly Hopkins* (Paterson, 1978), but as Gilly matures and learns to love, we start to understand her and care about her. The reader shares Gilly's heart-wrenching goodbye as she leaves a loving foster home and solemnly recognizes that it was Gilly's behavior that forced the move. When the grandma learns to read in *The Wednesday Surprise* (Bunting, 1989)—like Anna, the little girl who taught her—we feel a mixture of pride and tenderness.

Perspective   The perspective, or point of view, chosen by the author is critical in the quality of a story. Who tells the story influences how it is understood. When Hadley and Irwin choose to tell a tragic story of incest from the point of view of the young girl's boyfriend in *Abby, My Love* (Hadley & Irwin, 1985), the story is intensified. It allows a certain distancing from the actual details; the reader and Chip experience the same outrage and anger when Abby shares her terrible secret. Hearing a teenage boy tell Abby's story protects her and reinforces a powerful message: Abby was a victim, and like other victims, she is still worthy of being loved.

When the family dog narrates the tale in *Bunnicula* (Howe & Howe, 1979), the elements of modern fantasy are strengthened. Insight into the behavior of the family cat and the vampire bunny have more credibility when they are given by a fellow pet. Regardless of who a writer choses to tell a story about, the point of view must remain consistent and should play an essential role in developing the characters and carrying forth the plot.

Conflict Conflict is the driving force that makes all things happen in literature (Stewig, 1988). The problems and plights of the main characters keep us glued to the pages as we are drawn into a world created by the author. Excitement mounts when we experience a struggle vicariously. We gear up for solutions to sometimes insurmountable problems and look forward to the conclusion that will tie up most loose ends.

Children have definite plot preferences. They like action that helps them find out what has happened and they like the story to be carried forth with incident and dialogue (Sebesta, 1979). Children like fast-paced plots, warm characters, and a variety of story structures. The conflict must be believable, understandable, and convincing, and the resolution must logically follow what the author has set forth (Lukens, 1981).

It is the conflict in a story that keeps us glued to the pages. Most of us can recall stories we read in one sitting, simply because we had to know how they ended. When Naya Nuki is kidnapped with her childhood friend, Sacajawea, and escapes to make her solitary journey back home, across wintery Montana, every adventure and challenge forces the reader, like Naya Nuki, to forge onward (*Naya Nuki, Girl Who Ran* [Thomasma, 1983]). As it becomes clear that the beloved pet in *Charlie Anderson* (Abercrombie, 1990) really belongs to two families, the reader looks for a logical conclusion along with the main characters and, with them, finds poignant contentment when the story ends.

Setting The setting of a story—its location in time and place—is essential in helping the reader identify what is happening to the main characters (Norton, 1991). Although in the case of many stories, particularly traditional tales, setting is as vague as "once upon a time, a long time ago," the reader still needs to have a comfortable context for a story. Writers are often challenged by bringing setting to children without overwhelming them with facts for which they have little understanding.

Prairie Visions: The Life and Times of Solomon Butcher (Conrad, 1991) is the story of the famous photographer whose pictures captured life on the prairie for all future generations. Mixing factual information with narrative, Conrad helps her young readers envision life in a soddy: "When Solomon and Lillie's son Lynn was born in 1883, they moved out of his father's soddy and into this muddy, bright photo gallery. It wasn't too bad except when it rained and the roof leaked" (p. 12).

In order to make the Holocaust real, Jane Yolen transports her reluctant, self-absorbed main character, along with the reader, to Poland during World War II in *The Devil's Arithmetic* (Yolen, 1988):

The older people were pushed into the boxcars first, then the women and the girls. Someone shoved Hannah from behind so hard, she scraped her knee climbing up. She could feel the blood flowing down and the sharp gritty pain, but before she could bend over to look at it, someone else was behind her. Soon there were so many people crowded in, she couldn't move at all. It was worse than the worst subway jam she'd ever been in, shopping with her Aunt Eva in the city (p. 77).

Theme Theme is the enduring bit of a story that remains in our hearts long after a story has ended. It is the kernel of insight or bit of informtion with which we are left as the details fade. Theme has also been referred to as "the underlying idea that ties the plot, characters, and setting together in a meaningful whole" (Norton, 1991, p. 98). Theme goes beyond what a reader may have learned from a story to include how the person is different, even in nearly imperceptible ways.

When we see a book we read a long time ago, the feelings that surface are usually tied to the theme. One only has to see the imp of a mouse on the cover of *If You Give a Mouse a Cookie* (Numeroff, 1985) to recall how the whims of that little rascal wore out the little boy. We are reminded of the responsibility of caring for another. Hearing the title *Sounder* (Armstrong, 1969) recalls to mind the human suffering, family love, and enduring loyalty of the African-American characters. Memories of the potential cruelty of peer groups floods us when we hear someone talk about the events in *Blubber* (Blume, 1974). The courage and strength it took Omatu to face what he feared most in the world are recalled when we see the opening pages of *Call It Courage* (Sperry, 1940). All of these feelings are tied to the theme in a story.

Style How authors select words and sentence structure, much in the way that illustrators select artistic style and media, contributes to the overall effectiveness of a story and carries forth the mood and theme. Judith Viorst prefers the long, run-on sentences so common to young children in her books.

Style is one way we differentiate authors. Just as our physical features make us identifiable, the written features of their work make writers recognizable. It is often a particular writing style that makes certain writers our favorites.

Focusing on Story Grammar
The teacher can point out the elements of style in anything students read and can help them fine-tune their recognition of these story structures. The following items help children understand what the elements of story grammar are and how they come together.

ACTIVITY: STORY BEGINNINGS

For each of the stories below, read the introduction and list what we find out about each of the elements of story grammar.

- *Esteban and the Ghost.* Adapted by Sibyl Hancock. Ill. by Dirk Zimmer. New York: Dial, 1983.

Long ago in late October a merry tinker named Esteban came to a village near Toledo. It was All Hallows' Eve, and he had heard a tale that excited him to no end. Nestled in the golden hills of Spain stood a dark dwelling called Gray Castle, and it was said to be haunted" (unpaged).

1. Where does the story take place?
2. What clues does Sibyl Hancock give us that this story took place a long time ago?
3. Who is probably the main character?
4. What might this story be about?

- *How the Stars Fell into the Sky.* Jerrie Oughton. Ill. by Lisa Desimini. Boston: Houghton Mifflin, 1992.

When the pulse of the first day carried it to the rim of night, First Woman said to First Man, "The people need to know the laws. To help them, we must write the laws for all to see." "Write them in the sand," he told her. "But the wind will blow them away," she answered. "Write them on the water then," he said and turned to go, having more important matters on his mind.

1. How do we know that this is a traditional tale?
2. What is First Woman's task?
3. What do we know about the character of First Woman and First Man?
4. Think about the style of writing. What kind of words and sentences does the author use to tell this myth?

ACTIVITY: COMPARING VERSIONS

Compare the following versions of the same story.

- *The Fine Round Cake.* Arnica Esterl. Ill. by Andrej Dugin and Olga Dugina. Macmillan, 1991.
- *The Gingerbread Boy.* Paul Galdone. Seabury, 1975.

1. Draw an illustration from each book in a circle.

2. How are the two versions alike and different?
   a. Main characters:

   b. Point of view:

   c. Setting:

   d. Story events:

   e. Conclusions:

   f. Theme:

   g. Style:

Learning about Authors and Illustrators

As children learn more about specific authors and illustrators, they learn to appreciate the crafts of their artists. Focusing on writers and illustrators humanizes children's understanding of literature. Knowledge of these people not only enhances the reading experience but lends insight into what influences their work. Once children are aware of authors, illustrators, and dedications, they are soon careful to add those elements to their own writing and to forge the connection between the writing of others and their own writing.

Helping children learn about specific writers and illustrators is beneficial. Tomie de Paola is a favorite illustrator for young children and they know him better when they read this autobiographical story, *The Art Lesson* (de Paola, 1989). Knowing his Italian-Irish ancestry deepens our appreciation of the stories about his grandmothers, *Nana Upstairs and Nana Downstairs* (de Paola, 1973) and his folktales, *Strega Nona* (de Paola, 1975) and *Fin M'Coul* (de Paola, 1981).

The knowledge that Hans Christian Andersen felt unappreciated and unloved deepens our understanding of *The Ugly Duckling* (retold by Cauley, 1979). The realization that Chris Van Allsburg is also a sculptor and that David MacCaulay is also an architect explains the professional quality in the detail in their work.

Many video tapes and cassette tapes of authors and illustrators are now available for classroom use. A list of autobiographical books of the lives of these people is given at the end of this chapter. Children can also select a favorite author or illustrator to study and share with peers. Students can take the parts of these people for classroom interviews.

As seen below, thematic study of certain authors and illustrators can also be the focus of instruction.

ACTIVITY: ILLUSTRATOR STUDY

Trina Schart Hyman
   The Sleeping Beauty (Little, Brown, 1977)
   Little Red Riding Hood (Holiday House, 1983)
   Snow White (Heins)
   Hershel and the Hanukkah Goblins (Kimmel)

Personal information:

Style:

Media:

Examples of work:

What makes Ms. Hyman's work so recognizable?

How do Ms. Hyman's drawings add to the books she illustrates?

Learning about the Genres of Literature

Each genre of children's literature has specific, unique characteristics. When we read a traditional tale, we know the setting will be in the illusive past and that the story will contain quite a bit of action with very good main characters and completely bad villains. Whatever overwhelming odds face the miller's daughter in *Rumpelstiltskin* (Zelinsky, 1986), we know that somehow she will spin enough straw into gold to please her husband and not have to give her baby away to Rumpelstiltskin after all.

When we select another book in the *Little House* (Wilder, 1932, 1935) series by Laura Ingalls Wilder, we know that we will be sharing new pioneer adventures with Laura and Mary in sod houses and log cabins. Life in the late 1800s will come alive for us as we travel with the Ingalls family, and the family dog, Jack, from one early settlement to another by way of covered wagon.

When children become familiar with the intricacies of the genres of literature, they are joining the literary community shared by all people who love books. Knowing that each genre has certain predictable elements strengthens comprehension by reducing uncertainty. When children are aware of the criteria for excellence in each genre of literature, they are more able to judge for themselves whether books are worthwhile. The following activities focus on knowledge of the genres of children's literature.

ACTIVITY: GENRE DETECTIVE

1. A student in another class has to know what genre a book is before a test. He knows that it is either a traditional tale or modern fantasy. What will you do so that you can tell him, without a doubt, which genre the book is?

2. A student in the middle grades is reading a book but she doesn't know if it is science fiction or modern fantasy. What questions would you ask her in order to find out?

ACTIVITY: LIBRARY SEARCH

1. Using your school library, find examples of the following genres of literature. Explain why you know you have a good example.

     a. ABC book

     b. Counting book

     c. Modern fiction

     d. Wordless book

2. Tell what genres the following books are. Give your evidence.
   - *Zoo Doings.* Jack Prelutsky. Ill. by Paul O. Zelinsky. New York: Trumpet, 1983.

   Evidence:

   - *Christina Katerina and the Time She Quit the Family.* Patricia Lee Gauch. Ill. by Elise Primavera, New York: Putnam, 1987.

   Evidence:

   - *Where Was Patrick Henry on the 29th of May?* Jean Fritz. Ill. By Margaret Tomes, New York: Coward-McCann, 1975.

   Evidence:

Study Skills

Children not only need to learn specific information as they attend school but they need to learn how to learn. In the past, the memorization of facts and long verses was viewed as the ultimate academic accomplishment. Although we may still admire memory skills, we are now aware that learning in today's society is much more complex. The process of obtaining and synthesizing information is more important than memorizing it (Tonjes & Zintz, 1987). A focus on study skills helps equip children with the tools they need to acquire knowledge in a particular area (Farr & Carey, 1986).

The term *study skills* refers to several different processes: knowing how and where to locate information, knowing how to organize that information to enhance its recall, knowing how to use language or graphics to interpret information, knowing how to follow directions, and knowing how books are organized. Teaching study skills can begin in kindergarten and must continue throughout the elementary and secondary years. The information explosion in our country requires that its citizens know how to find out what they need to know. Independent learners know what they know, know what they do not know, and know how to find out.

Knowing How Information Is Stored

Knowing that information is often stored alphabetically saves us considerable time. When children can use the alphabet as a tool, they are on their way to becoming independent learners. To reinforce this information, children can compare the common objects in two alphabet books.

ACTIVITY

Read the following books:

- *Eating the Alphabet.* Lois Ehlert. San Diego: Harcourt Brace Jovanovich, 1989.

- *The Yucky Reptile Alphabet Book.* Jerry Pallotta. Ill. by Ralph Masiello. New York: Trumpet, 1989.

List the objects chosen by each author and illustrator to teach the alphabet. Draw the picture beside each.

	Eating the Alphabet	*The Yucky Reptile Alphabet Book*
Aa		
Bb		
Cc		

Dd

Ee

Ff

Gg

Hh

Ii

Jj

Kk

Ll

Mm

Nn

Oo

Pp

Qq

Rr

Ss

Tt

Uu

Vv

Ww

Xx

Yy

Zz

Knowing How to Organize Information

The research in schema theory tells us that information is better retrieved when it is stored in related chunks. Random ideas or bits of knowledge tend to be forgotten since they are not connected with what we already know. As soon as children enter school and are read to, they can learn to remember certain bits of information as a whole. Before reading a story to the class, the teacher can ask them to be paying attention to specific information so that they can later recall it. For example, prior to reading *Yummers!* (Marshall, 1973), children can be asked to listen for clues to the cause of Emily's stomachache at the end of the story.

Once children can write, they can complete brief study guides as the teacher reads. Early experiences with note taking will pay off in later years. The following guide accompanies *The Quicksand Book* (de Paola, 1977).

ACTIVITY

1. Who is in the quicksand?

2. Is quicksand a special kind of sand?

3. Does quicksand pull you down?

4. Name three places quicksand can be found.

5. What happens to each animal in quicksand? Match Column A to Column B.

Column A	Column B
HORSES	struggle and sink
MULES	rabbit hop
COWS	tuck feet underneath

6. What is the second thing you should do if you step into quicksand?

Following Directions

Following directions requires close reading and the ability to apply what has been read to actual situations. Starting in kindergarten, children can participate in activities that depend on their ability to complete work in sequential steps. In Lois Ehlert's colorful book about the life of a maple tree, *Red Leaf, Yellow Leaf* (1991), the directions are given for making bird treats. This is an especially effective, science-related activity for winter, when food may be scarce.

ACTIVITY

After listening to *Red Leaf, Yellow Leaf* (Ehlert, 1991), you may make your own bird treats.

Supplies
> bread
> heart-shaped cookie cutter
> pencil
> egg white
> pastry brush
> birdseed
> yarn or ribbon

Directions
1. Cut a heart shape from a slice of bread.
2. With the pencil, poke a hole near the top.
3. Brush the egg white onto the bread and pat the birdseed on it.
4. Let it dry.
5. Thread the yarn or ribbon through the hole and hang your bird treat in a tree for your feathered friends.

ACTIVITY

Mem Fox's book, *Possum Magic* (1983), is set in Australia. As Hush and her grandma try to find the right combination of foods that will make Hush visible again, they travel throughout Australia and sample the local food. As you lsiten to the story of Hush, trace her journey on your map of Australia. You may also enjoy finding out about some of the Australian animals mentioned in the story.

Foods	*Animals*
Anzac biscuits	Possums
Mornay and minties	Wombats
Steak and salad	Kookaburras
Pumpkin scones	Dingoes
Vegemite sandwiches	Emus
Pavlova	Koalas
Lamington	Kangaroos

Learning How to Interpret Graphics

Information and ideas in books are presented in a variety of ways. Teaching children how to gather details and concepts from diagrams, graphs, and charts will be an invaluable skill to them in later years. Children can also use graphics in their own writing.

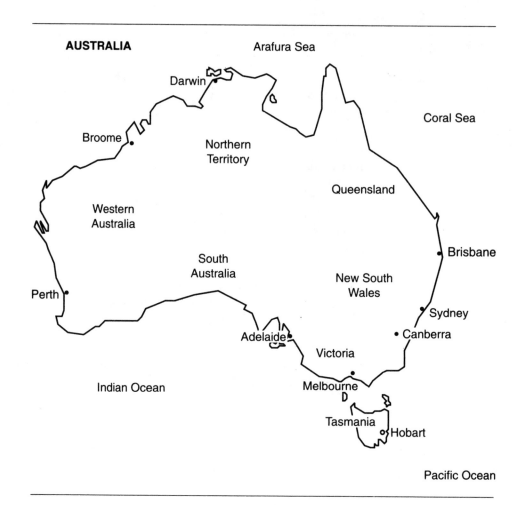

AUSTRALIA

Arafura Sea

Darwin

Coral Sea

Broome

Northern Territory

Western Australia

Queensland

South Australia

Brisbane

New South Wales

Perth

Adelaide

Sydney

Canberra

Victoria

Indian Ocean

Melbourne

Tasmania

Hobart

Pacific Ocean

ACTIVITY

- *Deadly Animals.* Martha Holmes. Ill. by Mike Vaughan. New York: Atheneum, 1991.

1. Before reading this book, make a list of four animals you consider the most dangerous on earth. Give your reason for each choice. Then read *Deadly Animals* to see how accurate your guesses were:
   a.
   b.
   c.
   d.

2. Using the chart from the glossary of the book (see Figure 8–2), answer the following questions.

Figure 8–2

Harpy Eagle
Bird of Prey

Height: 3 ft. **Weight:** female is heavier than the male and reaches weights of 20 lbs.

Home:
Forests in southern Mexico, eastern Bolivia, and Argentina.

Food:
Monkeys, sloths, and tree porcupines.

Family Life:
A pair of eagles mate for life. They build a big nest about 10 feet long at the top of a tree, as high as 160 feet. As far as we know they only have one egg every other year.

Superpower:
Speed and strength. It can fly straight upward. Few if any other birds can do that.

Did You Know?
It has the most powerful feet of any bird of prey.

Enemies:
It is threatened only by man's destruction of its jungles.

Spotted Hyena
Mammal

Length: 5 ft. **Height:** 30 ins. **Weight:** between 110 and 175 lbs.

Home:
Dry open grasslands and bush in many parts of Africa.

Food:
Eats almost anything alive or dead, from zebras to campfire rubbish.

Family Life:
They hunt and *scavenge* alone or in packs. Normally have 3 cubs which are looked after by the mother in a shared den. They live for about 25 years.

Superpower:
Teeth. Its front teeth are 1.5 inches long and can strip flesh from bones. The molars or back teeth then grind the bones down to a fine powder.

Did You Know?
It has a **digestive** system that can absorb almost anything.

Enemies:
Cubs are easy **prey** to many animals including male hyenas.

Killer Whale
Mammal

Length: 22 ft. but can grow as long as 35 ft. **Weight:** as much as 9,900 lbs. That's as heavy as 60 people.

Home:
All oceans.

Food:
Small whales, squid, dolphins, seals, and fish.

Family Life:
Live in groups called "pods" with one male plus a **harem** of 3–39 females. Pregnancy lasts 15 months and the babies are yellow and black. They can live up to 100 years.

Superpower:
Hunting in well-organized groups. They can stay underwater for 20 minutes, dive as deep as 1,000 yards, and leap into the air as far as 40 feet.

Did You Know?
Killer whales are dangerous in the sea, but can be trained to perform tricks in zoos.

Enemies:
Man.

a. How much does the spotted hyena weigh? Compare it to another animal about the same size.

b. What will hyenas eat?

c. What did you learn about hyenas from this book?

d. Who is the enemy of the harpy eagle?

e. Write two facts about these eagles that make them more powerful than other birds.

f. What is the superpower of killer whales?

g. How long can these mammals live?

h. Look through the remaining information about the enemies of these deadly animals. What did you learn?

ACTIVITY

- *Exploring the Titanic.* Robert D. Ballard. New York: Scholastic. 1988.

Use the diagram to help you understand how deep the *Titanic* was after she sank and how big the iceberg she hit was. Use a folded up piece of paper to make the comparisons.

1. About how many miles below the surface of the ocean was the *Titanic?*

2. How deep can scuba divers dive?

3. Compare the depth of the *Titanic* with the height of the Empire State Building.

4. The ice field the *Titanic* encountered was 78 miles long. Within that field was the iceberg that sunk the ship. Compare the iceberg with the size of the *Titanic.*

5. Now compare the iceberg with the size of the Empire State Building.

Understanding How Books Are Organized

As students focus on more detailed study within the content areas, they need to become familiar with the parts of a book so that they can quickly access the information they need. Beginning with informational picture books, the teacher can help children learn how books are organized.

The following terms should be familiar to children. The teacher can introduce each one and then show children examples in appropriate books:

Title
Author and/or illustrator
Publishing Company and Location
Copyright Date
Preface
Acknowledgments
Table of Contents
Index
Appendix
Glossary
Forward
Epilogue

ACTIVITY

- *Koko's Kitten.* Francine Patterson. Photographs by Ronald H. Cohn. New York: Scholastic, 1985.

Koko's Kitten is the story of a gorilla named Koko. A researcher taught Koko American Sign Language. The kitten who became Koko's pet is the focal point of the story. Use the picture book to answer these questions.

1. Who published *Koko's Kitten?*

2. When was this book published?

3. To whom does Dr. Patterson dedicate this story?

4. Whom does she acknowledge?

5. What does Dr. Patterson tell us about Koko in the preface?

6. What do we learn from the epilogue?

ACTIVITY

- *Buffalo.* Dorothy Hinshaw Patent. Photographs by William Munoz. New York: Clarion, 1986.

Use this informational book about buffaloes to answer the following questions.

1. To whom does the author dedicate this book?

2. Whom does she acknowledge?

3. List the topics found in the Table of Contents.
   a.

b.

c.

d.

e.

f.

g.

4. Look at the appendices on pages 70 and 71. List one organization to whom you could write to find out more about the buffaloes.

5. Where is the state closest to you where you could see buffaloes?

6. Which is the only foreign country where buffaloes can be found?

7. Look at the indices on pages 72 and 71. Where would you find information about the herd sizes of buffaloes?

8. On what page is there information about the two kinds of buffaloes?
   a. What are the two kinds of buffaloes?

   b. What are the main differences between these two kinds of buffaloes?

   c. Which of the two kinds of buffaloes is the most common?

Summary

Attempting to teach the skills of reading and writing with traditional methods has been frustrating and ineffective for both teachers and students. Oftentimes, worksheets are not connected to what the students are reading, reading and writing tasks are contrived, too many skills are taught in one lesson, and the children are required to do little thinking.

When teaching with literature, skills instruction takes on a completely different look. Skills are connected with what students are reading, and only one or two skills are focused on during a lesson that is teacher directed. Quality literature and poetry are the basis for instruction. Students do considerble writing that requires in-depth understanding of what has been read. The purpose of skills instruction is twofold: to help students master strategies that will make them independent readers and to involve them with quality literature.

The following skills are given emphasis in a literature-based program:

1. Vocabulary development
2. Decoding

    a. Gathering a sight vocabulary

    b. Using context clues

    c. Using phonetic clues

3. Literary skills

4. Study skills

(The skills of reading comprehension and writing are the focus of Chapters 4 and 5.)

References

Anders, P. L., & Vos, C. S. (1986). Semantic feature analysis: An interactive strategy for vocabulary development and text comprehension. *Journal of Reading, 29,* 610–615.

Beck, I. L., McKeown, M. C., McCaslin, E. C., & Burkes, A. M. (1979). *Instructional dimensions that may effect reading comprehension.* Pittsburgh, PA: University of Pittsburgh Learning Research and Development Center.

Berlyne, D. (1960). *Conflict, arousal and curiosity.* New York: McGraw-Hill.

Bond, G. L., Tinker, M. A., & Wasson, B. B. (1984). Reading difficulties: Their diagnosis and correction (5th ed.). Englewood Cliffs, NJ: Prentice Hall.

Bridge, C. A., Winograd, P. N., & Haley, D. (1983). Using predictable materials to teach beginning reading. *The Reading Teacher, 36,* 884–891.

Carbo, M. (1987). Reading styles research: What works isn't always phonics. *Kappan, 70,* 431–435.

Cullinan. B. E. (1989). *Literature and the child* (2nd ed.). San Diego: Harcourt Brace Jovanovich.

Davis, F. B. (1968). Research in comprehension in reading. *Reading Research Quarterly, 3,* 499–545.

Durkin, D. (1979). What classroom observations reveal about reading comprehension. *Reading Research Quarterly, 14,* 481–533.

Eeds, M., & Cockrum, W. A. (1985). Teaching word meanings by expanding schemata vs. dictionary work vs. reading in context. *Journal of Reading, 28,* 492–497.

Elley, W. B. (1989). Vocabulary acquisition from listening to stories. *Reading Research Quarterly, 24,* 174–187.

Farr, R., & Carey, R. F. (1986). *Reading: What can be measured?* (2nd ed.). Newark, DE: International Reading Association.

Hoskisson, K., & Tompkins, G. E. (1987). *Language arts: Content and teaching strategies.* Columbus, OH: Merrill.

Konopak, B. C. (1988). Using contextual information for word learning. *Journal of Reading, 31,* 334–338.

Lapp, D., & Flood, J. (1992). *Teaching reading to every child* (3rd ed.). New York: Macmillan.

Lukens, R. J. (1981). *A critical handbook of children's literature.* Glenview, IL: Scott Foresman.

MacGinitie, W. H. (1976). Research suggestions from the literature search. *Reading Research Quarterly, 11,* 7–35.

Mason, J. K., & Au, K. H. (1986). *Reading instruction for today.* Glenview, IL: Scott Foresman.

Meek, M. (1982). *Learning to read.* London: Bodley Head.

Morrow, L. M. (1988). Young children's responses to one-to-one story readings in school settings. *Reading Research Quarterly, 23,* 89–107.

Nagy, W. E., Herman, P. A., & Anderson, R. C. (1985). *Learning words meaning from context: How broadly generalizable?* (Technical Report No. 347). Urbana-Champaign, IL: University of Illinois Center for the Study of Reading.

Norton, D. E. (1985). *The effective teaching of language arts.* Columbus, OH: Merrill.

Norton, D. E. (1991). *Through the eyes of a child* (3rd ed.). New York: Merrill.

Sebesta, S. (1979). What do young people think about the literature they read? *Reading Newsletter, 8k.* Rockleigh, NJ: Allyn and Bacon.

Stahl, S. A., & Fairbanks, M. M. (1986). The effects of vocabulary instruction: A model-based meta analysis. *Review of Educational Research, 56,* 72–110.

Stewig, J. W. (1988). *Children and literature* (2nd ed.). Boston: Houghton Mifflin.

Tonjes, M., & Zintz, M. (1987). *Teaching reading/thinking/study skills in content classrooms* (2nd ed.). Dubuque, IA: William C. Brown.

Werner, H., & Kaplan, E. (1952). *The acquisition of word meanings: A developmental study.* Monographs of the Society for Research in Child Development, 51.

Children's Books

Abercrombie, B. (1990). *Charlie Anderson.* Ill. by M. Graham. New York: McElderry.

Aiken, J. (1963). *The Wolves of Willoughby Chase.* Ill. by P. Marriot. New York: Doubleday.

Aliki, (1983). *Medieval Feast.* New York: Harper and Row.

*Armstrong, W. H. (1969). *Sounder.* New York: Harper.

Asch, F. (1980). *The Last Puppy.* Englewood Cliffs, NJ: Prentice Hall.

Baker, L. (1987). *The Third Story Cat.* Boston: Little Brown.

Ballard, R. (1988). *Exploring the Titanic.* New York: Scholastic.

Blume, J. (1974). *Blubber.* New York: Bradbury.

Blume, J. (1974). *The pain and the great one.* Ill. by I Trivas. New York: Dell Yearling.

Browne, A. (1986). *Piggy book.* New York: Knopf.

Bunting, E. (1989). *The Wednesday Surprise.* Ill. by D. Carrick. New York: Clarion.

Byars, B. (1986). *The not-just-anybody family.* Ill. by J. Rogers. New York: Dell Yearling.

Carlson, N. (1983). *Loudmouth George and the sixth-grade bully.* New York: Puffin.

Cauley, L. B. (1979). *The ugly duckling.* San Diego: Harcourt Brace Jovanovich. (a Hans Christian Anderson tale)

*Coerr, E. (1977). *Sadako and the thousand paper cranes.* New York: Dell Yearling.

Cole, B. (1983). *The trouble with mom.* New York: Coward McCann.

Conrad, P. (1985). *Prairie songs.* New York: Trumpet.

Conrad, P. (1991). *Prairie visions: The life and times of Solomon Butcher.*

*Cross, G. B. (1986). *Mystery at Loon Lake.* New York: Atheneum.

Danziger, P. (1986). *This place has no atmosphere.* New York: Dell Yearling.

de Paola, T. (1973). *Nana upstairs and Nana downstairs.* New York: Trumpet.

*de Paola, T. (1975). *Strega Nona.* Englewood Cliffs, NJ: Prentice Hall.

de Paola, T. (1977). *The quicksand book.* New York: Holiday House.

*de Paola, T. (1981). *Fin M'Coul: The giant of Knockmany Hill.* New York: Holiday House.

de Paola, T. (1989). *The art lesson.* New York: Putnam.

Ehlert, L. (1989). *Eating the alphabet.* San Diego: Harcourt Brace Jovanovich.

Ehlert, L. (1991). *Red leaf, yellow leaf.* San Diego: Harcourt Brace Jovanovich.

Esterl, A. (1991). *The fine round cake.* Ill. by A. Dugin & O. Dugin. New York: Macmillan.

*Fox, M. (1983). *Possum magic.* Ill. by J. Vivas. Nashville, TN: Abingdon Press.

Fox, M. (1989). *Night noises.* Ill. by T. Denton. San Diego: Harcourt Brace and Jovanovich.

Fritz, J. (1975). *Where was Patrick Henry on the 29th of May?* Ill. by M. Tomes. New York: Coward-McCann.

Gag, W. (1928). *Millions of cats.* New York: Coward-McCann.

Galdone, P. (1975). *The gingerbread boy.* New York: Seabury.

Gauch, P. L. (1987). *Christina Katerina and the time she quit the family.* Ill. by E. Primavera. New York: Putnam.

Greene, C. C. (1976). *Beat the turtle drum.* New York: Dell Yearling.

Hadley, L., & Irwin, A. (1985). *Abby, my love.* New York: Signet.

Hancock, S. (1983). *Esteban and the ghost.* Ill. by D. Zimmer. New York: Dial.

Handford, M. (1987). *Where's Waldo?* Boston: Little, Brown.

Hastings, S. (1985). *Sir Gawain and the loathly lady.* Ill. by J. Winjngaard. New York: Mulberry.

Hendershot, J. (1987). *In coal country.* Ill. by T. B. Allen. New York: Knopf.

Holmes, M. (1991). *Deadly animals.* Ill. by M. Vaughan. New York: Atheneum.

Howe, D., & Howe, J. (1979). *Bunnicula.* Ill. by A. Daniel. New York: Avon.

Hutchins, P. (1968). *Rosie's walk.* New York: Macmillan.

Hyman, T. S. (1977). *Snow White.* Boston: Little, Brown.

Hyman, T. S. (1977). *The sleeping beauty.* Boston: Little, Brown.

Hyman, T. S. (1983). *Little Red Riding Hood.* New York: Holiday House.

Kasza, K. (1987). *The wolf's chicken stew.* New York: Putnam.

*Kimmel, E. (1985). *Hershel and the Hanukkah goblins.* Ill. by T. S. Hyman. New York: Holiday House.

*Kimmel, E. (1988). *Anansi and the moss-covered rock.* Ill. by J. Stevens. New York: Holiday House.

Kimmel, E. (1989). *Charlie drives the stage.* Ill. by G. Rounds. New York: Holiday House.

Lauber, P. (1988). *Snakes are hunters.* Ill. by Holly Keller. New York: Thomas Y. Crowell.

Maas, R. (1989). *Fire fighters.* New York: Scholastic.

Macaulay, D. (1977). *Pyramid.* New York: Trumpet.

MacLachlan, P. (1985). *Sarah, plain and tall.* New York: Harper and Row.

Marshall, J. (1973). *Yummers!* Boston: Houghton Mifflin.

National Geographic book of mammals. (1981). (Vol. 1). Washington, DC: National Geographic Society.

Numeroff, L. J. (1985). *If you give a mouse a cookie.* Ill. by F. Bond. New York: Harper and Row.

*O'Dell, S. (1960). *Island of the blue dolphins.* Boston: Houghton Mifflin.

*Oughton, J. (1992). *How the stars fell into the sky.* Ill. by L. Desmini. Boston: Houghton Mifflin.

Pallotta, J. (1989). *The yucky reptile alphabet book.* Ill. by R. Masiello. New York: Trumpet.

Parker, N. W., & Wright, J. R. (1987). *Bugs.* Ill. by N. W. Parker. New York: Mulberry.

Patent, D. H. (1986). *Buffalo.* Photographs by W. Munoz. New York: Clarion.

Paterson, K. (1977). *Bridge to Terabithia.* New York: Harper.

Paterson, K. (1978). *The great Gilly Hopkins.* New York: Harper.

Patterson, F. (1985). *Koko's kitten.* Photographs by R. H. Cohn. New York: Scholastic.

*Polacco, P. (1988). *Rechenka's eggs.* New York: Philomel.

Prelutsky, J. (1983). *Zoo doings.* Ill. by P. Zelinsky. New York: Trumpet.

*Rogasky, B. (1988). *Smoke and ashes.* New York: Holiday House.

Roy, R. (1986). *Big and small, short and tall.* Ill. by L. Cherry. Boston: Houghton Mifflin.

*Sperry, A. (1940). *Call it courage.* New York: Macmillan.

*Thomasma, K. (1983). *Naya Nuki: Girl who ran.* Ill. by E. Hundley. Grand Rapids, MI: Baker Book House.

Van Allsburg, C. (1992). *The widow's broom.* Boston: Houghton Mifflin.

Wilder, L. I. (1932). *Little house in the big woods.* Ill. by G. Williams. New York: Scholastic.

Wilder, L. I. (1935). *Little house on the prairie.* Ill. by G. Williams. New York: Scholastic.

Williams, V. B. (1988). *Stringbean's trip to the Shining Sea.* Ill. by J. Williams. New York: Scholastic.

Wood, A. (1984). *The napping house.* Ill. by D. Wood. San Diego: Harcourt Brace Jovanovich.

*Yolen, J. (1988). *The devil's arithmetic.* New York: Viking Kestrel.

Zelinsky, P. O. (1986). *Rumpelstiltskin.* New York: Dutton.

Poetry Cited in Chapter

Polacco, P. (1988). *Casey at the bat.* New York: Putnam. (originally by E. L. Thayer).

Prelutsky, J. (1983). *The Random House book of poetry for children.* Ill. by A. Lobel. New York: Random House.
"Leopard" (Kreps)

Wallace, D. (1978). *Giant poems.* Ill. by M. Tomes. New York: Holiday House.
"Giant's Delight" (Kroll)

*Indicates multicultural focus.

9

Assessment

Jessica Marie was a very serious kindergarten student. She approached each task with diligence, whether it was playing with clay or fingerpainting, and she was never satisfied that a job was complete until she was sure the work done was her best. Like most children who have participated in organized education, Jessica looked for the adult in control to confirm her own notions of what really *was* her best work. One particular day, Jessica had spent all of her free time coloring three picture versions of what she was going to be for Halloween. She carefully brought the pictures to the teacher and said, "Which one of these is the goodest?" The kind teacher recognized an opportunity to refine language development and to apply spontaneous evaluation with one fell swoop. She thoroughly examined each picture and then singled one out and handed it back to Jessica, "I think this one is the *best*." Jessica thought for a moment and then commented, "Well, whatever you say. But it looks like the goodest to me."

This anecdote demonstrates two facts about young children. First, their language development is a very gradual process in which form definitely follows function. *Goodest* was as effective as *best* for Jessica. Besides, the use of *goodest* was consistent with her development of other adjectives such as *long, longer,* and *longest.* The second fact, and the one pertinent to this chapter, is that children should play a key role in the assessment process and may even be the most accurate judge of the quality of their own work.

Traditional Assessment

Like Jessica's teacher, it is usually the teacher who is the final judge of academic excellence in the classroom and who decides when learning has occurred. The teacher chooses what each child needs to do, selects something that will measure whether this has occurred, assignes a value to what has gone on (typically a letter grade or a certain number of points), and reports the results to the child, the parents, and the school.

Even though the teacher's role in assessing reading should be to select a method of reporting individual progress that is consistent among grade levels, teachers, and even school districts, the result has instead been the strict adherence to a system that has gradually defined and dictated how reading is taught and evaluated. Unfortunately, assessment has often become the tail that wags the dog and consequently drives the reading process. Rather than being one integral facet of the reading program, assessment has become the determinant of what is taught and oftentimes how it is taught.

Once the concept of mastery learning was adopted by the educational community, reading was consequently viewed as the mastery of small, separate, enabling skills. This scope and sequence approach emphasized that to learn to read was to proceed down a path that was logically determined with certain tasks needing to be mastered before others could be introduced.

The flaws in traditional methods of assessing reading progress and skills are numerous:

- *The goals for the reading program are often taken directly from those selected by a basal publishing company.*

The goals established by publishers are generic; they are supposedly the best fit for the average student, in the average school, in the average town. Of course, no such person or place exists. Children in small, rural towns in the West are very different from children in cities the size of Miami. It is the responsibility of individual teachers and school districts to determine exactly what they want their children to do and know in reading. Only these people know enough about the children being taught to make these decisions.

- *Reading has been reduced to a set of skills that are easily tested.*

Every skill identified in the scope and sequence portion of a particular reading series can be broken down into units precise enough to test, whether these skills have to do with phonics, finding the main idea, or naming cause and effect. However, reading, like the performance of a symphony orchestra or the playing of an athletic game, is much greater than the sum of its parts. Letters and words come together in a way that can make us feel every human emotion. How we react to what has been read is unique; for some children, every dog story is a wonderful adventure. Other children would walk four blocks out of their way to avoid any dog.

- *Traditional assessment in reading makes few allowances for unique reactions or opinions.*

Children do not always agree with one another, much less with an adult or a book company about what they read. *Maniac Magee* (Spinelli, 1990) was given the Newberry Award in 1991, the most prestigious honor for literary accomplishment in books for children. Yet, when Elizabeth, a gifted fifth-grader who had just finished reading this book, was asked how she liked it, she said, quite simply, "It was weird and besides, kids don't act that way. And it wasn't written very well either."

Comprehension is individual; there is an infinite number of a acceptable responses to good high-level questions. Objective tests force responses to reading from set choices and limit individual reactions.

- *Instructional decisions are made based on what will be on standardized tests or basal tests.*

Although our notions of reading and writing have changed markedly in 20 years, the methods of assessment being used has not been affected by these new views of process writing and strategic reading (Valencia & Pearson, 1987). The very notion of reading and writing development proceeding in a convenient linear pattern has guided how these subjects have been taught and how competence in them has been measured. However, contemporary learning theorists have rejected such a simplistic premise. Instead, learning has been defined as a "process replete with plateaus, flashes of insights, apparent regressions, hypotheses, spurts, and unexpected outcomes" (Steinley, 1985, p. 319). Whereas scope and sequence charts lay out a step-by-step procedure by which reading will be learned, we now suspect it is not that tidy. Children, in particular, seem to learn in a highly individualistic manner that defies the confines of one logical, sequential pattern.

Because of pressure placed on teachers for their students to score well on tests, the tendency to teach to the test and emphasize what will be measured on tests during instruction is very real. Our goal is not assessment; assessment is a tool to be used to help us decide whether our goals are being met.

- *Assessment is treated as a result of reading.*

Traditional reading assessment takes a product approach. The consequence of having read something is what is measured. After-the-fact assessment denies the ongoing, dynamic nature of the reading process. If, during a reading conference, the teacher discovers that a student has an inadequate background for understanding the story, then changes in instruction should be made before reading continues. (Many of the before-reading and during-reading activities described in Chapter 4 can be used as assessment tools.)

- *Most assessment is written.*

Since most measures of skill in reading are written, they may unfairly assess students for whom writing is not their best way of communicating what they know. Confining accomplishments in reading to a paper-and-pencil test is not only inappropriate for many children but it also limits and reduces what is really taken away from the reading experience. In many cases, oral responses would be a good measure of understanding. Students can also complete a project or craft, or select a mode of their choice to demonstrate knowledge gained.

- *Assessment is used to group and grade children rather than to modify methods of teaching them.*

In a traditional classroom, teachers are pressured to use assessment measures to judge students. Charts are kept for spelling test scores and the mastery of lists of sight words. If an assessment measure indicates that a particular child has not learned something, then the energy should be directed toward designing instruction that will move that child closer to achieving the goals.

- *Students are often unaware of their strengths, weaknesses, and progress in reading.*

Many children have no idea what kind of readers they are. Few of them can specifically name their own strengths in reading, they have no idea what they need to do to become a better reader, and they determine their success in reading by which group they are in (LaBonty, 1989). Teachers seldom conduct conferences with students throughout the year to inform them of their progress. Oftentimes, students are completely surprised by the grades on their report cards.

- *Parents may be aware only of the weaknesses of the child.*

Since contact between parents and the teacher are generally limited to conferences and report cards, the focus is often on areas of difficulty. In the process of justifying grades lower than an A, teachers often point out what the child is doing wrong. Parents are often as unclear as their children as to the child's development as a reader.

Cumulative folders follow most children from grade to grade and school to school. But these letter grades and test scores tell little about the uniqueness of each reader. Grading is always reductive; it takes something so complex and multifaceted as the ability to read and represents it with symbols that may mean very different things to different people.

- *Reading skill is reported with letter grades.*

A more obscure fault of traditional methods of assessment lies in our notion that learning to read and reading somehow fit on the normal curve, hence the assignment of letter grades (A, B, C, D, F) to the work done during reading. Since the philosophy of many schools is to meet the individual needs of each child, it seems counterproductive to continually compare children to one another and either punish or reward them based on those comparisons.

The flaws of using letter grades to report accomplishments for reading are easily exposed. What letter grade do we assign students who are reading successfully but below their grade level? How do we grade students reading challenging material above their grade level? What assessment accurately reflects the student who can read but never chooses to? How does receiving a failing grade help a student learn what he or she needs to do to succeed?

- *Goals remain static.*

Reading goals should be under constant revision. As children change, then what is planned for their learning must change. If a teacher discovers that none of the children in his or her fourth-grade class is aware of how to use reference materials (a skill that should be mastered by then), then that teacher will certainly need to adjust the reading goals so that this skill is given emphasis. If a group of third-graders has already mastered all the decoding skills on the goals list, then the teacher can deemphasize those goals for those students. Much of our time in reading is spent teaching skills to children that that they already know or are not ready to learn.

- *Traditional assessment has preset standards: this average amount sets expectations.*

An additional side effect of traditional methods of assessment is a compliance to minimum standards. Once children find out exactly what the teacher wants and how it will be graded, they typically do only what is required and focus only on the particular aspects of their work that will be graded. If a book report must be 250 words, then students will painstakingly count words to make sure they do not exceed the teacher's requirements. If spelling is a major factor in their grade, then they will choose only words they can spell. Not only are we stifling an individual approach to learning, we are *not encouraging* students to become independent life-long learners.

- *The teacher takes on full responsibility for assessment: the student is not involved.*

When teachers become the sole dispensers of grades in a classroom, they assume complete responsibility for what goes on with each child. Since one of the goals of a quality reading program is that students will emerge from it as independent, strategic readers who can read for information and pleasure, then they must share the responsibility along the way of seeing that this happens.

Certainly, children cannot be given free rein in deciding what will happen during reading. These are the same children who, if given the choice, would wear the same shirt two weeks in a row, stay up until midnight every night, live on pizza and potato chips, and never brush their teeth. However, within the confines of the reading program children can make choices and set goals. If the teacher is focusing on poetry in order to meet a literature goal, then children may choose which poems they would like to read. If the teacher wants to emphasize reading for pleasure, students can set their own goals for which magazines, which sections of the newspaper, and how many books they would like to read.

Changing How We Assess Reading

Changing the methods by which we teach reading dramatically affects how we will assess students. While working with a school system that recently adopted children's literature instead of a basal reading series, the question of assessment reared its predictable head. One fifth-grade teacher summarized the concerns of all the teachers in the district when she asked, "How do I give a letter grade in reading when all of my students do the work? They all read the novels, they all write in their journals, they all participate in group discussions, and they all do any of the follow-up activities I design. Do they all get an A?"

Although many teachers enthusiastically embrace the concepts of whole-language and literature-based reading, a black cloud on the horizon—assessment—typically enters in to dim the enthusiasm. Teachers, many of whom have known in their hearts what researchers are now confirming about reading and writing, still harbor unanswered questions that could doom a new approach to teaching the language arts before it gets going: How will I grade my students? How will I know what they have accomplished? What will I report to parents? How will my students do on the standardized tests to which our district is committed?

Much of the criticism of changes in assessment stems from the question of accountability. One of the reasons that standardized procedures for reporting student progress were adopted in the first place was because they appeared to overide individual teacher bias and the confusion of letter grades. Obviously, new approaches to assessing the reading progress of children must be trustworthy. There must be clear methods for gathering the information, for evaluating the quality of the information, and for interpreting behaviors during reading class (Valencia, 1990b).

We need a procedure for assessing student achievement that carefully matches assessment to instruction and that holds both teachers and students accountable for achieving the predetermined reading goals (Valencia, 1990b). Once these measures of assessment have been gathered, then the results must be communicated openly to the student, the parents, and the school in a manner that gives a true picture of each student as a reader (Valencia, 1990b). Since reading behavior is extremely complex, we will want to gather our information from a variety of sources in order to get as clear a picture as possible.

Characteristics of Effective Assessment

The change to literature-based reading requires teachers to make changes in how they think of assessment. As opposed to evaluation that occurs at the end of a reading task and measures a small, discrete skill, authentic reading assessment would have the following characteristics (Valencia, 1991a):

1. It would develop from authentic reading instruction and reading tasks.
2. It would be continuous and ongoing.
3. It would sample a wide range of texts and a variety of purposes.
4. It would assess various cognitive processes, affective behavior, and literacy activities.
5. It would provide for active, collaborative reflection by both the teacher and the student.

Assessment and Evaluation in a Literature-Based Reading Program

When using literature to teach children to read, assessment becomes an integral part of the curriculum (Goodman, 1989). The teacher does not look at assessment as something that goes on *after* reading happens. Assessment should never be viewed as an end; it must be part of a dynamic process by which the teacher makes decisions about instruction and about students. Assessment is not used to pigeon-hole or to categorize students but to help determine their competencies, their weaknesses, and their accomplishments. It becomes one method by which teachers assess their own teaching and plan for what will happen next.

Integrating assessment into a literature-based reading program can follow this procedure:

1. A teacher or a group of teachers determines what students would need to do and know to become mature, enthusiastic, strategic readers.
2. Materials and tasks are selected and designed that will assist in reaching these goals.
3. Unique differences between children are taken into account.
4. Methods of assessment are chosen that would best reflect whether the goals were being met.
5. Children are involved in the assessment process.
6. Based on assessment, the knowledge of the teacher, and the accomplishments of and input by the student, instruction is modified to further guide the students in meeting the predetermined goals.

7. The student, the parents, and the school are aware of individual strengths, weaknesses, and progress.

8. This information is reported in many ways.

9. Reading and writing goals are continually be refined.

Reading Goals

By assessment, the teacher determines whether his or her goals for the reading program are being met. These predetermined goals guide the experiences that the teacher plans for the students and help to assure that children are becoming the readers they will need to be.

The most prominant goal (Goal 1) in the reading program should be to instill in children a desire to read. The conclusive research on the relationship between reading success and attitude toward reading is unarguable (Quandt & Selznick, 1984). It is useless to teach children to learn to read if, by our methods, we are killing any desire they have for the task. Children who are able to read but do not, are too far ahead of those can are unable to read.

A fifth-grade teacher related a story about one of his students he had the first year he began using only children's books to teach reading. One of his students who had always received grades of A and B in reading came up to him with a paperback copy of *The Cay* (Taylor, 1969) and said, "This is the first book I have read." The teacher misinterpreted his remark and said, "Well, that's great, it's only the end of September and you've already read one whole book." The boy shook his head, "No," he said, "You don't understand. It's the first *whole* book I've ever read. In my life."

In our zeal to excite children for the task of reading, teachers must employ any methods that work. We must surround the children with wonderful books and poems. Teachers themselves must model a love for reading (Mays, 1990). Children must be taught to read using only quality materials: books written and illustrated by people for whom writing for children is a talent. Any professional musician could tell you precisely which instruments were the best and why. They would never presume to convince you that any old violin was as good as another. One only has to watch the luge run during the Winter Olympics competition to realize the value the athletes place on the tools of their sport. Entrants encase themselves, rather unattractively, in spandex since they are steadfast in their belief that their performance will be only as good as their equipment.

The specific academic goals (Goals 2 through 7) would be what we would expect from the ideal reader at each grade level. Teachers would ask themselves exactly what they would want their students to accomplish in each of the six areas by the end of the year. For example, a literature goal for third-graders may be that students will know the elements of story grammar (setting, characterization, plot, theme, and style). A decoding goal for second-graders may be that they will know the most efficient ways to sound out unfamiliar words.

A quality reading program would have goals in the following areas for each grade level:

1. Reading for pleasure
2. Reading comprehension
3. Vocabulary development

4. Decoding skills

5. Writing

6. Literature

7. Study skills

Selecting Assessment as a Part of Planning

As the teacher plans a reading lesson, he or she can select the goals that would most effectively be taught during class. If fourth-graders are beginning a study of folktales, it would be a good time to focus on the elements of story grammar and to teach the characteristics of folktales. If first-graders are reading several books by Donald Crews, they may want to write letters to him, thereby focusing on some of the goals for writing. Fifth-graders who read *The Castle in the Attic* (Winthrop, 1985), a book about medieval times, can conduct further research (meeting a goal for studying) about heraldry and life in castles.

Once the goals have been identified and incorporated into the lesson, the teacher can decide how individual progress will be assessed the most efficiently. If one of the teacher's goals was to teach the elements of story grammar, the completion of a simple story map (see Chapter 4) should reflect whether or not children can identify these characteristics. Oral assessment may be the most efficient method for determining how children approach unfamiliar words encountered in their reading. Armed with a list of 10 nonsense words, the teacher can meet with individual children. The teacher can ask the children to "talk through" their approach to decoding each word.

Fourth-graders can write their own folktales and dramatize them or rewrite folktales taking the perspective of a different character. Letters to Donald Crews could be written using process writing, and students could keep a folder of their drafts and the final copy. After finishing *The Castle in the Attic* (Winthrop, 1985), students can design their own Coats of Arms to display during a Renaissance Fair. Cooperative learning groups can also make scale drawings of castles using MacCaulay's (1977) book, *Castle*, as an additional resource.

Methods of Assessing Reading

We will want to assess achievement in reading by using both a process and a product approach. When focusing on the reading process, the teacher will be observing and recording students' attitudes about reading and their approaches to reading tasks. The second aspect of reading that would be assessed concerns the products of reading. Using specific tools, the teacher gathers as much information as possible about the child as a strategic, effective reader.

Measuring a skill as complex and abstract as reading is extremely difficult. The use of brief measures infers that each question represents a larger body of knowledge. For example, it would be quite simple for us to write a 10-item test to measure the ability of a student to add double digit numbers. There is only one right answer for addition problems and it is much easier to generalize from the performance on a brief math exam to the total ability of the child. A 10-item test to assess reading comprehension would be much more difficult to write. It is simple to write a good addition problem; writing good comprehension questions that measure more than rote memorization is very challenging.

Comprehension skill is influenced by numerous variables: background information, attitude, interest, motivation, as well as the peculiarities of the text itself. This skill varies tremendously from person to person and story to story. Oftentimes, there is more than one right answer to good, higher-level questions and the responses are much more subjective. Even the makers of standardized tests have difficulty writing reliable, valid questions that allow generalization about the total reading skill of each child. For these reasons, we need many samples of different types to paint a true picture of one child as a reader. One measure should never be weighted too heavily. Rather, the teacher can make determinations about strengths and weaknesses by looking at daily work and assessment tools.

There are a variety of ways a teacher can gather data about the process and products of reading: conferences, classroom observation, samples of work, and checklists are some examples (Hoskisson & Tompkins, 1991).

Conferences

Conferences with students can be spontaneous or planned and can occur at any point in instruction. Teachers may set aside one day a week for conferencing with children on an individual basis. In a private area, the teacher can tap into any aspect of reading. For example, if the teacher wants to know if a child can use a variety of decoding skills, he or she can have the child read work that is of moderate difficulty and monitor the approaches the child uses. If a child is completing an individual project or report, the teacher and child can check the progress. Teachers may also conference with small groups that are working cooperatively. The following guidelines will keep conferences running smoothly:

1. If a conference is to be scheduled, let students know ahead of time so that they will be prepared. If they will need to bring certain materials (book, papers, or projects) with them to the conference, it should be announced.
2. Keep the conference brief. It may be a good idea to have children sign up for certain times.
3. Bring a notebook to the conference to make notes about each child. Date the entries.
4. On occasion, these conferences may be taped and the tapes played for parents. Each child can be assigned a blank cassette for conferences throughout the year. Children should be able to listen to these at any time.
5. Keep the conferences private. Children appreciate confidentiality.
6. Be positive.
7. Give the child an opportunity to ask questions or express concerns about reading class.
8. Share your reading assessments with the child. The child should have access to this information before the parents or school system do.

Classroom Observation

During reading time, the teacher can observe the behavior of the class as a whole and the behavior of individual children. Approximately twice a month, the teacher should spend time just watching the children and recording observations. Consider the following guidelines:

1. Observe the whole class. Do children tend to task immediately?
2. Are children seated in an productive way that is conducive to learning?
3. Is there a minimum of unnecessary talking?
4. Observe the individual child. Does he or she tend to task immediately?
5. Is the child attentive for a length of time?
6. Does the child exhibit signs of reading stress (nervous behavior)?

Samples of Work

A collection, or portfolio, of the products of reading for each child will not only yield invaluable information but will be an artifact that children will value in the years ahead. Each child can be given a notebook, an expandable file, or any type of container at the beginning of the year. Periodically, the child will select work to place in the portfolio. It should be emphasized to children that they choose the works they think are their best, that they enjoyed the most, or that they want to keep. At least once a grading period, the teacher and the child should review and update the portfolio. It will also yield considerable information to parents during conferences. The following items can be considered for inclusion in the portfolios:

1. A list of all the books read
2. A copy of favorite poems
3. A selection of stories that have been written
4. Projects related to reading
5. Individual goals

Checklists

Using a variety of checklists and measures, the teacher can assess children's progress toward the remaining goals of the reading program. These tools can be modified for any age. Checking the competence of each student three times during the grading period for each of the six goals should be sufficient. These assessments can be shared with the child, then kept for parent-teacher conferences.

Goal 1: Reading for Pleasure

A main concern of every reading teacher must be to determine what the child's interests in and attitudes toward reading are and to do everything he or she can to enhance those interests and attitudes (Mays, 1990). By giving students a Reading Interest Inventory and an Attitude Inventory at the beginning of the year, the teacher will have an idea of what each child likes. Depending on the abilities of the students, the teacher may read the Interest Inventory to the class. Younger children may draw their responses.

ACTIVITY

Interest Inventory

1. I like to watch movies about _____.
2. I like to look at pictures of _____.
3. An interesting pet would be a _____.
4. An exciting place to visit would be _____.
5. An interesting job would be _____.
6. If I could travel back in time, I would visit _____ in the year _____.
7. If I could travel forward in time, I would go to _____.
8. If I could meet a famous person, it would be _____.
9. If I could meet a famous person from the past, it would be _____.
10. I like to collect _____.
11. I like to draw pictures of _____.
12. I like to listen to stories about _____.
13. I am curious about _____.
14. The best story I ever heard was _____.
15. The best book I ever read was _____.
16. Besides watching TV, after school I like to _____.
17. My hobby is _____.
18. The most interesting place on earth would be _____.

Check the kinds of stories you like:

fairy tales	biography
joke books	informational books
poetry	science fiction
modern fiction	scary books
riddle books	historical fiction
mysteries	series books

ACTIVITY

Attitude Inventory

1. Does the child choose to read during free time?
2. Can the child choose a book of the appropriate level of difficulty?
3. Does the child finish a book once it is started?
4. Does the child attend to reading and stay on task during Sustained Silent Reading?

5. Does the child listen attentively during story time?

6. What does the Interest Inventory reveal about the attitudes of the child toward reading?

7. Does the child check books out of the school library and take them home?

8. Does the child ever order books from book clubs?

9. When asked, can the child name a favorite author and/or illustrator?

10. When asked, can the child name a favorite genre of literature or a favorite topic about which to read?

Questions for Parents

1. Does the child enjoy being read to?

2. Does the child choose to read during leisure time at home?

Goal 2: Reading Comprehension

Obviously, comprehending what has been read is the purpose of reading; therefore, comprehension is a goal that is given top priority. The teacher will want to design tasks that accompany reading that require students to undertand what they read. Direct teaching time will also be spent teaching students exactly how to comprehend a variety of printed materials.

The following checklist for comprehension can be given orally during a conference time. Questions can be tailored to what has been read. This checklist requires brief responses by the teacher.

ACTIVITY: READING COMPREHENSION

Name _____

Date _____

Title of book _____

1. Can the child answer literal·questions about the story?

2. Can the child answer interpretive questions about the story?

3. Can the child answer applied questions about the story?

4. Can the child retell the story?

5. Can the child sequence key events from the story?

6. Can the child discuss the elements of story grammar as they apply to this story?

characters _____   theme _____

setting _____   style _____

plot _____   point-of-view _____

7. Can the child ask two high-level questions from the story?

Although focusing on specific elements of reading comprehension (for example, perceiving cause-effect relationships or sequencing) are important, it is the larger picture to which we want to attend. Understanding what is read is very personal and goes beyond the details or the organization of a story.

Goal 3: *Vocabulary Development*

Vocabulary is linked to reading comprehension. Understanding what is read is dependent on facility with the words the author uses. Increasing the vocabulary of students is necessary for them to become skilled readers. We also want to focus on the ability of the students to infer meaning of unfamiliar words from context and to increase their knowledge of the morphology of our language.

Learning how to use context clues is a powerful tool in vocabulary development. The following activity helps determine how skilled children are at using syntactic and semantic clues to determine word meaning.

ACTIVITY: VOCABULARY DEVELOPMENT—USING CONTEXT CLUES

- *The New Kid on the Block.* Jack Prelutsky. Ill. by James Stevenson. New York: Greenwillow, 1984.

1. Sort the underlined words from "Happy Birthday, Dear Dragon" into two categories: Creatures and Actions.

Creatures   *Actions*

2. How does the poet use the different styles and sizes of type to give us an idea of the size of the guests at the party?

    a. Who was the smallest guest?

    b. Who was the largest?

3. What is a basilisk? (Hint: Prelutsky gives a clue by the way the basilisk says, "hooray".) Check with the dictionary.

We also want children to develop their understanding of the morphology of our language. This includes recognizing compound words. The teacher can make a tape of "The Creature in the Classroom" (Prelutsky, 1983). Students can follow along with their own text of the poem and can underline the compound words.

Goal 4: Decoding

Decoding skills are necessary for students to become independent readers. Students should have at their disposal a variety of tools for decoding words unfamiliar to them. The two most effective methods for recognizing novel words have been discussed previously: reading for pleasure, which increases the sight vocabulary, and teaching students to use context clues, the next most efficient method for unlocking the pronunciation of new words. Phonetic clues can also be helpful. All assessment of phonetic skill must be oral. We must hear what the child reads in order to know whether his or her mistakes are due to a lack of phonemic awareness or merely mispronunciation.

The following tasks assesses students' ability to recognize beginning sounds. Either the teacher or the child can read the first part of the page to provide background for the activity.

ACTIVITY: DECODING–CONSONANT SOUNDS

- *The Hungry Thing*. Jan Slepian and Ann Seidler. Ill. by Richard E. Martin. New York: Scholastic, 1967.

When a Hungry Thing wanders into a small town with a sign around his neck that says "Feed Me," the townspeople have trouble figuring out exactly what he wants to eat since he talks in rhyme. Children can read the first page of the story to get a sense of the writing style and then can read the lists of foods orally. The teacher can add more food riddles and then ask children to write a set of their own:

1. *mopcorn*   *mapes*   *smeggs and smoast*
   flopcorn   *bapes*   *(eggs and toast)*
   (popcorn)   *(grapes)*

2. Write a set of food riddles for the Hungry Thing.

The next activity helps the teacher measure a student's ability to read medial vowel sounds. Again, the predominant use of nonsense words helps detect decoding skills since we can observe a child's attempts to sound through words.

The teacher can read the first stanza of "Ping Pong" by Eve Merriam and then ask children to continue. After discussing the pairs of words Merriam selects, the children can complete the following tasks on their own.

1. Write your own word pair for the following words:
   bip
   kink
   muff

2. Now write a word pair for the following medial vowels:
   /a/   /i/
   /u/   /e/
   /o/   /e/

Goal 5: Writing

Writing is given top priority in a quality reading program. We want students to be aware of the stages of the writing process, to be able to write for a variety of purposes, and to use a variety of types of writing. The use of portfolios recognizes the importance of the ongoing, developmental aspects of writing.

Students can keep drafts of their writing in a folder and discuss their progress from time to time with the teacher. Spur-of-the-moment writing may be an unfair measure, so children should be given adequate time to perfect the writing samples that will be used for assessment and will be included in their portfolios.

ACTIVITY: WRITING–SKILLS ASSESSMENT (PUNCTUATION)

Use your writing folder and a book of your choice to complete the following task.

Title of book _____

Find an example of each of the following types of punctuation in the story (1.) and from something in your own writing (2). Write the sentences containing the samples and underline it.

Period
1.

2.

Question Mark
1.

2.

Exclamation Mark
1.

2.

Quotation Marks
1.

2.

Apostrophe
1.

2.

Comma
1.

2.

Colon
1.

2.

Parentheses
1.

2.

ACTIVITY: WRITING–WRITING PROCESS

Explain the following stages of the writing process. What do you do at each step?

Prewriting

Drafting

Revising

Editing

Sharing

ACTIVITY: WRITING–CREATIVE WRITING

- *Deep in the Forest.* Brinton Turkle. New York: Dutton, 19786.

Write a story to accompany this wordless picture book.

ACTIVITY: WRITING—POETIC WRITING

The following poem is a cinquain. It does not have to rhyme: the rhythm comes from the number of syllables in the poem (about 22). Study the example and then try one of your own.

Spider
Creepy, black
Spinning, crawling, eating
He is waiting for harmless prey
Tarantula

Line 1: a word for the subject
Line 2: four syllables describing the subject
Line 3: six syllables showing action
Line 4: eight syllables expressing a feeling or observation about the subject
Line 5: two syllables describing or renaming the subject

Goal 6: Literature

The literary heritage we share is not privileged information; it is the right of all children to be exposed to all genres of literature and to a variety of poetry. Children should become familiar with authors, artists, and poets. They should be able to identify the parts of a book and to discuss both artistic style and literary style.

Children can set their own goals for recreational reading each quarter. These goal sheets can be kept in their portfolios. Once the goals have been set, the students can finalize them with their teacher so that he or she can make sure the child has access to the books, newspapers, or periodicals.

ACTIVITY: LITERATURE–READING GOALS

Name _____

Date _____

Books I will read:

Magazines and newspapers I will read:

Poetry I will read:

Favorite Authors   *Books*

Favorite Artists   *Media*   *Style*

Favorite Poets   *Poem*

One of the elements of literary style that poets use is alliteration, which is the repetition of consonant sounds (for example, *big, bad, bear*). Children can underline the examples of alliteration in the following Mother Goose rhymes.

Diddle Diddle Dumpling

Diddle diddle dumpling, my son John
Went to bed with his breeches on,
One stocking off, and one stocking on;
Diddle diddle dumpling, my son John.

Sing a Song of Sixpence

Sing a song of sixpence,
A pocket full of rye;
Four-and-twenty blackbirds
Baked in a pie!

When the pie was opened
The birds began to sing;
Was not that a dainty dish
To set before the king?

The kind was in his counting-house,
Counting out his money;
The queen was in the parlor,
Eating bread and honey.

The maid was in the garden
Hanging out the clothes;
When down came a blackbird
And snipped off her nose!

Goal 7: Study Skills

Instruction in study skills can begin in first grade. Children can gradually develop their ability to take notes, use reference materials, follow directions, alphabetize, and to locate and recall information.

ACTIVITY: STUDY SKILLS—USING TABLE OF CONTENTS AND INDEX

- *Wild Animal Families.* Margaret Davidson. Ill. by Fran Stiles. New York: Scholastic, 1980.

1. On what book pages is there information about the following animals?

   Beaver _____   Racoon _____

   Fox _____   Walrus _____

   Hamster _____   Wolf _____

   River Otter _____

2. Explain why page numbers are printed in either brown or black.

3. What is the difference between the Table of Contents and the Index?

ACTIVITY: STUDY SKILLS – FOLLOWING DIRECTIONS

CONTENTS

INDEX

Page numbers in brown mean there is only a little bit of information about the animal on that page. Page numbers in black mean there is more complete information.

Baboon, 26, 40, 41

Bear, 8, 19, 26, 38, 40, 41, 42, 45–46.
   See also Polar bear.

Beaver, 25

Chimpanzee, 25, 38–40, 45

Coyote, 9, 18, 36–38

Deer, 6

Dolphin, 8, 11, 12, 27–28, 40, 41, 42, 45

Elephant, 6, 9, 12, 22, 29–31, 45

Fox, 18–19, 38

Gazelle, 16

Giraffe, 9

Hamster, 6

Kangaroo, 19–22

Lion, 9, 22, 34–36, 40, 41

Monkey, 9, 22, 42, 43–44. *See also*
   baboon and chimpanzee.

Mountain goat, 42

Mouse, 45

Otter,
   River otter, 32–33, 42
   Sea otter, 16–17

Polar bear, 13–14

Prairie dog, 14–15

Rabbit, 12, 18 36–37, 45

Raccoon, 13

Seal, 10, 23–24

Sheep, 22

Shrew, 18, 38

Walrus, 9–10

Whale, 6, 11, 16, 25, 45

Wolf, 6, 7–8, 13, 18, 45

Zebra, 16

ACTIVITY: STUDY SKILLS–ALPHABETIZING

- *A My Name is Alice.* Jane Thayer. Ill. by Steven Kellogg. New York: Trumpet, 1984.

1. Use the book to complete the sentences. Then write them in alphabetical order.

Polly is a _____.

Zach is a _____.

Olivia is a _____.

Yolanda is a _____.

Luke is a _____.

Alice is a _____.

Fifi is a _____.

Ivan is a _____.

Emily is a _____.

Keith is a _____.

Bob is a _____.

Maude is a _____.

2. Write an alphabet sentence for your own name using this pattern:

_____ My name is _____ and my husband's (wife's) name

is _____. We come from _____ and we sell

_____.

Reporting to the Child

It is important that children be aware of their strengths, weaknesses, and progress in reading. All assessment should be returned to the child; the child should be the first person who sees his or her report card. Since children oftentimes have difficulty making the connection between daily work, tests, and a final grade, it may be a good idea to have children keep their own sheets upon which they record all their grades. At a conference close to grading period, these sheets can be the focus of discussion with the teacher. After the grading period, the child and the teacher should spend a few minutes setting goals for the next nine weeks that include specific plans for improvement and a summary of areas of strength.

Communicating with the Parent

Traditional parent-teacher conferences are one vehicle for communicating progress for individual students. It is important that the teacher be positive but very specific when discussing areas of strengths and weaknesses. It is probably best if teachers do not become too dictatorial about what parents should do to help their children with reading. Taking time to read to children, listening to them read, providing paper and pencil for writing, and providing a quiet study area are sufficient demands. Homework is really a contract between the child and the teacher; the less it requires parental supervision, the better.

The portfolio is an excellent focus for the conference since it provides examples of the child's work. The teacher may also have one or two of the books or magazines the child is reading for recreational reading so that parents can get an idea of what type of material their child selects to read. Many parents may appreciate a copy of the Interest Inventory since some children are frustratingly closed-mouthed about what they like.

Most schools have access to video equipment. A tape of the reading period that includes a variety of activities will give a picture of what goes on during the day. Many parents have work schedules that prevent them from visiting school during the day, but few people can resist watching a movie of their children.

Cassette tapes are also a means of giving parents additional insight into their child as a reader. The tape can be cumulative and can contain samples of the child's oral reading and excerpts from conferences. These tapes can be sent home at the end of the grading period.

Making parents feel comfortable when visiting the school is essential. They are not intruders; at the very least, they are taxpayers wondering where those dollars for education go and voters who will pass or defeat budget legislation. An open invitation to parents (or other reltives) should be extended at the beginning of the year. These people can also serve as excellent resources. The following survey will provide information invaluable to the teacher as the school year progresses and he or she begins to seek resource personnel for classroom visits.

ACTIVITY: PARENT SURVEY

We will be studying a variety of topics throughout the year that can be enriched by visiting speakers. Please complete this survey so we can add your talents and interests to our list.

Name _____

Daytime Phone _____

Evening Phone _____

Occupation _____

Hobbies _____

Art/Crafts/Collections

Do you play a musical instrument? (Please list)

Have you traveled outside the area? (Please list)

Do you speak another language? (Please list)

Thank you!

Sending letters home on a regular basis will give parents an idea of what is going on in their child's reading class. The following information can be included:

1. Books the children are reading
2. Reading projects being worked on
3. Guests who will be visiting
4. Field trips that will be taken
5. Plays that will be performed
6. New acquisitions to the library

Grading

It is impossible to discuss assessment without addressing concerns about grading. Educators are usually quite interested in unique approaches to determining what their students know and do not know, but they are very aware that, in the final analysis, they will have to report to the parents. Traditionally, this reporting has been through the use of letter grades and report cards. Whether we are talking about the use of *S* for *Satisfactory, U* for *Unsatisfactory,* or the more conventional grades of A, B, C, D, and F, everyone expects some symbol to represent the student's skill in a particular subject.

Even though checklists, tapes, and samples of work reflect student performance, most parents still want to know what it all means. Certainly, teachers do not want to yield to pressure by grouping and labeling students just because it was done in the past. A clearly understood summation of progress is not unwarranted, but a reliance on outdated modes of grading are not beneficial. The traditional use of A, B, C, D, and F is based on the assumptions implied by the normal curve—that children's skills at reading and writing are distributed normally within the population and that there must be a wide range of performance.

Obviously, some attributes do fit nicely on the normal curve: height, weight, age, and income, for example. However, most of us would not go so far as to conclude that everything concerning humans could be compared so easily. Walking, talking, and eating seem to be skills that most people in our society manage quite well. Given typical experiences, most of us can learn to express ourselves orally, to get from one place to another by foot, and to eat in public places. In fact, few people would attempt to design a test that would separate adults into groups ranking from A to F on their ability to talk on the phone, walk to their cars, or eat a hamburger. These are necessary skills for survival in the modern world.

It is our philosophy that reading and writing skills are essential skills for participation in our literate, highly technological society. We cannot accept an assumption that grades of D and F are allowable. Furthermore, we find the grade C very difficult to understand. We do not knowingly allow people with failing driving skills out and about; we cannot let children with poor or barely adequate literacy skills graduate from our schools. Therefore, our goal is that all children have performance on literacy-based tasks that is either Excellent or Good. Nothing else is appropriate. Substandard performance should indicate that the student either does not understand what needs to be done or is attempting reading material that is too difficult. Adjustments in instruction need to be made in these cases.

Whether a child is reading or working on, at, or above some rather mysterious "grade level" is irrelevant. We all learn at different paces; what is important is that we do learn. If a child takes longer to make the transition from reading predictable books to reading all picture books, that is not important. Our goal is to teach reading, however long it takes. Children cannot be penalized because they take more time than their classmates. We don't punish babies who walk or talk later; we know that it is a matter of time.

It is also unacceptable that children obtain grades of C, D, or F because they choose not to do their work or do it poorly. Children may be given many opportunities to select what they like to read or what they want to write about, but they may never be allowed to choose not to do their work in reading and writing. It is too important to be left to the whims of children. A fourth-grader is not old enough to decide to quit school, get married, and buy a car; he or she is certainly not mature enough to decide that reading and writing are not important enough to be given serious attention.

Fortunately, we can state that teachers who change to teaching reading with children's books and poems do not report that children refuse to do their work or do it poorly. We may have forgotten, after years of using traditional textbooks, that people love to read. Losing oneself in a wonderful book is a pleasure for which most people wish they had more time. Reading is not a hateful task that children should need to be coerced into performing. Given the right materials to read and a supportive teacher, students warm to reading and often must be asked to put their books away so something else can be done.

In a literature-based classroom, all children are reading and writing. Assignments are completed carefully or are redone until the learning objective is met. For example, if a child turns in an incomplete story map, he or she does it again. All children are participating in group discussions and cooperative learning activities. No one is left out or allowed to drop out. With the tremendous variety of books and poems available, there is something that appeals to everyone. By doing away with endless workbook pages, children can give careful attention to the work that is assigned.

The following guidelines can help translate achievement in a literature-based reading program to a rating:

1. The teacher determines what qualifies as either "excellent" or "good" performance in his or her class based on the reading goals.

2. The teacher communicates to children what will be considered "excellent" or "very good" performance. He or she clearly explains that no other work will be acceptable.

3. A simple reporting sheet with categories to check is designed to share with the students and the parents. Obviously, checks in the "Always" column infer "excellent" work. A mixture of checks signify "good."

Example of Reporting Sheet:

Skill	*Always*	*Most of the Time*
1. Chooses book for SSR of appropriate difficulty		
2. Participates in discussion groups		
3. Completes written work accurately		
4. Completes projects		
5. Demonstrates the skills of reading		
6. Meets self-selected goals for reading		

Summary

One of the most dramatic changes that results from a change to literature-based reading is modification in our view of assessment. Rather than using tests and other evaluations to judge, label, and track students, assessment has as its primary purpose the evaluation of curriculum and the monitoring of individual student progress toward predetermined goals. Assessment does not drive reading instruction; it is one facet of it. Ideally, assessment tools are predominantly teacher made, are based on authentic text, and measure a variety of skills.

The following ideas summarize the information presented in this chapter:

1. The shortcomings of traditional reading assessment are numerous. Textbooks have driven the process, emphasizing low-level responses to sequential tasks. Assessment is treated as a result of reading and is predominantly written. The teacher assumes full responsibility for student performance and reports achievement to both the child and parents with letter grades.

2. Authentic assessment involves work with natural texts and a variety of skills and processes.

3. Teachers, not textbooks, determine reading goals, design tasks to teach those goals, match assessment to instruction, and use the results of assessment measures to modify instruction.

4. A variety of methods of assessment are available to classroom teachers: conferences, classroom observation, samples of student work, and checklists.

5. Teachers must set the highest standards in reading achievement for their students. Poor and barely adequate performance in such an essential area is unacceptable.

References

Alexander, J., & Filler, R. (1976). *Attitudes and reading.* Newark, DE: International Reading Association.

Atwell, N. (1988a). *In the middle.* Portsmouth, NH: Heinemann.

Atwell, N. (1988b). Making the grade: Evaluating writing in conference. In T. Newkirk & N. Atwell (Eds.), *Understanding writing: Ways of observing, learning, and teaching, K–8* (pp. 236–244). Portsmouth, NH: Heinemann.

Bean, W., & Bouffler, C. (1987). *Spell by writing.* New South Wales, Australia: Primary English Teaching Association.

Glasser, W. (1990). *Quality school.* New York: Harper & Row.

Glazer, J. I. (1991). *Literature for young children* (3rd ed.). New York: Merrill.

Goodman, K. S. (1989). Preface. In K. S. Goodman, Y. M. Goodman, & W. V. Hood (Eds.), *The whole language evaluation book* (pp. xi–xv). Portsmouth, NH: Heinemann.

Graves, D. H. (1983). *Writing: Teachers and children at work.* Portsmouth, NH: Heinemann.

Harp, B. (1988). When you do whole language instruction, how will you keep track of reading and writing skills? *The Reading Teacher, 42,* 160–161.

Hoskisson, K., & Tompkins, G. E. (1991). *Language arts: Content and teaching strategies* (2nd ed.). New York: Merrill.

LaBonty, J. (1989). Metalinguistic interviews with elementary students. Unpublished data.

Mason, J. M., & Stewart, J. P. (1990). Emergent literacy assessment for instruction and assessment. In L. Morrow & J. Smith (Eds.), *Assessment for instruction in early literacy* (pp. 155–175). Englewood Cliffs, NJ: Prentice Hall.

Mays, F. B. (1990). *Reading as communication: An interactive approach* (3rd ed.). Columbus, OH: Merrill.

Norton, D. E. (1992). *The impact of literature-based reading.* New York: Merrill.

Pikulski, J. J. (1989). The assessment of reading: A time for change? *The Reading Teacher, 43,* 80–81.

Quandt, I., & Selznick, R. (1984). *Self-concept and reading.* Newark, DE: International Reading Association.

Steinley, G. (1985). Reading to learn in life and school: Some changes we could live with. *The Clearing House, 58,* 318–321.

Tiedt, I. M., Gibbs, R., Howard, M., Timpson, M., & Williams, M. Y. (1989). *Reading/Thinking/Writing: A holistic language and literacy program for the K–8 classroom.* Boston: Allyn and Bacon.

Tompkins, G. E. (1990). *Teaching writing: Balancing process and product.* Columbus, OH: Merrill.

Turbill, J. (1985). *No better way to teach writing!* New South Wales, Australia: Primary English Teaching Association.

Valencia, S. W. (1990a). A portfolio approach to reading assessment: The whys, whats, and hows. *The Reading Teacher, 43,* 338–340.

Valencia, S. W. (1990b). Alternative assessment: Separating the wheat from the chaff. *The Reading Teacher, 44,* 60–61.

Valencia, S. W., & Pearson, P. D. (1987). Reading assessment: Time for a change. *The Reading Teacher, 40,* 726–732.

Children's Books

Bayer, J. (1984). *A my name is Alice*. Ill. by S. Kellogg. New York: Trumpet.

Birdseye, T. (1988). *Airmail to the moon*. Ill. by S. Gammell. New York: Holiday House.

Davidson, M. (1980). *Wild animal families*. Ill. by F. Stiles. New York: Scholastic.

MacCaulay, D. (1977). *Castle*. Boston: Houghton Mifflin.

Merriam, E. (1986). *A sky full of poems*. Ill. by W. Gaffney-Kessell. New York: Dell Yearling.

"Ping-Pong" (Merriam)

Prelutsky, J. (1984). *The new kid on the block*. Ill. by J. Stevenson. New York: Greenwillow.

"Happy Birthday, Dear Dragon" (Prelutsky)

"The Creature in the Classroom" (Prelutsky)

Slepian, J., & Seidler, A. (1967). *The hungry thing*. Ill. by R. E. Martin. New York: Scholastic.

*Spinelli, J. (1990). *Maniac magee*. New York: Scholastic.

*Taylor, T. (1969). *The cay*. New York: Doubleday.

Thayer, J. (1984). *A my name is Alice*. Ill. by Steven Kellogg. New York: Trumpet.

Turkle, B. (1976). *Deep in the forest*. New York: Dutton.

Winthrop, E. (1985). *The castle in the attic*. New York: Bantam-Skylark.

*Indicates multicultural focus.

Index